Globalisation, Domestic Politics and Regionalism

Globalisation, Domestic Politics and Regionalism analyses the relationship between globalisation and regionalism through a detailed examination of the ASEAN Free Trade Area (AFTA) project.

The book argues that AFTA encompasses the features of both open and developmental regionalism due to the political significance of foreign and domestic capital, illustrating the more general point that the domestic political economy, which mediates between globalisation and regionalism, can be used to explain the evolution of AFTA between 1991 and 2002. Despite being triggered by the pressures of globalisation, it was the tussle between the imperatives of growth and domestic distribution that shaped the way AFTA unfolded.

Nesadurai's concept of developmental regionalism breaks new ground, supplementing existing models of the globalisation–regionalism relationship. She also offers an account of how universal structural pressures arising from global capitalism are played out in different regional and country settings. It should appeal to all those interested in the manner in which the global and the local interact in processes of regionalism, particularly in settings outside North America and Western Europe.

Helen E.S. Nesadurai is Assistant Professor at the Institute of Defence and Strategic Studies, Nanyang Technological University, Singapore.

Routledge/Warwick Studies in Globalisation

Edited by Richard Higgott and published in association with the Centre for the Study of Globalisation and Regionalisation, University of Warwick.

What is globalisation and does it matter? How can we measure it? What are its policy implications? The Centre for the Study of Globalisation and Regionalisation at the University of Warwick is an international site for the study of key questions such as those in the theory and practice of globalisation and regionalisation. Its agenda is avowedly interdisciplinary. The work of the Centre will be showcased in this new series.

This series comprises two strands:

Warwick Studies in Globalisation addresses the needs of students and teachers, and the titles will be published in hardback and paperback. Titles include:

Globalisation and the Asia-Pacific
Contested territories
Edited by Kris Olds, Peter Dicken, Philip F. Kelly, Lily Kong and Henry Wai-chung Yeung

Regulating the Global Information Society
Edited by Christopher Marsden

Banking on Knowledge
The genesis of the global development network
Edited by Diane Stone

Historical Materialism and Globalisation
Edited by Hazel Smith and Mark Rupert

Civil Society and Global Finance
Edited by Jan Aart Scholte with Albrecht Schnabel

Towards a Global Polity
Edited by Morten Ougaard and Richard Higgott

New Regionalisms in the Global Political Economy Theories and Cases
Edited by Shaun Breslin, Christopher W. Hughes, Nicola Phillips and Ben Rosamond

Routledge/Warwick Studies in Globalisation is a forum for innovative new research intended for a high-level specialist readership, and the titles will be available in hardback only. Titles include:

1 **Non-State Actors and Authority in the Global System**
Edited by Richard Higgott, Geoffrey Underhill and Andreas Bieler

2 **Globalisation and Enlargement of the European Union**
Austrian and Swedish social forces in the struggle over membership
Andreas Bieler

3 **Rethinking Empowerment**
Gender and development in a global/local world
Edited by Jane L. Parpart, Shirin M. Rai and Kathleen Staudt

4 **Globalising Intellectual Property Rights**
The TRIPs Agreement
Duncan Matthews

5 **Globalisation, Domestic Politics and Regionalism**
The ASEAN Free Trade Area
Helen E.S. Nesadurai

For my parents, Esther and Victor Nesadurai

Globalisation, Domestic Politics and Regionalism

The ASEAN Free Trade Area

Helen E. S. Nesadurai

Routledge
Taylor & Francis Group
LONDON AND NEW YORK

First published 2003
by Routledge
11 New Fetter Lane, London EC4P 4EE

Simultaneously published in the USA and Canada
by Routledge
29 West 35th Street, New York, NY 10001

Routledge is an imprint of the Taylor & Francis Group

Typeset in Baskerville by
Integra Software Services Pvt. Ltd, Pondicherry, India
Printed and bound in Great Britain by
Antony Rowe Ltd, Chippenham, Wiltshire

British Library Cataloguing in Publication Data
A catalogue record for this book is available from the British Library

Library of Congress Cataloging in Publication Data
Nesadurai, Helen Sharmini.
Globalisation, domestic politics and regionalism : the ASEAN Free Trade Area / by Helen E.S. Nesadurai.
p. cm.
Includes bibliographical references and index.
1. Free trade—Asia, Southeastern. 2. Asia, Southeastern—Commercial policy. 3. Regionalism—Asia, Southeastern. 4. Globalization—Economic aspects—Asia, Southeastern. 5. Globalization—Political aspects—Asia, Southeastern. 6. Asia, Southeastern—Economic integration. 7. Asia, Southeastern—Foreign economic relations. 8. ASEAN Free Trade Area. I. Title.

HF2330.8.Z7 N47 2003
337.1′5—dc21

2002153797

ISBN 0–415–30800–3

Contents

Illustrations

Figure

Tables

Acknowledgements

Many people and institutions have made possible the completion of this book, which is based on my doctoral dissertation completed in 2001 at the Department of Politics and International Studies at the University of Warwick, UK. I am deeply grateful to my dissertation supervisor, Richard Higgott for his encouragement, support and guidance throughout the PhD. I especially appreciate his understanding and patience in allowing me the intellectual space to explore varied lines of research, and for wisely guiding me back whenever I strayed too far. To him I owe my most sincere thanks.

My research also benefited enormously from my affiliation as ASEM/Chevening Fellow at the Warwick/ESRC Centre for the Study of Globalisation and Regionalisation (CSGR). The Centre offered a stimulating intellectual environment in which to work, and a friendly and lively atmosphere as well that made writing the dissertation that much more enjoyable. Additionally, I wish to express my gratitude to the UK Foreign and Commonwealth Office, which, through its Chevening Award provided full funding for my three years of PhD research. I would also like to record my appreciation to the Institute of Strategic and International Studies (ISIS) in Malaysia for granting me leave from work to read for the PhD. The final draft of this book was completed at the Institute of Defence and Strategic Studies (IDSS), Nanyang Technological University, Singapore where I am currently based. For his support and encouragement to complete the book manuscript, I would like to thank Barry Desker, Director of IDSS.

A number of research institutes in Southeast Asia also greatly facilitated my field research in the region. ISIS Malaysia in Kuala Lumpur and the Centre for Strategic and International Studies (CSIS) in Jakarta kindly hosted my research visits to Malaysia and Indonesia respectively during July–September 2000. My thanks, too, to the Library of the Institute of Southeast Asian Studies (ISEAS) in Singapore for its welcome and the help extended to me. I am also indebted to Mushahid Ali, then with the Ministry of Foreign Affairs, Singapore and currently my colleague at IDSS, for his help in securing appointments with Singapore government officials.

To the more than 30 people who graciously consented to be interviewed for this project, I would like to extend my gratitude. Their patient and candid responses to my myriad questions helped me considerably in interpreting the dynamics of AFTA, although they may not fully agree with the views expressed in this book, which are, of course, entirely my own.

Shaun Breslin and David Camroux, my dissertation examiners, offered valuable suggestions on converting the dissertation into a book, for which I am grateful, as I am to the two anonymous reviewers for their constructive feedback on the book proposal. At Warwick, I benefited from the discussions with Chris Hughes, while Diane Stone helped me gain better insights into my own research by inviting me to collaborate with her in writing on Southeast Asian think tanks and regional cooperation. Participants at the May 2000 Graduate Students' Workshop at the University of California, San Diego provided useful feedback on portions of my dissertation. My thanks, too, to the workshop participants at the International Symposium on Southeast Asian regionalism organised by the Southeast Asian Research Centre, City University of Hong Kong in January 2002 who made useful comments on the material that is incorporated in this book.

I am deeply indebted to Cho Kah Sin of the ASEAN Secretariat who was not only instrumental in securing all my appointments at the ASEAN Secretariat, but was a very generous host as well in Jakarta. Susan Teoh, Director of the ISIS Malaysia Library, went out of her way to help me fill in the gaps in my references, responding with patient good humour to my e-mail pleas during the final write up. Both Kah Sin and Susan have remained extremely supportive of this book project, and I am grateful for their encouragement, help and friendship.

Some of the material in this book first appeared in an article titled 'Attempting Developmental Regionalism through AFTA: The Domestic Sources of Regional Governance' published in *Third World Quarterly*, 24(2), 2003, while parts of Chapter 6 first appeared in a book chapter titled 'Cooperation and Institutional Transformation in ASEAN: Lessons from the ASEAN Free Trade Area (AFTA) Project, in Andrew T.H. Tan and J.D. Kenneth Boutin (eds), *Non-Traditional Security Issues in Southeast Asia*, published by the Institute of Defence and Strategic Studies, Singapore in 2001. I am grateful to both Taylor & Francis (www.tandf.co.uk), publishers of *Third World Quarterly*, and the Institute of Defence and Strategic Studies, Singapore for granting me permission to use material from those articles. My thanks also to Heidi Bagtazo at Routledge, who has been extremely helpful in steering the book to final production, as well as to Grace McInnes, also of Routledge, for all her help.

If writing the PhD dissertation was less onerous than I had initially feared, it was largely because of the company of fellow students and colleagues at Warwick – Liliana Pop, Fernanda Tuozzo, Paola Robotti, Shigeko Hayashi, Hitesh Patel, Titipol, Fransisco Huanacune, Denise

Hewlett, Domenica Scinaldi and Jill Pavey. Lee Hock Guan, Khalid Mehta, Patrick Pillai and Ong Hong Cheong in Singapore and Kuala Lumpur took time to write humorous letters and keep me up-to-date with developments back home. The task of writing the final draft of the book in Singapore during 2002 was made more pleasant by the cheerful atmosphere at IDSS.

Close friends and family played an especially critical role. I am deeply grateful to my dear friend, J.N. Mak, for his constant friendship and unfailing support. My sister, Anita, and her family – Jose and baby Alexander – provided me with a 'home away from home' in London during my PhD where I spent many happy hours, the memories of which will always remain with me. My final thanks go to my parents, Victor and Esther, whose work as teachers inspired a lifetime love of learning, and for their total encouragement for this and all my other quests in life.

Abbreviations

ABL-72	Alien Business Law, 1972 (*Thailand*)
AEM	ASEAN Economic Ministers
AFAS	ASEAN Framework Agreement on Services
AFTA	ASEAN Free Trade Area
AIA	ASEAN Investment Area
AICO	ASEAN Industrial Cooperation
AIJV	ASEAN Industrial Joint Ventures
APEC	Asia-Pacific Economic Cooperation
ASEAN	Association of Southeast Asian Nations
BBC	Brand-to-Brand Complementation
BPPC	Clove Support and Marketing Board (*Indonesia*) (*English translation*)
BULOG	National Logistics Agency (*Indonesia*) (*English translation*)
CBU	Completely Built Up Units
CEPT	Common Effective Preferential Tariff
CKD	Completely Knocked Down Units
CSIS	Centre for Strategic and International Studies (*Indonesia*)
DSM	Dispute Settlement Mechanism
EFTA	European Free Trade Area
FDI	foreign direct investment
FTA	Free Trade Area
GATS	General Agreement on Trade in Services
GATT	General Agreement on Tariffs and Trade
GDP	Gross Domestic Product
GLC	government-linked corporations (*Singapore*)
HS	Harmonised System
IMF	International Monetary Fund
IPE	international political economy (*the scholarly field of study*)
IR	international relations (*the discipline*)
JETRO	Japan External Trade Organisation
MAI	Multilateral Agreement on Investment
MFN	most-favoured nation
MNC	multinational corporation

NAFTA	North American Free Trade Area
NEP	New Economic Policy (*Malaysia*)
NIEs	Newly Industrialising Economies
NTBs	non-tariff barriers
OECD	Organisation for Economic Cooperation and Development
PAP	Peoples' Action Party (*Singapore*)
PAS	Pan-Malaysian Islamic Party (*Malaysia*) (*English translation*)
PE	polyethylene
PNB	National Equity Corporation (*Malaysia*) (*English translation*)
PP	polypropylene
PVC	polyvinylchloride
SEM	Single European Market
SEOM	Senior Economic Officials Meetings
TNC	transnational corporation
TRIMS	Trade Related Investment Measures
UK	United Kingdom
UMNO	United Malays National Organisation (*Malaysia*)
UNCTAD	United Nations Conference on Trade and Development
US	United States of America
VDP	Vendor Development Programme (*Malaysia*)
WTO	World Trade Organisation

Introduction

Ambiguities and contradictions in AFTA

Considerable scepticism greeted the 1991 announcement by the leaders of the Association of Southeast Asian Nations (ASEAN)[1] that they had decided to form the ASEAN Free Trade Area (AFTA). Those within ASEAN, including scholars and the business community, as well as those outside ASEAN were not convinced of the project's likely progress, even in its initial limited form. The project was originally designed to lower tariffs on manufactured goods and processed agricultural products to between 0 and 5 per cent by 2008 over a fifteen-year period beginning in January 1992. The economic incentives for forming a free trade area (FTA) in ASEAN seemed far from overwhelming to sustain the regionalist project, especially since member countries were not 'natural trading partners' and were, instead, far more closely linked through trade and investment flows with countries outside the ASEAN grouping (Ariff 1994; Ravenhill 1995: 866).[2] As a result, significant welfare losses for many ASEAN member countries were expected due to trade diversion. Many believed that this outcome, coupled with the project's distributional effects, both within and between member countries, would threaten AFTA's success (Ariff 1994: 20; Means 1995; Low 1996: 201–2). These early doubts over AFTA's future did not appear to be misplaced in view of the considerable setbacks experienced in regional trade liberalisation during its initial years and the disputes between member countries that emerged during the project's course. ASEAN's previous failed attempts at regional economic cooperation during the late 1970s and 1980s as well as the continual rejection, by most members, of the idea of a regional free trade area, the most recent in 1987 at the Third ASEAN Summit, added to the misgivings many had about AFTA's viability.[3]

Yet, the AFTA project has not merely persisted, its pace was accelerated and its scope expanded from what was initially planned. Its six original or core members[4] agreed to bring forward the date of AFTA's completion to 2002/2003 when tariffs on all manufactured products and processed agricultural products are to be at the 0–5 per cent level while a zero tariff ASEAN for the six original AFTA signatories is due in 2010. In addition, the scope of AFTA has been expanded to include unprocessed agricultural products, services, and investment, all potentially contentious issue areas that member governments had initially excluded from AFTA. Thus, AFTA has now become a composite project of ASEAN economic regionalism comprising three component programmes. The Common Effective Preferential Tariff (CEPT) scheme governs liberalisation of goods trade, the ASEAN Framework Agreement on Services (AFAS) governs liberalisation of services trade, and the ASEAN Investment Area (AIA) scheme governs investment liberalisation. A wide range of ambitious commitments in these different component programmes was negotiated, timetables and rules governing liberalisation were firmed up, and additional programmes in trade facilitation to support these primary liberalisation agreements were adopted.[5]

Despite these significant advances in commitments, implementation has had mixed success. On the one hand, tariff reductions on manufactured goods are essentially on schedule, with almost 96 per cent of total tariffs already in the 0–5 per cent band in 2002. In addition, many of the tariff reductions negotiated under AFTA were extended to products originating from non-ASEAN sources on a most-favoured nation (MFN) basis, although the MFN–CEPT differential widened after 2000. On the other hand, Malaysia excluded automobiles from the CEPT schedule of tariff liberalisation, ostensibly for a temporary period of time although all manufactured goods had been scheduled to come under AFTA disciplines from 2000. The deadline for trade liberalisation in key unprocessed agricultural products was also pushed back to 2010 from the original 2003 while a number of exceptions to the end tariff rate of 0–5 per cent were allowed for particular agricultural items. Negotiations in services liberalisation have been slow, especially in the financial services and telecommunications sectors.

Apart from the more cautious approach to AFTA in these areas, the other curious development was the distinction initially made in the investment liberalisation programme between ASEAN and non-ASEAN or foreign investors. The ASEAN member governments pledged to remove all exemptions to national treatment and market access for ASEAN investors by 2003 in the manufacturing sector and 2010 in other sectors while offering these concessions to foreign (non-ASEAN) investors only in 2020.

How do we interpret these rather ambiguous trends in AFTA? That the ASEAN member governments agreed to ambitious commitments, especially on potentially contentious items, is in itself significant irrespective of the implementation record. It indicates the willingness of these governments to submit these areas to joint decision-making. Disjuncture between commitments and implementation is not uncommon in international cooperation, and this is usually attributed to changing domestic political dynamics or because external conditions change (Lipson 1991: 518; Chayes and Chayes 1993: 195–201). If the ASEAN member governments voluntarily agreed to the commitments in AFTA and if the implementation is problematic, we also need to ask why this is the case and how member governments sought to overcome these problems. Merely explaining this as 'protectionism' is insufficient, as it explains little of the dynamics underlying these trends.

Research questions

These ambiguities in AFTA between 1991 and 2002 raise at least three sets of interrelated empirical questions that this book attempts to answer. The first set of questions relates to AFTA's establishment and its evolution in terms of the commitments made. Why did the ASEAN countries, already committed to open trade and investment regimes since the end of the 1980s and which were already trading extensively worldwide and participating in international investment flows, form a regional free trade area? Why were potentially contentious issue areas such as agriculture, services and investment that member governments initially excluded from AFTA subsequently incorporated within the project in the mid-1990s? To what extent have neoliberal norms and practices emphasising free trade, open markets and reduced state intervention in the economy underwritten the evolution of AFTA, generally regarded as an instance of open regionalism[6] aimed at integrating its members with the global economy? Ravenhill (1995: 855) suggests that AFTA's formation reflects, and was facilitated by, a shift in thinking at the domestic level towards the neoclassical free trade paradigm while Bowles (2000) makes the stronger case that AFTA is underwritten by a neoliberal ideology. These arguments, however, need to be evaluated more carefully in the light of seemingly opposing trends within the regionalist project, which form the basis for the next two sets of questions.

The second set of questions relates to AFTA's investment liberalisation component programme and its discrimination of foreign investors compared to ASEAN national investors. Why did member governments decide to offer full national treatment and market access privileges to ASEAN investors at least ten years earlier than foreign investors in the AIA programme?[7] Although member governments removed this particularly discriminatory clause in September 2001, the fact that a distinction between foreign and ASEAN or domestic investors was adopted and maintained for a three-year period warrants explanation. If, as the current literature suggests, AFTA was primarily motivated by the desire to attract global investment capital, then the privileging of ASEAN investors over foreign investors is rather curious. Is it sufficient to attribute this move to 'policy inconsistency' or information deficiencies on the part of ASEAN policymakers in view of essentially liberal national foreign direct investment (FDI) regimes in ASEAN, or is there a more rational explanation? Does this move also deny the idea of AFTA as a project of open regionalism informed by neoliberal ideas?

The third set of questions deals with implementation processes in AFTA. What accounts for the shift to a more cautious programme of implementation in sectors like agriculture, petrochemicals, automobiles and services despite the ambitious commitments originally made in these areas? Was the initial scepticism about the long-term viability of AFTA borne out by such trends? Why was implementation only a problem in a limited number of sectors and products and how did member governments deal with non-compliance at the regional level? Does the exclusion of certain products and sectors from regional liberalisation challenge the open regionalist character of AFTA and the free trade credentials of its members? These questions have yet to be answered satisfactorily in the literature.

While the primary purpose of this book is to provide a coherent account of the emergence and evolution of AFTA between 1991 and 2002 using these questions as a guide, the book also seeks to answer a conceptual question that has broader analytical significance: how does economic regionalism relate to globalisation? The growth of economic regionalism,[8] or regional economic cooperation, worldwide since the mid-1980s against the backdrop of globalisation has generated considerable interest in the relationship between them, with students of regionalism regarding this phenomenon to be in some way related to globalisation, a key structural condition of the world economy in the 1990s.[9] Nonetheless, it is also necessary to ask to what extent structural factors in the world economy are primarily responsible or whether local dynamics, both intra-state and intra-region, also influence the course of regionalism. These are the broader analytical issues that students of contemporary regionalism are called on to address (Breslin and Higgott 2000). They are also the questions that this book aims to answer through its study of AFTA.

Single case studies are worthwhile because they provide empirically rich insights into particular phenomena in social science and enable dynamic effects to be captured as trends are traced over a period of time. On the other hand, they make generalisations rather more difficult compared to the comparative method. The latter offers especially useful insights into how particular local variables shape the nature and course of different regionalist projects worldwide despite similar international level or structural influences, a key question in the study of contemporary regionalism as noted above. In this instance, however, the contradictions between AFTA's investment and tariff liberalisation programmes provide sufficient variation within AFTA itself to explore how distinct local variables affect the course of regional cooperation. Thus, the limitations of the case study approach for theorising are to some extent overcome in this instance, while the book gains considerably from the rich empirical insights provided through in-depth analysis of a single case. In any case, the empirical material and insights gathered from this study form a ready base from which one can attempt comparative regionalism in the future.

In fact, a distinctive feature of this book is its *comprehensive* analysis of AFTA that allows dynamic effects to be captured. It provides a detailed narrative discussion of AFTA from 1991, when the project was initiated, to 2002, on the eve of AFTA's completion for its original members. The book not only examines the commitments made in AFTA in all three of its component programmes – liberalisation of tariffs and non-tariff barriers, services and investment – but also analyses their implementation. To date, this has yet to be done for AFTA. One of the most notable trends in AFTA has been the disjuncture between the ambitious commitments that were made and its ambivalent implementation. The common explanations for this state of affairs are 'lack of political will' and/or 'protectionism'. Yet, these explain very little. This book attempts to fill a gap in the existing literature on AFTA through its politically informed analysis of *both* the commitments made in regional cooperation and their implementation record.

A useful exercise, then, would be to first examine how existing works on AFTA have explained the developments in the regionalist project since its inception in 1991. What theoretical approaches do these works draw on and why have they been unable to fully account for the contradictions and ambiguities described above? Additionally, a brief review of the literature on contemporary regionalism allows this study to be placed in the broader context of theorising about regionalism. The rest of this introduction, therefore, concentrates on critically reviewing the literature on AFTA as well as on contemporary regionalism and concludes with a discussion of the book's conceptual framework.

The literature on AFTA – strengths and limitations

Although there is a substantial body of works on AFTA, much of this is either atheoretical or adopts an economistic approach that pays little attention to the political dynamics behind AFTA. Despite their lack of explicit theorising, these writings can, nevertheless, be grouped into three broad categories of implicit theoretical approaches. A large portion of the early literature on AFTA adopted a neoclassical framework of analysis that essentially sought to assess the project's net welfare benefits. These writings are less able to provide plausible explanations for why AFTA was established, both on theoretical and empirical grounds. Works that moved away from a pure neoclassical model of trade but that continued to stress the key role of economic incentives have fared better, particularly those focusing on investment rather than on trade flows. Some writings adopt an implicit realist interpretation of AFTA, seeing AFTA as a means by which the ASEAN member governments sought to attain strategic goals in the regional and international system. A third set of writings adopts a political economy approach that integrates economic and political dynamics in attempting to account for AFTA.

Neoclassical approaches

Neoclassical analyses of regionalism draw on customs union theory that focuses on the net welfare gains arising from the balance between the trade creation and trade diversion generated by regional liberalisation to justify such projects.[10] Narrowly concerned with these net welfare gains, neoclassical trade theory pays scant attention to the political choices and conditions shaping regionalism. In this rational choice model, the comparative advantage of a country is externally given, and policymakers who act rationally will adopt the 'correct' economic policies in line with this pre-determined comparative advantage. This line of argument makes it rather difficult to justify a regional trading arrangement since a key theoretical insight from customs union theory is that a global union is the superior or first best option rather than a regionalist scheme as the former avoids all trade diversion. Regionalist schemes are second-best options in neoclassical thinking.

Early studies of AFTA, based on neoclassical trade theory, reveal that unilateral or globally negotiated trade liberalisation would yield far superior income gains compared to AFTA, thereby confirming this particular tenet of neoclassical trade theory and consequently raising questions about the rationality of engaging in such a project.[11] ASEAN's core trading links were with the non-ASEAN world, and any shift in trade patterns towards the region as a result of AFTA was expected to be detrimental to the growth prospects of the ASEAN economies (Ariff 1998: 8–9). For this reason, the wider Asia-Pacific Economic Cooperation (APEC)[12] forum established in 1989 was felt to be a far more viable project of regional economic cooperation compared to AFTA owing to the greater economic benefits APEC offers to the essentially export-oriented ASEAN member countries (Mattli 1999: 171). Net welfare gains were calculated to be higher in APEC than in AFTA (Low 1996: 200–5). This is unsurprising, as among APEC's members are the two major markets for exports from the ASEAN countries, namely the United States and Japan.

Although some dynamic gains from exploiting scale economies in AFTA were expected to boost the project's overall welfare gains (Ariff 1994; Low 1996), an insight that also comes from customs union theory, the scale economies argument by itself cannot be sustained on theoretical grounds. There is no logical necessity for a regional arrangement to exist before scale economies can be exploited, provided global markets in general are not closed (Panagariya 1999: 121). When local production is expanded in order to reduce costs, whatever is not consumed locally may quite easily be exported. Thus, Oman (1994: 23) notes that the scale economies argument by itself does not provide a rational justification for ASEAN economic regionalism, since member countries have extensive trading links with other countries. The successful conclusion of the GATT Uruguay Round negotiations in 1994 reinforced Oman's point, however uncertain the prospects for an open, multilateral trading system had seemed just three years earlier.

Thus, approaches based on neoclassical trade theory are hard put to fully account for the ASEAN decision to engage in regional trade liberalisation as a rational policy choice. Key shortcomings include the model's central emphasis on the trade effects on income and welfare, the neglect of political factors in analysis and the assumption of a narrow form of economic rationality based solely on the calculations of expected net welfare gains to explain what is essentially a political decision to cooperate.

In the neoclassical model, trade is privileged while other forms of economic interactions, notably investment flows that are equally, if not more, salient in the present context are neglected. Despite their acknowledgement that contemporary regional trading arrangements may be more significant in stimulating investment than in stimulating trade between partners (Ethier 1998), economists continue to focus on the latter when analysing the welfare effects of regional arrangements. Computable general equilibrium (CGE) modelling employed in such analyses is not easily adapted to deal with foreign direct investment (FDI) effects, a problem compounded by the limited availability of systematic investment data (Scollay and Gilbert 2001: 19). The tendency in economic analysis is, therefore, to continue to focus on traditional trade effects based on customs union theory despite shifting dynamics in the real world. Nevertheless, economists like Bowles and MacLean (1996) and Athukorala and Menon (1997) have provided useful insights into AFTA by shifting beyond neoclassical trade theory's trade focus to also consider the investment dimension.

Moreover, traditional trade theory's underlying assumption of perfect markets,[13] where firms are price takers, tends to marginalise activities that hinge on firm behaviour like production, foreign investment and technological development (Helpman and Krugman 1985: 39–40; McCulloch 1993: 39). This perspective thus says little about the role of the very large firms that undertake much of the world's production, trade, investment and technological innovation (McCulloch 1993: 39). It is difficult, therefore, to use neoclassical theory to analyse the globalisation–regionalism relationship, since one of the key features of globalisation is the growing dominance of large firms and multinational/transnational corporations (MNCs/TNCs) in the world economy.

The traditional emphasis in neoclassical trade analysis on the notion of segmented national economies linked to each other by trade flows is similarly limiting. In these models, an economy or a country is regarded 'as a basket of resources' – capital, labour, land and raw materials – which collectively constitute its comparative advantage, and which are 'assumed to stay within its borders' (Petri 1997: 191). In the contemporary world economy where capital flows often surpass the flow of goods, economic growth depends less on what factors a country is originally endowed with than on what factors it is able to attract through the world economy.[14] This points to the crucial role of FDI in the contemporary period. It also suggests that there may be a role for an activist government in creating the conditions that can draw in FDI, a conclusion that may be at odds with neoclassical thinking on 'getting prices right' and minimal state intervention in the economy except to provide public goods, including training and infrastructure.

Neoclassical theory regards the economic and political domains as two separate spheres of activity with their own distinct dynamics. The market is viewed as an impersonal device that allocates resources based on the price mechanism, and by extension is seen as apolitical, while the state is regarded as a collective set of political actors and institutions likely to interfere with the self-regulating market and the adoption of technically efficient, or 'rational' economic policies. This view of a state or political authority essentially distinct from and anathema to the self-regulating market or economy is conceptually incorrect and inconsistent with reality (Polanyi 1944: 71). The market has historically been given form by political authority, shaping the course of economic development in different societies through influencing the political and social environment even if direct intervention in economic matters is minimal (Rodan 1989: 4). Moreover, the market has long been employed by the state to achieve particular social and political outcomes. This is applicable in the Southeast Asian context (Beeson and Jayasuriya 1998: 316) as it is virtually true for other parts of the world as well (Samuels 1981; Underhill 2000).

The state–market relationship is better conceptualised in the scholarly field of International Political Economy (IPE), which emphasises the reciprocal connection between the control of economic resources in the market economy and the exercise of political power (Underhill 2000: 4). Markets are not merely mechanisms that enable the efficient allocation of economic resources, they also allow the allocation and consolidation of political power. This suggests that political leaders and policymakers will evaluate any development that affects the economy not merely in terms of its economic effects but also for its political implications. In such a context, the decision to engage in regionalism and the course of regionalism as well are likely to be driven by the interaction of both economic and political imperatives.

Neoclassical economic theory does not reject the close relationship between economics and politics, in fact, partly attributing departures from the narrow economic rationality suggested by neoclassical models to political factors, the other being misinformation on the part of policymakers. The problem with this approach is that it leaves much of the real-world developments unanswered because it abstracts from the political dimension of the market. Pressures that might have prompted a turn to regional economic cooperation arising from the location of policymakers within distinct domestic social and political contexts and within the world political economy are absent from the model. It is, thus, not surprising that many economists writing on AFTA are compelled to step outside the neoclassical framework in order to explain why governments agreed to cooperate in forming AFTA. They generally list a range of economic and strategic pressures arising from the external environment that prompted this move in 1991 (Imada 1993; Low 1996; Petri 1997; Ariff 1998; Chia 1998). Apart from the need to create a larger market to attract FDI to regional economies, the other reasons cited emphasise the strategic rationale.

The strategic realist interpretation[15]

The strategic realist interpretation, because of its emphasis on power, security and survival as central variables, points to the formation of regional groupings as strategic responses to power political competition, with no difference between political/strategic regionalism and economic regionalism (Hurrell 1995: 49). Stephenson's argument that AFTA is pursued 'more for foreign policy and strategic reasons than for economic reasons' reflects this line of thinking (quoted in Pangestu 1995: 136).

Thus, AFTA is explained as the economic instrument that ASEAN members adopted to give ASEAN new political purpose after the end of US–Soviet confrontation and the resolution of the Cambodian crisis, and to provide the foundation for Southeast Asian regionalism in the 1990s (Buszynski 1997: 557). In this realist interpretation of events, waning superpower confrontation between the United States and the Soviet Union from the late 1980s reduced not only the strategic significance of ASEAN to external powers, particularly the US, it also weakened the utility of the association to its own members. AFTA, it was argued, would provide the means through which ASEAN members could maintain ASEAN's identity as a purposeful and viable regional organisation in a post-Cold War era (Soesastro 1991: 2; Ariff 1994: 31–2; Ravenhill 1995: 853). This was all the more urgent amidst fears that APEC would marginalise ASEAN in regional affairs as well as drive a wedge between ASEAN members due to their divergent positions on APEC (Bowles and MacLean 1996: 340; Buszynski 1997: 566–8).

Additionally, the very real possibility in 1991 that the Uruguay Round negotiations of the GATT would fail, coupled with the turn towards regionalism in North America and Europe, was believed to have stimulated the decision to form AFTA. AFTA was regarded as an insurance for the ASEAN countries, should the world economy become either carved up into closed regional blocs or turn protectionist. In conjunction with this, AFTA was also seen as a possible means towards greater bargaining power in the ASEAN countries' economic and political relationships with other countries and regional groupings.

These diverse reasons accounting for the decision by the ASEAN governments to form AFTA are certainly plausible. Public policies, including foreign economic policies are usually formulated with multiple objectives and a range of anticipated eventualities in mind. Nevertheless, with the benefit of hindsight, it is clear that these factors are less able to explain why the project was sustained and indeed expanded further as many of these initial reasons cited for AFTA's formation were no longer salient. For instance, the Uruguay Round negotiations were successfully concluded in 1994. By 1995, APEC had become far less threatening than in 1993 through the grouping's decision to adhere to the principles of voluntarism and non-binding commitments. Moreover, it was clear by this time that Europe and North America were not turning away from free trade into protectionism.

The strategic interpretation of AFTA is limited by the realist tendency to regard the state as a black box in analysis. Domestic dynamics are ignored, while the actions of state actors are regarded as driven purely by systemic forces. Once the black box of the state is opened up it becomes difficult to see how AFTA could have been sustained and in fact, expanded in terms of its agenda purely as a strategic project. The economic policy shifts required to implement AFTA would inevitably have introduced material changes to the respective economies of the core ASEAN countries. One economic study, for instance, found that AFTA would accelerate industrial restructuring within member economies (Low 1996: 203). The policy changes required to implement AFTA, therefore, had the potential to alter domestic distributional arrangements, especially in the new issue areas like agriculture, services and investment, all of which had been used by one or more of the core ASEAN governments to achieve domestic social and political objectives. The tendency to treat the state as a black box in much realist analyses obscures these crucial domestic dynamics that are likely to influence the political responses to regionalism.

It is, therefore, not unreasonable to argue that political leaders would not have accepted the material changes that a regionalist policy like AFTA would have introduced into their national economies unless these changes were desired in themselves. Otherwise, it would have been difficult for the ASEAN countries to sustain AFTA, important though the strategic goal of ensuring ASEAN's future may have been. The core ASEAN countries have always placed great emphasis on domestic economic needs, and continued to do so well into the 1990s (Kurus 1994: 38).[16] Strategic imperatives arising from the end of superpower confrontation between the United States and the Soviet Union, worries over APEC and the concerns stemming from the Uruguay Round impasse may have been partly responsible for the initial decision by the ASEAN policymakers to establish AFTA. It is also clear, however, that we need to understand more precisely the role of AFTA in the domestic political economy calculations of the ASEAN member countries, if we are to explain the evolution of the project through the decade.

Political economy approaches

A number of studies have attempted to explicitly or implicitly link economics and politics in their explanations of AFTA, using insights from a range of theoretical traditions in International Relations (IR) and International Economics.

Trade-centred explanations

One explicitly political economy approach is that of Walter Mattli (1999). Mattli employs a model of regional integration based on transaction cost economics (or the new institutional economics) and neoliberal institutionalism from IR to predict that AFTA is likely to fail (Mattli 1999: 169). His rather pessimistic and perhaps premature pronouncement on AFTA is based on his central argument that regional integration is more likely to succeed if there is strong market-led pressure for cooperation arising from the significant 'potential for economic gains from market exchange within a region' (Mattli 1999: 42). AFTA does not meet this critical demand-side pre-condition for successful economic cooperation because the volume of trade in the ASEAN/AFTA region remains low. For instance, intra-ASEAN trade in 1985 was 18.6 per cent of the total trade of the six core ASEAN countries, falling marginally to 17.4 per cent in 1990 although it rose to about 20 per cent in 1995 (Ariff 1993: 2; Tongzon 1998: 50). Thus, following Mattli's line of argument, there is little incentive for business leaders in ASEAN to apply pressure on governments to promote regional cooperation to reduce the costs of cross-border exchange relations.

Mattli's approach, in locating explanations for economic regionalism in the context of the economic gains that accrue from regional cooperation, is a useful corrective to strategic realist interpretations that emphasise purely strategic rationales behind economic cooperation projects. Mattli, moreover, introduces the political and the domestic level into analysis through a pluralist model of domestic politics that explains governments' embrace of regionalist schemes in terms of business pressure on policy-makers. Nevertheless, his focus on exchange or trade relations as a source of those economic gains while neglecting the investment dimension is limiting, a point already made in the discussion on neoclassical approaches. Moreover, the neoliberal institutionalist assumption, that growing economic interdependence between countries is a necessary pre-condition for successful cooperation, is unduly limiting and raises more questions than it answers. At what level of interdependence are shared interests in collaboration, regional or otherwise, likely to emerge? Convergent preferences in favour of regionalism may well arise from other sources, from the international or systemic level for instance, despite low levels of regional economic interdependence. Globalisation can result in precisely similar pressures, prompting not only the initial turn to regional collaboration but could well sustain such efforts despite limited direct economic interactions among them. This raises the question of whether a generalised model of regional cooperation like Mattli's aimed at explaining regionalism across time and space is feasible, since such a model is not likely to capture historically unique structural conditions within which actors operate, such as globalisation in the present time. Even if there is business pressure on governments to engage in regional cooperation, as Mattli suggests, is this sufficient to explain regionalism as a policy choice in the light of evidence from case studies of domestic–international bargaining that leads Evans (1993: 403) to conclude that 'international initiatives in direct response to constituency pressure were surprisingly rare'?

FDI-centred explanations

In contrast to trade-centred explanations, other scholars interpret AFTA in terms of its role in attracting FDI. The single regional market project was regarded as a means of the ASEAN countries to attract FDI that, at the beginning of the 1990s, appeared in danger of being diverted to other newly emerging markets (Ravenhill 1995: 854; Bowles and MacLean 1996: 336; Hay 1996: 267–8; Low 1996: 198; Chia 1998: 218). The growing importance of FDI-sponsored growth in the different ASEAN countries made AFTA a perceived necessity. Economists who had previously regarded AFTA as an inferior exercise in welfare terms and inconsistent with global free trade have now come to accept this interpretation.[17] AFTA, in these accounts, is regarded as an instrument through which investment diversion from the ASEAN region would be avoided, rather than as a means to trade creation as in neoclassical approaches (Petri 1997). It is, thus, the political economy of foreign direct investment that is salient to understanding the development of AFTA (Higgott 1997: 261).

The FDI-centred explanation is, however, incomplete. Most importantly, it does not explain why foreign investors, ostensibly the main actors AFTA is purported to attract, are treated less favourably in the AFTA investment liberalisation programme than domestic investors from the ASEAN countries. The latter are scheduled to receive full national treatment and market access privileges by 2003–10 while foreign investors are to receive these benefits only by 2020. The wisdom of such a policy move has, in fact, been questioned (Menon 1998: 18; Tham 1998: 32–3). While AFTA may be a response to the growing international competition for foreign investment, it is also clear that we need to consider other dynamics centred on the distinction between domestic- and foreign-owned capital if we are to account for this inconsistency in the AFTA project. It is likely that the answer lies in the *political* significance of domestic-owned capital in member countries.

Emphasising domestic politics

Two papers that explicitly consider the domestic level in explanation are Bowles and MacLean (1996) and Stubbs (2000), who focus on shifts in domestic coalitions to explain why governments in ASEAN agreed to form AFTA. Bowles and MacLean (1996: 337–9) emphasise the growing influence of reform-minded domestic business interests and the prior adoption of neoliberal economic reforms in removing any serious political opposition to AFTA. Stubbs (2000) similarly accords primary explanatory importance to the shift in the domestic balance of power from economic nationalists in government and the bureaucracy who had thus far adopted inward-looking economic policies to the liberal reformers/technocrats who favoured economic liberalisation. While advancing our understanding of the domestic political dynamics underpinning AFTA, these accounts are incomplete.

Although the internal developments emphasised in the two papers explain why it was politically feasible to establish or sustain AFTA, they do not account for the decision to engage in *regionalism* in the first instance. These domestic political changes are just as likely to have led the ASEAN governments to engage in unilateral trade liberalisation or to focus exclusively on multilateral or even APEC trade liberalisation. Explanations of AFTA's formation that emphasise the domestic political ascendancy of reformers favouring a more liberal economic regime also do not explain why member countries agreed in 1998 to treat foreign investors less favourably than domestic investors from the ASEAN countries when offering full market access and national treatment privileges. The shift towards economic liberal policies in the ASEAN countries was also not unequivocal. Both sets of policies co-existed during the 1990s in these countries, though to different extents. These complexities are likely to have substantial implications for the conduct of regional economic cooperation.

Accounting for implementation: the role of regional-level political processes

Stubbs (2000) and Mattli (1999) fill a gap in the literature on regional economic cooperation by emphasising the importance of implementation processes that are as necessary to secure successful international cooperation as are convergent preferences. The analysis of regionalism all too often focuses on the initial decision to establish a particular regionalist project and fails to ask how the commitments made are implemented, or if they are not, why, and how non-compliance is dealt with at the regional level by the grouping's members. While Stubbs focuses on the cultural norms and processes derived from constructivist approaches, Mattli draws on both hegemonic stability arguments and institutionalist theory.

Stubbs (2000) suggests that the regional political culture – the 'ASEAN Way' – that emphasises flexibility, informality over formal rules, consultative processes and consensus-building played a significant role in helping to move AFTA forward.[18] This argument, however, neglects the growing attempts by ASEAN members to develop a more rules-based regime for AFTA, as the discussion in Chapter 6 reveals, which is a clear departure from ASEAN's normative preference for informality. Stubbs, nevertheless, is correct to emphasise the role of consultations, compromises and flexibility in helping to advance AFTA, although one could challenge his argument that this was due to adherence by member governments to ASEAN norms. On the contrary, these processes could well have been driven by interests, an argument this book makes in Chapter 6. After all, many international agreements are advanced through similar processes – consultations, compromises and flexibility – including those in the highly institutionalised European Union (Jonsson and Tallberg 1998), a point that weakens the cultural basis of these processes in ASEAN.

Mattli, in contrast, views things in a different light from Stubbs. He argues that the absence of a dominant regional power especially, and to a lesser extent centralised institutions, for ensuring implementation of AFTA commitments does not augur well for the future of this project, particularly for deeper integration beyond regional trade liberalisation.[19] First, a dominant power is seen to be crucial in easing distributional problems by acting as the regional 'paymaster' providing side payments. Second, a regional leader is needed to overcome the coordination problems arising from divergent domestic standards and technical arrangements by providing its own standards and policies as the focal point around which regional standards and policies will be constructed. Although the importance of leadership in advancing regional cooperative processes cannot be ignored, whether alternative mechanisms other than a leader to ease distributional problems are feasible is a pertinent question in the light of arguments that distributional functions may be performed through institutions.[20] In the case of AFTA, we also need to ask whether a regional leader is needed as a normative focal point since the ASEAN countries have opted to harmonise regional standards and regulations to international norms where these exist, a logical move given their predominantly global economic focus. Mattli's argument that a dominant power is a necessary supply condition for successful regional integration is undermined by one of his own case studies that reveals how resistance to American hegemony in Latin America prevented the creation of a Pan-American commercial union in the early 1890s (Mattli 1999: 131). Hegemony, or leadership as Mattli calls it, does not necessarily result in cooperative outcomes despite the arguments of hegemonic stability theory, which in any case have been criticised on both theoretical and empirical grounds. Moreover, Mattli's Euro-centric view that only supranational or centralised institutions for monitoring and enforcement matter (Mattli 1999: 54) is somewhat at odds with Kahler's (1995) conclusion drawn from his study of international institutions that successful implementation is not always achieved through centralised institutions. Diplomacy and inter-governmental bargaining may well be more useful mechanisms to advance cooperation in situations where conflicts of interest arise.

Building on these political economy studies

Despite their limitations, these political economy studies are a substantial improvement over the more common economistic studies of AFTA as well as those that see essentially strategic imperatives driving economic regionalism in ASEAN. They offer at least three valuable insights. First, a number of the studies emphasise other forms of economic interactions and activities that are far more salient in the contemporary world economy such as investment flows and, therefore, are potentially able to enhance understanding of the turn to economic regionalism in the 1990s. Second, many of the writings explicitly seek to relate system-level structures and processes to the political decision to engage in regionalism made within the context of domestic political and social structures and processes. These interactions remain under-conceptualised in these studies, however. Third, at least two authors point to the need to consider how regionalist projects are sustained and advanced further once established.

Drawing on the wider regionalism literature

While much of the literature on AFTA lacks explicit theorising, there is a large and growing IPE literature that offers useful insights into theorising about contemporary regionalism.[21] Traditional IR approaches – neorealism and neoliberal institutionalism – that respectively privilege material power captured in hegemonic stability theory and rational-choice based institutions in explaining cooperation have been subject to a wide range of criticisms, both theoretical and empirical. The link between power and regionalism is an ambiguous one (Hurrell 1995). There is no clear *a priori* relationship between hegemony and cooperation, as cases from history support contradictory claims that hegemony facilitates regional collaboration and also that it hampers cooperation (Ravenhill 2001: 11). A more fundamental criticism is that the theory of hegemonic stability cannot be transposed in mechanical fashion to the regional level due to the difficulties in ensuring that the collective gains from the regional project accrue only to the project members (Lake 1993). In any case, this approach is of limited utility in explaining cooperation in non-hegemonic settings such as ASEAN. Apart from the limitations of rational choice institutionalism already discussed, an added criticism is that its functionalist underpinnings may not operate in settings where domestic socio-political logic often overrides the efficiency logic in policy choices, as in ASEAN.

In a recent work, Ravenhill (2001: 15) cites the contagion effect as a possible explanation for regionalism, whereby regionalism in one part of the world leads to governments in other parts of the world opting for similar projects. The defensive motivation – to defend domestic interests that are somehow threatened by other regionalist projects – may well explain the mushrooming of regional cooperation efforts, not only in the present time but historically as well, a point also emphasised by Mattli (1999: 59–64). The domestic level, however, must remain a key part of the explanations emphasising contagion effects although such projects may result purely from power political competition among strategic rivals. For countries that are not in the game of strategic competition, it is at the domestic level that the externalities of other regional arrangements are likely to be experienced. Whether and how governments perceive and respond to these external effects, which can include market access problems and investment diversion, will depend on the extent to which these externalities affect domestic coalitions as well as domestic economic, social and political arrangements. Similarly, ideas, leadership and interdependence, three other systemic variables emphasised in IR theorising on cooperation are also likely to influence the course of regionalism through their domestic effects, through altering domestic coalition arrangements and consequently, government preferences (Ravenhill 2001: 23). The domestic level, in short, is a key level of analysis, a central insight of IPE approaches.

The systemic level, however, cannot be ignored simply because there are no 'self-contained' regions in the contemporary period wholly isolated from external influences (Hurrell 1995: 46). More specifically, many contemporary works on regionalism from the IPE literature argue that regionalism cannot be explained without explicit reference to globalisation.[22] Nevertheless, these authors avoid focusing on a single level of analysis.[23] It is the interaction between systemic-level variables central in the notion of globalisation and domestic-level variables that interests students of contemporary regionalism. Their focus is on how domestic state–society relations mediate the external impulses associated with globalisation in shaping the course of regionalism.

Empirical evidence suggests that most of the recent moves towards regionalism originate within the policy elite in the countries concerned, with little popular input into and pressure on policy choices (Gamble and Payne 1996a: 253). Nevertheless, it remains important to consider the domestic social and political context within which such elite decisions are made when theorising about regionalism (Coleman and Underhill 1998a; Grugel and Hout 1999; Breslin and Higgott 2000: 339). Rarely do state/political elites make policy decisions that do not, in some way, reflect societal needs although direct constituency pressure may not be sufficient to trigger a foreign economic policy response, as Evans (1993: 403) suggests. Policymakers and political leaders are rarely 'policy neutral' to the degree portrayed in strict pluralist models of domestic politics where domestic groups jostle to influence policymakers who are neutral over which policy to adopt provided their chances of retaining office are assured.

This is a call, therefore, to reject the methodological individualism found in economics and in some traditional approaches to IR in which domestic structures and processes are presumed to be irrelevant in shaping interests, with essentially atomistic actors acting solely to maximise a universal notion of material self-interest or of the national interest.[24] Attention to the complexities of domestic social and political interrelationships offers us a way to understand how in distinct domestic settings interests and preferences are formed, the manner in which competing interests are addressed, as well as when and under what conditions domestic socio-political goals override the logic of efficiency. This is not to suggest that the state does not matter. What is important is the *interrelationship* between the state or political actors and other domestic social groups – citizens more generally and business actors more specifically.

Other authors cite ideological forces in accounting for regionalism. The various chapters in Gamble and Payne (1996b), for instance, focus on how ideological power is employed to construct distinct regions, thus explicitly bringing in questions of regional identity in explaining the nature and form that regionalism takes. There is merit, however, in shifting the analysis away from a sole focus on regional identity towards ideational forces at the global level and asking how the ideologies associated with globalisation, *and* the perceptions and images that actors hold about this phenomenon, shape incentives for regionalism.

There is, however, no *a priori* theoretical relationship between the neoliberal ideology of globalisation and forms of regionalism. While those like Bowles (2000) see a positive link between contemporary regionalist projects and the neoliberal ideology, Stubbs (1998), in contrast, suggests that regionalist projects can also emerge to challenge the neoliberalism inherent in globalisation. Which process dominates remains an empirical question, and clearly depends on how actors located within domestic political contexts respond to these systemic impulses. Also, the images and perceptions that actors increasingly hold about globalisation itself, whether shared or otherwise, are likely to shape their policy choices and behaviour (Palan and Abbot 1996: 32). What this also implies is the need for a more precise conceptualisation of globalisation, one that goes beyond the idea of globalisation as economic interdependence between states and societies to include its ideational/cognitive dimension. Interdependence is clearly an outcome of globalisation, but globalisation cannot be reduced to it (Scholte 1997b: 431). Extending our understanding of globalisation will have implications for how we explain its relationship to regionalism.

In the previous section, we saw how atheoretical analysis of ASEAN economic regionalism left many fundamental questions about AFTA unanswered. The discussion in this section suggests that the particular theoretical or conceptual approach adopted to theorise about regionalism is equally important. We have already seen how Mattli's attempts at constructing a generalised model able to explain regionalism across time and space led to flawed conclusions about AFTA. One may be tempted to dismiss this last criticism by pointing to the insignificance of AFTA when compared to the model's predictive power for the European Union and North American free trade area (NAFTA), two very large regionalist projects in the world economy. Yet, it is precisely because of such anomalies that scholars have called for more attention to be paid to local context by analysing regionalist projects outside the European and North American settings (Payne 1998). Breslin and Higgott's (2000: 341) call for a 'marriage between the disciplinary approaches of the theorists of regionalism and the richer empirical work which recognises the importance of specific historical and political contexts' is one that this book takes seriously.

The book in outline

What insights can we draw from our survey of both the literature on AFTA and the more conceptual work on contemporary regionalism? It should be clear from the above discussion that four factors should inform our study of AFTA, at least three of which point to an IPE mode of analysis.

First, states are central actors in international politics, but they are not the only ones whose decisions and actions matter. This is clearly seen once we conceptualise the state as 'Janus-faced', looking both inward to domestic society as well as outward to the external environment (Hobson 1997: 253). Thus, it is how state actors interact with citizens and domestic social groups including business actors on the one hand, and with other states, international organisations as well as global corporations at the systemic level on the other hand that must be considered in the explanation. By conceptualising the state in this way, we address the domestic–international interaction that is central to an IPE approach. This still leaves open the question of how to conceptualise the systemic and domestic levels.

Most authors writing in the IPE tradition regard globalisation to be the most salient characterisation of the systemic level in the 1990s, as well as the principal explanation for contemporary regionalism. This book is no exception, locating its study of AFTA within a theoretical framework that explores the relationship between globalisation and regionalism. This is discussed in some detail in Chapter 1. Best regarded as structure, globalisation provides the operating environment for state and non-state actors and consequently imposes constraints on some forms of action as well as creates opportunities for others. Structure, however, is not a causal variable, and by itself cannot explain outcomes unless it is conceived of as a process, 'set in motion by agents whether individual or collective actors' (Underhill 2000: 17). Globalisation is manifested and reproduced through agency, through the actions of its key agents including state elites, business actors and multilateral organisations. How these actions lead to and shape the course of regionalism is a key question this book aims to answer.

While it is the interaction of international pressures and domestic politics that is key to the explanation, the domestic level must be accorded analytical priority. Political/state elites who make external policy decisions do so on the basis of domestically-derived interests and priorities. Their interests are not determined solely in relation to international structure. Their location within distinct domestic social and political contexts is assumed to influence how they interpret external events – globalisation – and in the choices they make in response to these impulses. This is not the same as saying that their choices are solely dictated by the demands of powerful domestic constituencies. Nevertheless, the degree of support political elites enjoy and their political legitimacy depend on how they meet the needs of a variety of domestic groups, including social and ethnic groups, business actors, and citizens more broadly.

For this study of AFTA, the domestic level is best conceptualised in terms of elite governance politics. As Chapter 1 shows, this enables the analysis to overcome the conceptual constraints posed by the diversity of political systems in ASEAN by focusing on the underlying nature of political relationships at the domestic level. Domestic politics in elite governance systems is best characterised in terms of the tussle between priorities centred on growth of the economy broadly defined and priorities emphasising distribution of wealth to particular segments of domestic society. This conflict between maximising wealth in the economy as a whole and maximising the wealth of particular groups is not unique to elite governance systems as in ASEAN, and is also a useful characterisation of domestic politics in general. Nevertheless, the domestic social and political context determines which particular groups are privileged, which will, of course, vary across states.

The approach to conceptualising the state outlined above also addresses a second key tenet of the IPE mode of analysis – the interaction between politics and economics, or more specifically between the state and market. The state–market interrelationship is reflected in the manner in which state authority controls the domestic market, as well as by its control of the degree of engagement of the domestic market with global market forces. This is implicit in the notion of the state as 'Janus-faced', and therefore facing domestic and global market actors. But, why state actors are driven to exert more or less control over market actors depends on the particular domestic social and political context. For those sympathetic to the IPE approach, the short answer is because the control of economic resources through the market is intimately related to the exercise of political power (Underhill 2000: 4). The three main theoretical perspectives on IPE – the liberal economic, the economic realist and the structuralist perspectives – adopt distinct views of this relationship, which will be discussed in some detail in Chapter 1. This book adopts an economic realist theoretical perspective integrated with a model of domestic politics to explore the relationship between globalisation and regionalism. In the economic realist view of the state–market relationship, the 'tendency of government is to restrict, to channel, and to make economic activities serve the perceived interests of the state and of powerful groups within it' (Gilpin 1987: 11).

The third factor that informs the study, and which is related to the previous two points, is the emphasis placed on capital and production rather than on trade and exchange as central concerns of state elites in the contemporary world economy (Murphy and Tooze 1991: 19–20). Moreover, capital or business actors are regarded as a part of social wholes and rooted in domestic society rather than as atomistic units, which consequently alter their relationship with state actors in ways that are likely to be significant for regionalism. Treating business actors as a part of domestic society and politics also allows us to make an explicit distinction between domestic-owned and foreign-owned capital, notwithstanding the practical difficulties in doing so. Otherwise, the tendency in much of the analyses is to distinguish business in terms of its market orientation, either towards the global market or the domestic market, which derives from the competitive position of business actors in the world economy rather than in terms of their ownership.[25]

While the previous three points place the study clearly in the field of IPE, it is also clear from the review of the literature that inter-state politics at the regional level must be taken into account as the fourth factor in the book's framework of analysis. Only then will we be able to explain how and why individual governments, responding to both systemic- and domestic-level pressures and priorities, decide to come together to cooperate as a way to respond to these pressures, as opposed to adopting unilateral measures.

These four factors then constitute the key elements of the analytical framework that informs the book's study of AFTA. Existing accounts of AFTA are limited because they have neglected one or all of these factors, or they have not incorporated them in a conceptually consistent manner. The incorporation of these four factors as part of the study's framework of analysis should help this book to advance a more robust explanation for developments in AFTA during 1991–2002, one that is able to explain dynamic trends in the regionalist project as well as to account for some of its seeming contradictions. Nevertheless, these four factors do not in themselves constitute a theoretical argument. That will be developed in the next chapter. They merely point to the manner in which explanation must be constructed by identifying relevant levels of analysis, key actors, their interrelationships and how their interests and preferences should be defined.

Main arguments and chapter outlines

The next chapter develops the book's theoretical argument in some detail. It explains the limitations of the two main models of the globalisation–regionalism relationship found in the IPE literature, namely open regionalism and the resistance to globalisation model. The former underwritten by the liberal political economy perspective on IPE offers a limited view of politics at the systemic and domestic levels, while the latter, although more sensitive to the domestic level, nonetheless offers a characterisation of domestic politics that is somewhat Euro-centric. These limitations were overcome by adopting the economic realist perspective on IPE and by paying closer attention to the nature of domestic state–society relations. The latter influences political choices between maximising wealth in society and maximising the wealth of selected groups and/or individuals.

As a result, the book advances two additional models of the globalisation–regionalism relationship. In developmental regionalism, which is also informed by strategic trade theory from the International Economics discipline, regionalism is employed as a means to nurture domestic-owned capital through temporary and partial resistance to global market forces. The conceptual approach adopted also enabled a subtle distinction to be made within the dominant open regionalist model between a neoliberal variant and an FDI model. Economic realist thinking is clearly evident in these additional models of the globalisation–regionalism relationship, namely developmental regionalism and the FDI model. In both of these 'new' models, self-interested governments, realising that they are unable to individually ensure that advantageous processes of economic growth and capital accumulation necessary to meet their (domestically-derived) interests are located within their respective territories, turn to cooperation with other governments to achieve these aims. Which particular type of regionalist project ultimately emerges out of the pressures of globalisation – the chapter identifies four such ideal-type models – will depend on how political elites choose between interests centred on the search for growth/efficiency and the domestic distributive impulse.

These conceptual insights enable a more nuanced reading of the empirical trends associated with AFTA, which are detailed in Chapter 2. While the current literature explains AFTA as a project of open regionalism focused on the need to attract FDI to the region, this book advances the argument that AFTA encompasses the features of *both* open and developmental regionalism due to the political significance of *both* foreign and domestic capital in the domestic political economy. In Chapter 3 we see how open regionalism, which is centred on the CEPT and which displays only limited neoliberal features, was the means employed by the ASEAN governments to offer foreign investors, who were increasingly practising a regional division of labour, an alternate regional space for production vis-à-vis China, ASEAN's primary competitor for FDI in the Asia-Pacific region.

Notwithstanding the importance of foreign capital for economic growth, Chapter 4 makes the point that a few ASEAN governments were prompted to advocate the idea of developmental regionalism through the AIA component of AFTA due to their concern over the future of emerging domestic capital. ASEAN leaders were confronted with the possibility of new multilateral rules that would privilege foreign firms and disadvantage fledgling domestic firms. Their views and perceptions of an unrelenting globalisation involving intense competition with foreign/global firms exacerbated these anxieties. Developmental regionalism was the outcome of these concerns, and it accounts for ASEAN's puzzling offer of earlier market access and national treatment privileges to domestic/ASEAN investors ahead of foreign investors in the AIA, which governments hoped would stimulate the growth of internationally viable domestic firms and regional/ASEAN conglomerates in a partially (and temporarily) sheltered expanded regional market.

Nevertheless, despite their keen interest in pursuing both open and developmental regionalism through AFTA, the ASEAN governments seemed ready to renege on their original commitments in particular instances as they sought to protect the interests of individuals or firms with close ties to the political elite or which political leaders considered crucial for the security and stability of ruling regimes. Chapter 5 elaborates this argument, that domestic distributive concerns were sometimes so overwhelming that they overrode the concern with growth and led to setbacks in AFTA. While the first portion of this chapter focuses broadly on the implementation of regional liberalisation commitments in manufactured goods, investment and services, the rest of the chapter presents three specific cases of disputes over implementation – in petrochemicals, agriculture and automobiles.

These setbacks invariably led to disputes within ASEAN, leading member governments to engage in inter-governmental bargaining processes, to find ways to address the growth-distribution tension within, and consequently between, member countries. This is discussed in Chapter 6. More specifically, the ASEAN governments engaged in compliance, or post-agreement bargaining, which explains why the commitments initially adopted were often altered subsequently. Two specific disputes in AFTA – over agriculture and automobiles – are analysed in detail to reveal how bargaining over implementation led to both the downward revision of original commitments and institutional strengthening, both processes helping to sustain the AFTA project while taking care of domestic political priorities centred on the distributive imperative.

The concluding chapter draws together the various arguments advanced in the book, and also asks whether this story of AFTA, and in particular the book's conceptual innovations, offer new ways to think about regionalism more broadly, as well as to interpret recent empirical trends in wider Asia-Pacific regionalism more specifically.

The arguments advanced in the book were evaluated through empirical research covering the 1991–2002 period using a wide range of sources. Secondary material in the form of official documents and newspaper archives as well as primary information from semi-structured interviews conducted during July–September 2000 and December 2001 provided a rich source of empirical material that enabled construction of the narrative of AFTA between 1991 and 2002 as well as development of the book's central arguments. The use of a range of empirical sources also enabled cross-verification of the information obtained. Although AFTA is a project involving all ten ASEAN members, empirical analysis of the domestic-level dynamics focuses on five of the six core or founding members of AFTA.[26] Indonesia, Malaysia, Singapore, Thailand and to a lesser extent, the Philippines were responsible for not only initiating the AFTA project, they were also instrumental in determining the way the project evolved through the decade.

Moreover, major disputes or disagreements in AFTA over compliance and implementation were between two or more of these countries. Although the research attempts to integrate domestic politics into the analysis, the book takes neither a single country nor a comparative approach. Instead, it attempts to locate explanations for developments in AFTA in broad patterns of domestic politics in the five core ASEAN countries named above, focusing in particular on how domestic and international structures and processes interact in shaping the course of economic regionalism.

1 Globalisation and economic regionalism

Although globalisation has been defined in a variety of ways,[1] a common theme is that it generates increasingly intense interactions between nation-states and societies through flow of goods, money, people, ideas, images and information, in the process making territorial boundaries less salient (Hurrell 1995: 54). This makes the recent growth of economic regionalism amidst globalisation rather a paradoxical phenomenon, and has generated considerable scholarly interest in the relationship between them. While globalisation tends to de-emphasise boundaries, regionalism appears to be an attempt by state actors at re-imposing them at a different level, consequently creating a new, larger space out of smaller territorial spaces bounded in nation-states although the larger space is rarely, if ever, a new political unit or super-state.[2] How do we explain a relationship between two seemingly opposing phenomena?

Recent works in IPE identify two ways in which regionalism might emerge as an outcome of, or a response to, globalisation, depending on whether the relationship is conceived of as being accommodating or antagonistic. The former – open regionalism – is the dominant model in the literature, conceptualising regionalism as a way station to globalisation, a means through which policymakers enhance the participation of their respective national economies in globalisation processes. It is a model that is informed by the liberal political economy perspective on IPE. A contrasting model, privileging domestic political dynamics, explains regionalism as an attempt by state or other domestic actors to resist the negative effects of globalisation. The main aim in this case is to preserve domestic social, including distributive agendas that are threatened by globalisation. Although providing considerable insight into developments in the contemporary world economy, these ideal-type models suffer two weaknesses, which consequently have implications for how they allow for the interpretation of empirical trends. Briefly, these models lack an adequate conception of the relationship of the state to domestic society on the one hand and to global market actors and other states on the other. These limitations, however, can be addressed by using a more appropriate theoretical tool, namely an analytical framework that integrates the economic realist theoretical perspective on IPE with domestic politics. This approach, which is discussed in detail in this chapter, offers substantial analytical purchase in explaining *why* regionalism may emerge out of globalisation and the *forms* it might take.

Before embarking on this discussion, it is necessary as a first step to advance a conception of economic globalisation that will help to extend our understanding of how globalisation might relate to regionalism as well as provide a frame of reference when operationalising the concept for empirical analysis. In the next section, globalisation is conceived of as a multi-dimensional structural phenomenon, which takes us beyond the still fairly common but rather narrow, liberal economic interpretation of globalisation as the extent and depth of economic integration between countries.

Conceptualising globalisation

In conceptualising economic globalisation, three key features are salient. The first stresses the notion of globalisation as structure. Structure, as was discussed in the previous chapter, asserts or manifests its effects on actors through agency, or the policy choices and actions of a variety of agents – governments, businesses, international organisations and individuals. Not only does this particular characterisation reject the idea of globalisation as an inexorable economic force, it also introduces into the equation the scope for human agency to resist, control or manage globalisation.

The second emphasises the multi-dimensional nature of globalisation, involving not just material economic factors but also ideational/cognitive and institutional forces operating in the world political economy (Higgott 2000: 70). Consequently, the pressures of globalisation are not solely manifested through the material economic changes associated with global market competition, such as shifts in prices, market shares or profit rates, they can also emerge through cognitive and ideational influences as well as through institutional prescriptions and proscriptions. The interplay between these three dimensions of globalisation – the material, ideational and institutional – constitutes the 'context of habits, pressures, expectations and constraints within which actions take place' (Cox 1981/96: 97–8). Governments, businesses and other social groups have to respond to these forces in one way or another, but they cannot ignore them. In other words, even if states participate only marginally in world economic activities, that does not mean that they are not 'part' of globalisation, or unaffected by it. They are still very much subject to the forces of globalisation, which structure the environment in which these states are located. Conceptualised in this manner, globalisation is clearly much more than the sum of economic interactions and interdependencies between countries.

The third feature of globalisation, emphasised by Scholte (1997b: 431), is its tendency to disengage human activity from territory. Hughes (2000: 4) suggests that globalisation is qualitatively distinct from internationalisation and liberalisation, two phenomena often conflated with globalisation, because of its potential to 'reconfigure social space away from and beyond notions of delineated territory' (Hughes, 2000: 4). It is important, however, to avoid the 'hyper' globalisation thesis that the world is moving inexorably towards a borderless world.[3] The 'de-territorialisation' that some argue to be the essential feature of globalisation is still a limited phenomenon, with national borders continuing to constrain the unfettered flow of global market forces.[4] 'De-territorialisation' is perhaps confined largely to the world of global financial flows and the internet where finance and information flow instantaneously around the globe unconstrained by territorial borders and removed from territorial space. Nevertheless, Hughes raises a crucial point about the tendency of globalisation to reconfigure social, including economic space beyond prevailing notions of territoriality, namely nation-states. But, what exactly is it about globalisation that has the potential to reconfigure economic space? More specifically, how is economic space being reconfigured and how might this relate to regionalism? A closer look at the constituent dimensions of globalisation is instructive in this regard.

The material dimension: the changing dynamics of competition

Historical similarities exist in patterns of trade, finance and production between earlier periods and the present, post-1970s world economy, which is argued to represent most clearly the globalisation period (Oman 1994: 33).[5] Yet, many students of globalisation point to the sharp differences in the volume, scope, speed, clustering and depth of the processes and interactions in the world economy between the two periods (Petrella 1996: 64–6; Sjolander 1996: 605–7; Higgott 2000: 70). More to the point, contemporary global linkages are argued to be 'organically different' due to changes in the 'manner in which firms organise production and both cooperate and compete with each other'.[6] This is a valuable point, because it draws attention to the underlying firm-level dynamics that underpin globalisation processes and which drive the tendency to reconfigure economic space.

One of the most important driving forces of globalisation is the diffusion and adoption of the post-Fordist or flexible model of corporate and industrial organisation, particularly in the post-1970s world economy (Oman 1994: 83–99).[7] Flexible production systems increasingly underpin the growing prominence of functionally integrated transnational production patterns that has been noted in the contemporary period (Dunning 1993: 4; Oman 1994: 97; Dicken 1998: 175). Governments and firms concerned respectively about economic growth and profitability find themselves having to respond in one way or another to the implications of the shifts in the way production is becoming increasingly organised.

First, the growing turn to more flexible modes of production has been accompanied by a shift in the sources of wealth creation from natural assets such as unskilled or low-skilled labour, land and natural resources to 'created' assets centred on information, technology and management/organisational competencies (Dunning 1993: 6). Although broad generalisations need to be made with care, since natural assets remain important in a number of economic sectors, it is also evident that technology and skills have become crucial in manufacturing and service sectors, particularly in the higher value-added segments (Dicken 1998). Created assets, which tend to be firm specific and thus, potentially mobile, lend considerable structural power to global capital. Governments concerned about high value economic growth are increasingly reliant on the firms that possess these created assets to establish production activities in or involving their respective economies, underscoring the crucial importance of FDI, particularly for the developing world, and the intense competition for it among governments (Stopford and Strange 1991: 1).

Production decisions remain, however, within the purview of the global firms that governments are increasingly trying to attract (Petrella 1996: 74). Competition for FDI among countries has, therefore, become far more intense since governments are all courting essentially the same types of firms to their respective economies than in previous times, having adopted broadly similar export-centred economic policies. The worldwide liberalising trend has widened the location choice available to the firms that own these mobile assets (Stopford and Strange 1991: 1; Dunning 1993: 13–15). Storper (1997) suggests that particular geographic locations are entirely substitutable apart from nominal cost differences. It seems as though economic space worldwide is becoming increasingly homogenised with regard to economic policy (Biersteker 1992). Although this homogenising trend should not be exaggerated, the point remains that coupled with technological advances and the deregulation of financial flows worldwide, production can now be located worldwide with considerably more ease than in previous decades. This makes competition for FDI likely to be more intense than ever, even if the ability of a firm to relocate, once established, is more restricted than is commonly presumed. Governments will more than ever compete with each other to attract these mobile assets before they become location bound once production is established.

Apart from governments, firms too are compelled to respond to the new competition. Globalisation has led to a more complex business environment for firms and more intense competition, particularly as the 'coordination and configuration of production chains has become the key to creating and sustaining competitive advantage' (Dicken and Yeung 1999: 118). This imposes an enormous burden on emerging firms, especially in the developing world, that are new to the game and which also usually lack the ownership-specific assets to compete with well-established global corporations from the advanced countries in global competition (Stopford and Strange 1991: 1–5).

Apart from this, the growing turn to flexible production methods also has implications for the manner in which economic space might be reconfigured. On the one hand, it would seem logical for firms to have an inherent preference for a global division of labour in line with the expansionary logic of capitalism. The turn to flexible production systems, however, may well be contributing to a phase of economic agglomeration through global capital's need for the spatial concentration of production activity. The agglomeration logic arises because the flexible modes of production are highly dependent on physical proximity between producers and suppliers on the one hand, and between producers and customers on the other (Oman 1994: 17; Dicken 1998: 241). Thus, globalisation processes may help to re-define economic spaces beyond existing notions of territoriality, namely the nation-state, but not necessarily towards a global economic space. In short, both centrifugal forces (expansionary logic of capitalism) and centripetal tendencies (the agglomeration logic) co-exist in globalisation. Although this does not in any way imply in deterministic fashion particular forms of geographical clustering of production activities, it does explain the growing prominence of regionally, as opposed to globally, integrated production in the world economy (Oman 1994; Dicken 1998: 216–17). In an interesting case study, Studer-Noguez (2000) documents how Ford Motor Company's global corporate strategy shifted from one based on a single global production chain dispersed worldwide, which proved unworkable, to one that relied on setting up self-contained regionalised production chains replicated in different parts of the world. Ford's revised global corporate strategy was, therefore, premised on a number of distinct regional production operations located worldwide.

These new forms of production, driven by the shifting corporate strategy of global firms, are different from the cross-border economic activity that was prevalent during the 1960s and 1970s. Then, MNCs had exploited low labour costs in offshore production sites, producing for export to markets outside the region, usually to the industrial world and the MNCs' home markets. Although involving cross-border economic interactions, this form of internationalised economic activity did not involve any fundamental reconfiguration of production space. Production was still organised *multi*-nationally on the basis of territorial nation-states, even if cross-border economic interactions were prominent. Since then, the dynamics of global production have altered towards an increasingly *trans*-national production pattern with different segments of a single production chain established in a number of sites, often straddling or crossing state boundaries. Critics of the globalisation thesis point to the regional clustering of economic activity as evidence against the emergence of a single global market place, and thus of globalisation as a meaningful or salient phenomenon.[8] On the contrary, this chapter argues that these regionalising tendencies are the very outcomes of globalisation, emerging out of the shifting micro-economics of production.

Where such regional clusters emerge depends both on the policies adopted by governments as well as on the corporate decisions of firms. Because much of the assets required for production are located within firms themselves, firms are theoretically able to relocate worldwide, provided local conditions meet their production needs. Walter (2000: 65) notes that foreign investors privilege, among other factors, market size and 'access to large regional markets' when deciding where to locate their investments. Interestingly, governments may be able to meet firms' growing need for proximity to regional markets through participating in regional cooperation schemes.

The ideational and institutional underpinnings of globalisation

Far from being purely a material phenomenon, globalisation is sustained and reinforced by a coherent set of, by now, widely practised neoliberal economic ideas, which are increasingly institutionalised through the rules and practices of multilateral institutions, notably the World Trade Organisation (WTO).[9]

The dominant neoliberal ideas underpinning globalisation emphasise and advocate, among other things, a free market economy with limited government involvement in and control of economic activity through policies of liberalisation, deregulation and privatisation, as well as the ideal of market competition. These ideas have become especially prominent from the middle of the 1980s, and are widely practised in both the industrial and developing world (Biersteker 1992), although they do not go unchallenged (George 2000). In fact, part of their appeal lies in the seemingly simple and effective recipe for growth and wealth creation they offer to governments, compared to the failed interventionist alternatives tried during the 1960s and 1970s. Then, a variety of economic ideas prevailed, ranging from neoclassical ones about free trade and free markets, interventionist approaches to economic management, to more radical dependency thinking that emphasised withdrawal from the exploitative processes of the world economy. The extensive adoption today of neoliberal ideas globally facilitates the worldwide spread of economic activity, allowing corporations the flexibility to organise production in whatever spatial configuration that best maximises their goals. Although there is growing opposition to these neoliberal ideas and practices, they nonetheless retain their considerable influence on state actors, and, consequently, play a substantial role in reinforcing the material dimension of globalisation.

While neoliberal ideas are a crucial component of globalisation and sustain it, at a more fundamental level it is perhaps the growing instantiation of 'globalisation' itself and of global economic competition especially that influences how people respond to global economic change. Mittelman (2000: 4) notes that 'globalisation has become normalised as a dominant set of ideas'. Palan and Abbott (1996: 32) argue that the perception of globalisation is possibly the main cause for changing patterns of behaviour today. Actors, in their view, respond not only to actual external pressures or changes, they are increasingly responding to *perceived* environmental change. This is not an unusual point. Perceptions are, after all, of considerable importance in practical politics and policymaking (Barry Jones 1995: 7). Policymakers, as do corporate actors, may respond in an anticipatory fashion to perceived global market competition to stay one step ahead of the game even if there are no immediate or serious market pressures on the economy. We should, however, reject the suggestion that only one kind of behaviour is possible – that which accommodates to globalisation. Not all governments wish to act out the 'neoliberal script' underpinning globalisation. Ultimately, actors will respond to these perceptions in ways that are also governed by their location within distinct domestic social and political contexts.

While governments may be attracted to neoliberal economic ideas that promise simple recipes for creating economic wealth for societies – liberalisation, deregulation and privatisation – it is becoming difficult for governments to select particular elements from this package of policy prescriptions while ignoring others, or even to reject them altogether, should they wish to do so. It is increasingly the case that international organisations, especially the World Bank, the International Monetary Fund (IMF) and the WTO underwrite globalisation processes by developing neoliberal rules to which national governments eventually have to conform. Either these rules are binding on governments if they are members of the WTO, or governments have to subscribe to the neoliberal policies dictated by the IMF or the World Bank in return for financial assistance during economic crises. In short, the post-World War II period of 'embedded liberalism' (Ruggie 1998: 72–6) has given way since the 1970s to what Hoogvelt (1997: 135) terms 'unembedded liberalism'.

Embedded liberalism allowed governments to intervene in the domestic economy to safeguard domestic social stability, provided border barriers to international trade were progressively reduced. This compromise, which effectively allowed governments to deny market access and national treatment to foreign firms if they so wished, began unravelling over a period of time beginning from the early 1970s (George 2000). It was only from the mid-1980s, however, that new rules in world trade were adopted that redefined or more precisely markedly reduced the purposes for which the government could legitimately intervene in the domestic economy, including restricting or discriminating against foreign firms. The new rules consequently advanced the interests of the transnational corporations (TNCs) that are key agents of globalisation. In short, the neoliberal ideas associated with globalisation have been increasingly institutionalised through a multilateral rule-based framework that has substantial authority over national governments, especially through the WTO.

To date, the WTO, previously the General Agreement on Tariffs and Trade (GATT), has been perhaps the pre-eminent institutional agent of globalisation, having a more extensive reach both in terms of geographical coverage and ever widening scope compared to other global institutions. Unlike the IMF, which enters the scene during times of economic distress when governments need emergency financial assistance, the WTO is a more constant influence or constraint on national governments and firms. Not only does the WTO boast 144 contracting parties with others awaiting entry,[10] its functional scope has dramatically expanded and its authority strengthened compared to the GATT.

Since the GATT Uruguay Round negotiations of 1986–94 that launched the WTO, disciplines addressing intellectual property rights protection, negotiable market access and national treatment for foreign service firms, as well as trade-specific investment measures were explicitly incorporated into the multilateral trade regime. Rules on domestic competition and investment liberalisation are expected to eventually fall under the ambit of the WTO. In these new issue areas, rules are expected to prescribe market deregulation while proscribing state intervention in the market, thereby constraining government direction of the economy. While the WTO is constructed in a way that provides ample opportunity for dissenting governments to veto its liberalisation agenda, there are costs to such recalcitrance. Valuable market access concessions from industrial countries might not be forthcoming while governments lose credibility in the eyes of the corporations that increasingly hold the key to wealth creation.

These trends raise expectations among governments, particularly in the developing world, that the new rules that will be written into the multilateral trading regime will increasingly restrict the rights of governments to intervene in the domestic economy even for what would have been previously considered to be legitimate domestic social purposes. While such rules will offer TNCs a global trading and production environment that is increasingly tailor-made to their needs to pursue 'maximum profit' (George 2000: 22), emerging firms from the developing world may become increasingly disadvantaged. Should these rules be adopted, developing country governments, while obliged to allow foreign firms domestic market access, will become increasingly constrained in providing preferential treatment to domestic firms. This, coupled with the competitive pressures discussed above, further reinforces perceptions in the developing world of globalisation as heightened global market competition. The fear that fledgling firms will suffer from direct competition with TNCs is a growing feature in many developing country policy circles.

Globalisation: structure, process and agency

Three points need to be kept in mind from this discussion. First, while globalisation involves the reconfiguration of economic space, this does not necessarily imply either re-definition towards a global economic space or a single global division of labour, or the absence of territoriality. Instead, the optimal economic space appears to be regional. This is not to suggest a functionalist line of explanation for the relationship between regionalism and globalisation. Nevertheless, the functional relationship between these two phenomena implies that corporate actors may respond positively to regionalism, particularly of the kind that further entrenches globalisation – open regionalism. Globalisation, in other words, opens up space for agency, particularly on the part of state actors to influence corporate behaviour.

The discussion also identified three sets of potential globalisation pressures that might result in the adoption of policies for regional cooperation – material economic pressures, cognitive influences and institutional rules. There is, however, no determining logic that points to open regionalism as the only policy response to globalisation. Countervailing tendencies may well result in other forms of regionalism, notably the resistance model. Much depends on how the actors located within domestic social and political contexts respond to the structural pressures associated with globalisation on the one hand and to domestic political and social imperatives on the other that may collide with the globalisation logic. There are today significant counter-currents in the world economy that challenge both the neoliberal discourse and globalisation itself (Hveem 2000; Mittelman 2000).[11] It is in this sense that globalisation is not a stable structure or a fully entrenched order, but one that can be challenged.

While it is true that globalisation is partly driven by technological innovations and the uncoordinated individual actions of rational economic actors out to maximise economic gains – the liberal economics reading – this is not the same as saying that globalisation is an inexorable economic force. It is necessary to recognise that globalisation is a process driven by the policy choices of a variety of actors – governments, corporations, international organisations and individuals – who put in place the necessary institutional structures that support globalisation processes (Higgott 1999: 27). What this also implies is the possibility for human agency, including that of governments, to manage the process or to attempt to shape it in preferred ways (Hirst and Thompson 1995). It is out of such attempts that regionalism emerges in response to globalisation.

Open regionalism: the liberal political economy interpretation

The preceding discussion suggests that the relationship between globalisation and regionalism may be complementary. The outward-looking nature of most contemporary regionalist projects leads many observers to surmise that these projects are designed to enhance the participation of member countries in global market activity (Gamble and Payne 1996a: 251–2). This is the notion of 'open regionalism', which is a striking contrast to the 'closed' regionalism of the 1960s and 1970s that had been aimed at insulating members from the world economy in line with dependency thinking (Grugel and Hout 1999: 10). Open regionalism is the dominant theoretical model of the globalisation–regionalism relationship in the literature, as well as the most common form of regionalist project found in the contemporary world economy (Mittelman 2000: 126).

Open regionalism, as the term was originally used, meant a form of regionalism based on the principles of unilateral liberalisation rather than formally negotiated liberalisation, as well as non-discrimination, meaning that regional concessions were offered to both members and non-members alike (Drysdale and Garnaut 1993: 187–8). While retaining these liberal economic underpinnings, the term is now used in a more general sense to characterise regionalist schemes that are fundamentally about engaging with globalisation and the global market. Therefore, in regionalist schemes characterised as open regionalism, the exchange of preferences among regional partners is not accompanied by the imposition of new barriers to non-partners (Gamble and Payne 1996a: 251). Some scholars also define an open regionalist project as one whose members are willing to admit new members into the grouping provided they conform to group rules and arrangements (Grugel 1996: 131; Mittelman 2000: 113).

Underwritten by the liberal political economy perspective on IPE, the primacy of economic incentives and the search for efficiency and competitiveness are emphasised in explaining open regionalism as a policy response to globalisation. Consequently, much of the literature explains open regionalism as a project of governments responding to the needs of corporate actors to improve competitiveness in global markets, using regional action as a means to engage with the global economy (Grugel and Hout 1999: 10; Hveem 2000: 70–4; Mittelman 2000: 121). The liberal interpretation also suggests that these projects are likely to include a strong neoliberal agenda requiring extensive domestic deregulation, apart from trade liberalisation, aimed at reducing the state's role in economic life in order to yield efficiency gains.[12] The effect of such actions is to markedly reduce transaction costs for firms engaged in transnational economic activities. In short, this form of regionalism – neoliberal regionalism – subordinates the economies of member countries to what are seen as the beneficial forces of the global market. Aimed at deep engagement with the process of globalisation, open regionalism is an instance of 'meso-globalisation'.[13] Open regionalism and neoliberal regionalism are often regarded as synonymous in the literature.[14]

This still leaves open the question of why corporate actors and national policymakers would advocate a policy of *regionalism* if their ultimate aim is to engage with the global market. While the discussion in the previous section suggests how globalisation may be functionally related to regionalism, this does not explain regionalism as a *political* choice. The liberal perspective underpinning the notion of open regionalism provides only limited answers to this question. A strict liberal interpretation would, in fact, see global liberalisation to be superior to regional liberalisation even if corporate strategies dictate regional production networks as the optimal configuration under flexible modes of production. Even if their preference is to organise production regionally, global liberalisation allows corporations maximum choice of where to invest and in whatever spatial configuration best accommodates the firm's needs. This is borne out by actual trends in the world economy, as the previous discussion made clear. While global corporations today tend to organise production on a regional basis, locating regionalised production operations in different parts of the world, this is usually part of a global strategy.

The regime literature (neoliberal institutionalism), a variant of the liberal perspective, provides an answer to the 'why regionalism?' question by suggesting that governments opt for regionalism because cooperation is easier to negotiate with smaller numbers than would be the case for negotiating global liberalisation (Oye 1985). Regionalism is a solution to the collective action problems that impede cooperation among large numbers. Moreover, by creating both an incentive and a potential bargaining tool for further negotiations, regional cooperation can potentially advance global liberalisation (Oye 1992). Liberal readings of regionalism thus see the phenomenon as a building block to global liberalisation. This particular interpretation suggests that we are likely to see ever-widening processes of regionalism, as more and more nation-states are brought into existing regional projects in an effort to build up global liberalisation (Mittelman 2000: 113). Regionalism, then, constitutes an efficient but possibly interim approach to global liberalisation.

Although providing useful insights into the globalisation–regionalism relationship, liberal interpretations of regionalism are, nonetheless, limited because they lack a deeper notion of international politics. The decision to participate in regionalism is made in order to subordinate the national economy to what are seen as the given and beneficial forces of the global market. In this liberal model, regionalism involves very little purposeful political action by governments of states to attempt to intervene in globalisation processes – in short, the absence of any notion of political struggle, both domestically and externally. Instead, governments acquiesce in and act in accordance with the logic of global market forces asserted through the pressure of market competition. This interpretation of regionalism is based on a somewhat simplistic characterisation of the international political economy, while it also privileges structurally derived interests in explanation. There is an implied coincidence of interests between state actors and those businesses in favour of (regional/global) liberalisation, with both sets of actors responding similarly to the pressures of global market competition. The liberal perspective is silent on domestic distributive issues, since in the liberal world the search for efficiency and the resultant economic growth leads to gains for all in the long run.

Like its circumscribed characterisation of the international political economy, the neglect of the distribution question is a serious limitation of the liberal political economy reading of regionalism. Moreover, its framing of the relationship between state and corporate actors is overly simplistic. In particular settings, the distinction between foreign-owned and domestic-owned capital is often the more salient one, rather than between inward-focused and outward-oriented businesses. Although broad generalisations need to be made with care, domestic-owned capital is often harnessed to attain vital domestic social and political goals aimed at by political leaders, while foreign capital addresses the broad growth priorities of national governments. For this reason, it is important to take seriously domestic distributive dynamics. In parts of Southeast Asia, for instance, domestic-owned capital is central to domestic distributive agendas. In settings such as this, governments may well respond to globalisation in ways that attempt to preserve and/or nurture domestic capital, particularly if emerging domestic capital that is also politically important is in danger of losing out to global capital in market competition. To the extent that such responses include regionalism as a policy choice, the nature of the regionalist project adopted is likely to differ from the liberal model of open regionalism.

Regionalism as resistance to globalisation: legitimacy and domestic politics

The second ideal-type model of the globalisation–regionalism relationship in the literature explicitly brings in the domestic level, and is thus a useful corrective to the basic model of open regionalism that focuses on systemic level forces only. Although encompassing a range of variations, the essential feature of the basic resistance model is that it seeks to preserve through regionalism particular forms of national policy instruments or domestic social and economic arrangements that are difficult to sustain individually amidst globalisation (Mittelman 2000: 116–30). The resistance model thus emphasises concern with non-economic or social values like distribution and social justice as the main driving force for regionalism, in contrast to the basic model of open regionalism that emphasises the search for efficiency and competitiveness as a key driving force. Although systemic forces – globalisation – do come into the picture, the response to them – resistance regionalism – is mediated through the domestic political economy.

Legitimacy is usually an underlying concern for policymakers contemplating this form of regionalism (Hveem 2000: 75–8; Mittelman 2000:

116–30). Governments, deriving political legitimacy from their capacity to undertake traditional social responsibilities for the societies they govern, may be compelled to turn to regional collective action as the only viable option to maintain national social/economic arrangements like the welfare state apparatus (Hirst and Thompson 1996: 162). Globalisation arguably makes such arrangements more costly to maintain at the national level. Kurzer, for instance, suggests that the future of national social democratic economic systems and re-distributive policies in European countries lies in a European regional project (Kurzer 1993: 254).

Notwithstanding the theoretical possibility of the resistance model, most instances of regionalism in the world economy today are examples of open regionalism, including the European Union (Mittelman 2000: 126).[15] Nevertheless, there is always the possibility of a dialectical process emerging out of globalisation to challenge the neoliberal trend in regionalism. The resistance model may consequently emerge as an empirical feature as regional projects originally designed to engage fully with globalisation are themselves challenged by domestic groups suffering the effects of regional liberalisation, particularly if social protection or compensatory measures are unavailable as a result of neoliberal approaches to market liberalisation (Higgott 2000: 80–1). Neoliberal regionalism consequently may challenge the authority and legitimacy of governments under these conditions. In such instances, governments may attempt to withdraw from the regionalist project, or alternatively seek to change the project's original terms and conditions. The tendency to use regionalism to ride on globalisation may not be a lasting one (Hveem 2000: 71). Regionalism should, therefore, not be viewed only in static terms as the outcome of a one-off decision to cooperate. New forms of regionalism could emerge from what was originally a neoliberal project, especially if the re-negotiation option is adopted rather than outright abandonment of the project.

Although offering an alternative to the model of open regionalism through emphasising the domestic legitimacy concerns of governments, the resistance model unfortunately imposes a separation of economics and politics by conceptualising growth or efficiency (economics), the primary goal of open regionalism, and legitimacy (politics) as opposed to one another. This is because the analysis of domestic politics in the resistance model does not extend to uncover the bases of legitimacy. Instead, this model adopts a somewhat Euro-centric understanding of legitimacy based on the European welfare state. If we explore the dynamics of political legitimacy in other settings, we are likely to find that in certain political contexts, growth/efficiency and legitimacy may be closely interrelated, and complementary rather than opposed. Much, therefore, depends on the sources of political legitimacy in a particular society.

The ASEAN case illustrates this point particularly well. In this setting, it is the governments' ability to deliver material economic well-being, in addition to social and political stability, that accords them legitimacy, rather than representation and process as in liberal, western democracies (Castells 1992: 59–60; Alagappa 1995: 330; Stubbs 2001: 50). In these countries, high rates of economic growth not only satisfy mass aspirations to material well-being they also allow elites to maintain their right to rule (Case 1996: 18). In such instances, the presumed tension between legitimacy and growth/efficiency is either relieved or, at least, reduced. Concern with legitimacy could thus entrench open regionalist projects if these contribute to growth, rather than result in challenges to them. Clearly, we need to pay closer attention to domestic state–society relations that help us to identify what the bases of legitimacy are, and the conditions under which growth or efficiency considerations prevail over distributive agendas, and vice versa.

Conceptual gains from the economic realist perspective on IPE

As already noted, the two models of regionalism offer a limited treatment of the *political* relationship between states and markets (both the domestic and the global market) as well as between states themselves. In open regionalism, global market forces are taken as a given and are regarded as benign, conferring benefits on all states in a positive-sum manner. State actors engage in regionalism because it is an *efficient* means of facilitating the integration of the national economy with the global economy. In the context of this book's study of AFTA, this model cannot explain why the ASEAN governments opted to make a distinction between foreign and domestic-owned capital in regional investment liberalisation, which is clearly an attempt to block the workings of (global) market forces, thereby contradicting the model of open regionalism. The resistance model, in contrast, explains regionalism as an attempt to block global market forces. This model is similarly unable to explain why the privileging of domestic-owned capital in AFTA's investment programme was only temporary and partial. How do other theoretical perspectives fare in modelling the relationship between globalisation and regionalism?

Alternative theoretical approaches – structuralism and economic realism in IPE – would dispute the liberal reading of the international economic order. Both these perspectives regard the global economy as an inherently political space in which economic interactions and activities reflect redistributive, zero-sum games (Barry Jones 1995: 19–43). By doing so, both perspectives allow for the possibility of human agency, as actors try and manipulate prevailing patterns of economic activity and economic relations in order to gain an increasing share of the benefits of global market activity. Nonetheless, the structuralist perspective is rejected as a useful theoretical model for this study because of its strong element of economic determinism. Actions and outcomes in international politics are driven by the logic of global capitalism, with the state acting as the instrument of capital. Although states are considered in analyses, they are not seen as political communities in their own right but merely as constituent units of a world capitalistic system (Hoogvelt 1997: 8). Domestic considerations and priorities stemming from domestic political constituencies are marginalised in structuralist approaches, which tend to focus almost exclusively on social groups derived from the capitalist mode of production – capital and labour, whether national or transnational – while ignoring other social groups that are significant in a number of ASEAN countries, ethnic groups for instance. Ethnicity often gives rise to vertical cleavages within capital and labour groups.[16]

On the other hand, the economic realist perspective offers greater scope for our analysis. Its view of nation-states as independent political communities, notwithstanding their interdependent relations with other states and with non-state actors, is one that accords with much real world dynamics (Gilpin 1987: 46). One of its central arguments is that 'states seek to influence markets to their own individual advantage', making the geographic location of economic activities their leading concern (Gilpin 1987: 47–9).[17] This implies that governments are likely to marshal power in an attempt to interfere in global markets to attain the interests of their respective states in competition with other states, or in response to non-state actors such as TNCs in the global system. For smaller, less powerful states, this can occur through cooperation between similarly situated states, for instance, in much the same way that alliance formation meets the shared strategic interests of a group of states vis-à-vis other state(s). This particular view of agency in the international political economy concurs with classical realist thinking. Morgenthau, for instance, acknowledged that states have the potential to transform the international system 'through the workmanlike manipulation of the perennial forces that have shaped the past as they will the future' (Morgenthau 1948/85: 12).[18] Economic realism recognises, therefore, that state actors can attempt to, and often do, manipulate inter-state politics to try and influence some aspect of the international political economy. While the actual success of such agendas may be limited, especially in the case of developing countries, nevertheless by allowing for the possibility of purposeful action, the economic realist perspective introduces a more realistic notion of politics into liberal frameworks of regionlism.

Modifying understandings of open regionalism: the FDI variant

As it was noted previously, the economic realist perspective offers valuable insights into the globalisation–regionalism relationship based on the notion that there is room for 'purposeful action to alter or transform prevailing patterns of economic capability and advantage' (Barry Jones 1995: 31). This point of view suggests that even in the case of open regionalism where governments seek to integrate their economies with the global economy, governments may be using regionalism in a purposeful manner to manipulate particular aspects of globalisation processes to benefit the state and its society, or particular members of the political community. It encompasses the idea that governments are not always totally helpless in the face of globalisation, and may find the space to engage in actions through cooperation that alter or interfere with global market outcomes in certain desired ways.

Mittelman (2000: 133) alludes to this when he suggests that the logic of global capital, namely its tendency to engage in regional production, offers nation-states an incentive to collaborate 'to attain market shares and augment trading and investment opportunities'. Regionalism, thus, presents one means to help re-direct beneficial global capital to the region in question through the carrot of the single regional market. As the previous discussion has shown, corporate actors are likely to respond positively to the presence of regional markets when deciding where to invest. In such instances, open regionalism is driven less by narrower concerns with economic efficiency and more by concerns with attracting FDI, which is a key source of economic growth for many countries. It is an agenda that is likely to appeal to developing countries.

Governments may respond to the structural power of transnational or global production capital[19] by actively using regionalism to attract new production capital to the region and through the process to individual national economies. Developing countries, usually with limited indigenous capabilities for global production, often look to attracting TNCs that do possess these assets to their respective economies. In a situation where FDI can theoretically locate in a variety of sites, developing countries will want to prevent the potential loss of these wealth-creating assets owned by TNCs to other locations. TNCs may not be involved in direct lobbying or bargaining with governments, but policymakers are likely to make policies with this thought – the need to attract or retain global capital – in mind. Although this may be accomplished through providing a more liberal national regulatory environment for investors, market size and access to large regional markets are among the main criteria now influencing the decision about where to invest.

Engaging in regional cooperation, thus, allows governments to exploit global capital's functional preference for regional markets. Policymakers are likely to respond with a policy of regionalism to external developments that are seen as having the potential to divert investment away from the national economy, provided they recognise the potential of regionalism in retaining or attracting production capital. They may become aware of the potential of regionalism as a magnet for FDI once they realise that foreign investors are registering strong interest in, and are actually investing in regionalist projects established elsewhere. This argument is in line with the contagion explanation of regionalism highlighted in the previous chapter.

Regionalist projects driven primarily by the desire to attract global capital are instances of open regionalism to the extent that they are about engaging with globalisation processes. In that sense both economic realist and liberal theoretical perspectives provide similar readings of regionalism. These contrasting perspectives offer distinct views on two issues, however – the precise form or features of the regionalist project and its likely future trajectory.

Regionalist projects designed primarily to attract FDI need not necessarily encompass the strong neoliberal, deregulatory agenda often associated with neoliberal regionalist projects driven by efficiency concerns. The overriding concern in the former is more broadly with economic growth.[20] Efficiency is attained to the extent that the incoming capital operates efficiently, but the regionalist project is not necessarily underpinned by neoliberal ideas nor associated with a strong neoliberal agenda. There is substantial empirical evidence that foreign investors privilege other factors above the policy regime when making investment decisions, although they would clearly prefer less rather than more government intervention in markets (Walter 2000). Provided key areas of economic life that are crucial for foreign investors are relatively unrestricted, such as trade flows and financial regulations on profit repatriation, investors appear able to live with some degree of government restriction in markets.[21] Regionalism primarily motivated by the desire to draw in FDI may therefore display only limited neoliberal characteristics. These projects are best termed 'embedded neoliberal projects'.[22] While they are, nonetheless, instances of open regionalism designed to remain engaged with global market forces, these projects are entirely consistent with a degree of government intervention in markets.

An economic realist reading of open regionalism also suggests that the prospects for extending the regionalist project to include new members will be contingent. Since regionalism is directed at offering global capital a distinct functional space of production, extending the project to new members could weaken the distinctiveness of the original regional project. This will be the case especially if the new member itself is a very attractive site for FDI, potentially able to draw in substantial amounts of incoming FDI with limited spillover benefits to other members in the project through vertical and horizontal production linkages. Although there is always an element of competition among the members of a regional project for incoming FDI, the presence of complementarities among members usually ensures that some form of balance is achieved. In contrast, regional projects involving a group of small countries may not necessarily benefit from the membership of a large country such as China, which itself effectively offers foreign capital a 'regional' site of production by virtue of its size and wide-ranging industrial complementarities. There is a strong possibility that foreign investors may prefer to establish production networks within the Chinese territory but trade the resultant output to the other members of the regional scheme, thus defeating the purpose of the regional exercise for its original members. The benefits of extending FDI-centred regional projects to new members are not unequivocal, unlike the case of efficiency-driven neoliberal regionalism.

Although the dominant open regionalist model emphasises globally oriented capital in analysis, with foreign capital a key focus in the FDI variant, domestic capital is thus far invisible. There is little attempt to consider the relationship between governments or political/state actors and fractions of capital distinguished by their ownership – domestic- or foreign-owned capital. The conventional focus in the literature has usually been on segments of capital distinguished by their market orientation, either towards the domestic market or the international market.[23] Although it may be increasingly difficult to distinguish business in terms of its nationality – the 'who is us?' question posed by Robert Reich (1991: 304) – such a distinction, nevertheless, remains relevant in particular political contexts where policymakers and politicians do consciously make this distinction for various political reasons. In these settings, and this is especially true for developing countries where domestic capital is usually not as well developed as foreign capital but often plays a crucial social/political role, governments may well respond to globalisation in ways that attempt to preserve and nurture domestic capital. Clearly, we need to consider theoretically plausible models of regionalism in which domestic capital is accorded analytical priority.

Developmental regionalism: privileging domestic capital

Making an analytical distinction between foreign and domestic capital reveals a fourth model of regionalism, what I call 'developmental' regionalism. Deriving from the notion of the developmental state, developmental regionalism encapsulates the developmental state idea of state intervention in markets to promote national development agendas,[24] in this case by adopting an approach to regionalism through which to nurture emerging domestic firms to eventually become internationally competitive. This is achieved through two instruments: one, the expanded regional market generated through inter-state cooperation and two, temporary protection or privileges for domestic capital in this expanded market. According to strategic trade theory from the international economics discipline, both measures can help to secure benefits for domestic firms over their foreign competitors.[25]

Insights from Paul Krugman's 'import protection as export promotion' strategic trade model reveal that when a domestic firm is given a privileged position in the home market, it enjoys an advantage in scale over foreign rivals that enables the firm to realise 'learning by doing' benefits (Krugman 1984). A larger protected home market offers greater dynamic scale and learning effects to the privileged firm. Thus, by employing selective protection or privileges for group members only and market expansion through regional cooperation, governments can use regionalism to help develop competitive domestic industries to survive global market competition and eventually become world market leaders, at least in theory.[26] Developmental regionalism is clearly in the economic realist tradition, encompassing as it does the idea of state activism in the international system, in this instance through inter-state collaboration to manipulate economic activity to serve the perceived interests of the state.

We may regard the concern with domestic capital as a preoccupation with distribution, or with the selective allocation of economic benefits including rents to domestic businesses, in contrast with the generalised growth/efficiency imperative that underpins open regionalism. Nevertheless, concern with growth is not entirely absent in developmental regionalism. Rather, the growth imperative is infused with distributive concerns. Developmental regionalism is, therefore, not about resisting globalisation completely, but neither is it about complete acquiescence to global market forces. Instead, it encompasses a period of temporary and limited resistance to aspects of globalisation through which attempts are made to enable domestic businesses to eventually participate in global market activities. This model of regionalism, therefore, allows us to consider departures from open regionalism as representing a distinct approach to regionalism rather than merely as inconsistencies in open regionalism or as instances of protectionism.

The question that remains, however, is why political actors would seek to nurture *domestic* capital. Why would they prefer to maximise the wealth of a segment of society instead of maximising the wealth and efficiency of society as a whole through full embrace of global corporations, arguably the primary source of wealth creation in the global economy? In fact, we should extend this question to also ask why and under what conditions state actors would opt for a form of regionalism that privileges FDI instead of the neoliberal or the developmental versions.

A strict realist interpretation would see state authorities seeking consciously to manipulate patterns of international economic activity for strategic, power-political purposes, and may arguably apply to the interactions of the major powers and potential strategic rivals like the US, Japan or the EU. It applies less well in other settings, developing countries included. The latter are more likely to be driven by concerns rooted in the domestic political economy rather than by a concern with inter-state power political competition. This line of thinking is not such a radical departure from the realist notion of national security. Security for developing states is generally framed in terms of the security of *domestic* political institutions and governing regimes (Ayoob 1995: 8). The realist tradition, after all, does not completely ignore the domestic level unlike its neorealist counterpart.[27] As such, it is conceptually consistent to argue that an economic realist external orientation is underpinned or driven by domestic regime security imperatives more specifically, and by domestic political determinants more broadly. This book, therefore, argues for attention to be paid to the domestic level in explaining the turn to regionalism. Although the FDI variant of open regionalism and developmental regionalism are both informed by economic realist insights, analysis moves beyond the strict realist conception of state interests in terms of security and survival of the state in inter-state power political competition. Instead, these interests are defined primarily in relation to domestic political dynamics. The question, of course, is how the domestic and international levels are related, to which the next section turns.

Incorporating the domestic level

Political actors everywhere are usually confronted by the choice of adopting policies that maximise wealth in society as a whole or that benefit particularistic interests; in other words, between concern over growth or over domestic distributive priorities. Distribution is defined in this book as the conscious allocation of income, rents and other economic benefits by governments to particular individuals, groups or firms who would otherwise not have received these gains through the workings of the free market.[28] Policy responses to external events, including choices about regionalism, are quite likely to involve tension between the growth and distributive imperatives. In most domestic settings, economic policies, including foreign economic policies, are influenced by these basic priorities, with policymakers driven by whichever goal best secures their chances of remaining in power. Which priority dominates – growth or distribution – will depend on the political costs to incumbent leaders of adopting policy choices that emphasise/de-emphasise one or the other goal, and thus, will be contingent on prevailing economic as well as political circumstances. It will also depend on the nature of political legitimacy.

This is best illustrated by exploring more closely the case of the ASEAN states, which may be characterised as elite governance political systems where political elites are preoccupied with maintaining both the prevailing regime or political system and themselves in power.[29] Many developing countries share similar preoccupations.[30]

Conceptualising domestic politics in ASEAN

Although political systems in ASEAN during much of the 1990s ranged from democracies to semi-democracies and authoritarian regimes, all the ASEAN countries shared the basic characteristics of elite governance political systems where political power was largely in the hands of elites despite the presence of mechanisms for citizen participation (McCargo 1998: 127).[31] The political elite was, however, not completely insulated from domestic society, and needed to respond to concerns arising from this level in order to maintain elite rule and its legitimacy, which remained fragile throughout the 1990s. In such settings, political elites depend on two key policy instruments – growth and distribution – to maintain themselves in power and to ensure stability of the domestic regime or political system.

On the one hand, political elites need the support of citizens to maintain their right to rule and to ensure political order, and this is largely achieved through creating material wealth for citizens – the notion of performance legitimacy, which remains relevant to date (Alagappa 1995: 330; Stubbs 2001). This explains the preoccupation of political leaders with securing and maintaining key sources of growth in the economy, of which FDI is pre-eminent in ASEAN. On the other hand, elite rule is also sustained by unity and accommodation between members of the elite/governing coalition (Haggard and Kaufman 1997). Political elites selectively distribute economic benefits to their elite partners as a primary means to achieve elite unity.

By the 1990s, it was the accommodation between the political elite and an emerging domestic business class that was crucial in much of ASEAN. The material and other forms of political support provided by domestic businesses helped incumbent political elites maintain their power base, while the former in turn received economic privileges through preferential policies instituted by the latter. In addition, domestic businesses were often privileged because they helped political actors fulfil broader social equity goals in society. This was especially clear in the Malaysian and Indonesian cases, where political legitimacy also rests on the capacity of the state to develop respectively an ethnic Malay and indigenous Indonesian domestic capital class, particularly to offset the dominance of ethnic Chinese capital.[32] There is also a wider distributive agenda in parts of ASEAN that may lead policymakers to privilege non-elite or broad social groups in policy choices, provided these represent key constituencies for ruling elites and vital to sustaining elite rule and the stability of the regime (see Figure 1.1).

The importance of the distributive agenda in maintaining elite unity does not imply that economic growth is unimportant in this process. Even though economic distress is not the primary source of factional or inter-elite conflicts, it is likely to exacerbate them. Fewer internal divisions within the ruling elite are likely when economic growth is strong. Declining economic performance often disrupts the political bargain rulers typically forge with other elite groups in the society (Case 1996: 17–20). Under these circumstances, political elites are unable to provide their elite partners with the basic conditions that support wealth creation, while the latter become unable or unwilling to continue to offer material and political support to the ruling incumbents. The end result is a weakening of elite cohesion and the power base of incumbent elites, while opposition groups gain from the defection of business and other elites

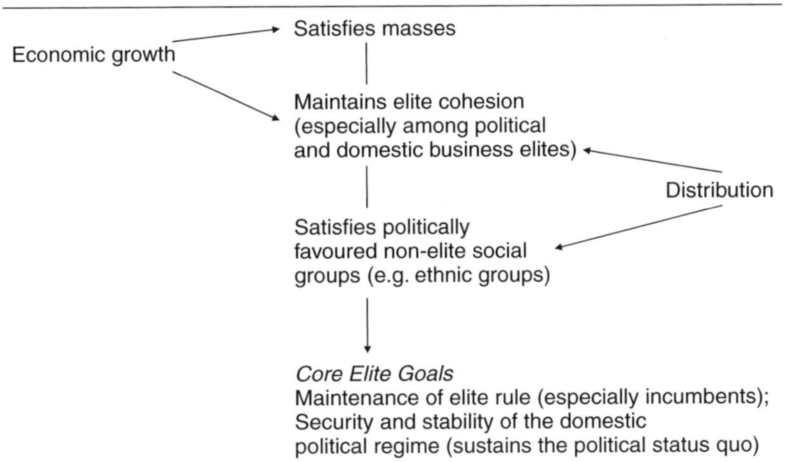

Figure 1.1 The role of growth and distribution in elite governance political systems.

previously aligned with the incumbents (Haggard and Kaufman 1997: 267–8).

The challenges posed to ruling elites by declining economic performance have been amply demonstrated in the case of Indonesia and Malaysia. In Indonesia, political turmoil and the ousting of incumbent ruling elites quickly followed financial and economic troubles as a result of the Asian financial crisis that began in mid-1997. Malaysia too has witnessed substantial elite cleavages as a result of the financial crisis, although an emergent mass challenge to the ruling incumbents has been contained (Khoo 2000). In short, while the selective distribution of economic benefits to elite partners is a primary means of maintaining elite cohesion, broad-based economic growth is not unimportant. Political elites often have to engage in difficult balancing acts in their policy choices, particularly when these involve significant trade-offs between the growth and distributive imperatives, or between maximising wealth and efficiency in society as a whole and maximising the wealth of a segment of society.

In much of ASEAN, foreign capital remains a key source of growth and exports, particularly in the high value-added and advanced sectors of the economy that virtually all governments are increasingly targeting, although domestic-owned firms are not entirely absent from this picture. A simplifying, though not unreasonable assumption made in this book is that the foreign capital governments are targeting is internationally-oriented and thus in favour of liberal market policies that maximise growth. On the other hand, the distributive imperative in ASEAN, where it exists, is usually aimed at privileging domestic-owned capital or segments of it that are also close allies of the political elite. Domestic capital may be either internationally oriented or emerging/inward focused. To the extent that both foreign investors and internationally oriented domestic-owned capital are likely to favour similar types of policies, essentially growth-centred, liberal market policies, little or no conflict should be expected between the growth and distributive imperatives even if internationally oriented domestic capital is closely allied to the political/state elite. It is when the political elite is closely allied to inward-focused or emerging domestic capital that the tension between growth and distribution becomes pronounced. Since this segment of domestic capital is not as well developed as foreign capital, policymakers may well adopt measures to protect, preserve and/or nurture emerging domestic capital vis-à-vis foreign capital if the former is to survive direct competition with the latter.

While government policies for distributing economic benefits to politically important individuals, firms or groups do not necessarily mean that the economy is on course towards economic decline, distributive policies may involve trade-offs with the growth imperative. Trade-offs are especially likely when economic rents are created through artificial restrictions on market competition by governments, which could undermine growth (Bhagwati 1982). When distributive policies involve restricting the domestic operations of foreign (or internationally oriented) firms, growth prospects may be weakened if the latter are significant agents of growth. Growth need not, however, be disrupted if the extent of distribution is limited, either to particular sectors or in terms of time. On the other hand, governments may find it necessary to limit their distributive agenda during times of economic distress, or expected economic hardship, which will affect citizens in general through unemployment, for instance, as well as threaten elite unity (Haggard and Kaufman 1997). By threatening the political future of incumbent political elites, economic decline, or the prospect of it, often compels governments to restore the conditions favouring growth, particularly since growth will allow distribution to take place with fewer costs than under conditions of generalised economic decline.

Although the discussion thus far has been framed in terms of how governments may be driven by concerns related to capital, it is important to note that these concerns are not derived from the logic of global capitalism, nor in relation to freeing up the market for business in some technical sense, but instead stem from domestically derived political priorities. Although the book focuses on the relationship between *capital* and state/political elites in explaining particular outcomes in regionalism, this is not to suggest a Marxist or neo-Marxist conception of capital and of state–capital relations. The discussion on the specific case of ASEAN illustrates how the relationship between state and capital in the ASEAN countries is one conditioned by the domestic political imperatives of elite rule rather than the imperative of capitalist production.[33]

Conclusion

The analytical framework adopted in this study that combines the economic realist perspective on IPE with a model of domestic politics offers substantial analytical purchase over liberal perspectives in explaining regionalism as an outcome of globalisation. The value of economic realism as a theoretical tool comes from its recognition that states continue to matter, and more importantly, that the governments of these states can, and often do, consciously manipulate inter-state relations to try and intervene in the international political economy in line with domestic interests. Regionalism can be interpreted as one such instrument for states to pool their resources in order to influence the international political economy. By using the economic realist theoretical perspective, it was possible to, first, identify two variants of open regionalism, and second, to advance a fourth ideal-type model of the globalisation–regionalism relationship in addition to the two existing ideal-types in the literature, namely developmental regionalism (see Table 1.1). These four distinct models differ in terms of how they engage with globalisation, their relationship with different segments of capital and with other social groups, whether driven by growth, efficiency or distributive concerns, and their key features.

Despite according attention to the systemic level, and the privileging of globalisation as a key explanation for regionalism, it is clear that attention must be paid to the domestic level as well. A key assumption of the study is that governments respond in the first instance to domestic political constituencies on whom they rely for political support and for their legitimacy. Therefore, it is dynamics operating at the domestic level that determine which of the four ideal-type models of regionalism outlined in this chapter will emerge in response to globalisation.

Hence, the central argument advanced in this chapter is that the type of regionalism that emerges as a result of globalisation is mediated by domestic political economy dynamics centred on the tension between growth/efficiency concerns on the one hand, and distributive priorities on the other, even in the case of regionalist projects that seek engagement with globalisation. Political and state actors interpret external events and developments – globalisation – through lenses grounded in domestic political priorities, which also influence their responses to these external impulses, including their particular approaches to regionalism. Drawing on this central argument, the chapter concludes with three specific propositions with regard to AFTA, which are developed in detail in the rest of the book.

The first proposition is that AFTA is likely to encompass the features of *both* open regionalism and developmental regionalism due to the political significance of *both* foreign and domestic capital in the domestic political economy of member countries. Although both forms of regionalism are

Table 1.1 Four models of the globalisation–regionalism relationship

Ideal-type models	*Relationship to globalisation*	*Key driving force*	*Key features*	*Relationship to foreign and domestic capital*
Neoliberal regionalism [A variant of open regionalism]	Engages with globalisation	Concern with efficiency	No new barriers to non-members imposed; Full deregulatory agenda contemplated; Also associated with agenda to reduce government's role in all aspects of economic activity; Hence the neoliberal credentials	Does not distinguish between foreign and domestic-owned capital; All globally oriented capital privileged
FDI model [A variant of open regionalism]	Engages with globalisation	Concern with attracting FDI, which is a crucial source of growth; Efficiency may be a primary or secondary concern	No new barriers to non-members imposed; Deregulation agenda could be extensive or limited; Ambivalent with regard to government's role in the economy; More likely to be an instance of embedded neoliberal regionalism	Foreign capital (FDI) is targeted
Resistance model	Resists globalisation	Concern with social/ distributive issues	Seeks insulation from global market forces; Dominant agenda is social/ distributive.	Other social groups, apart from capital privileged, notably labour
Developmental regionalism	Engages globalisation eventually, though initially has a period of limited and temporary resistance to it	An initial concern with domestic distribution, with growth a long-run aim	Employs temporary protection of, or temporary privileges for domestic capital; Distribution is thus directed towards domestic capital	Domestic capital privileged

the outcome of globalisation, and driven by a concern with economic growth and engaging with globalisation, domestic priorities centred on nurturing domestic capital infuse the growth imperative in the case of developmental regionalism, leading to departures from open regionalism in the design of regional cooperation. The balance between the two approaches to regionalism depends on the cost to ruling elites of privileging either foreign or domestic-owned capital vis-à-vis the other. Chapters 3 and 4 examine these arguments in detail.

The second proposition is that the distributive imperative may be so overwhelming in particular instances, despite initial commitments to cooperate driven by the growth dynamic, that governments opt to shield affected elements of domestic businesses from the liberalisation required under both open regionalism and developmental regionalism. Sectors most likely to be shielded are those in which politically important businesses are prominent. Disputes among regional members are likely to emerge, as governments renege on their original commitments as they attempt to balance growth and distributive concerns. Chapter 5 elaborates on this proposition.

This leads to the final proposition that implementation becomes a political process rather than a technical one of complying with commitments already made earlier. This requires some form of regional mechanism to address the tension between growth and distribution and to enable cooperation to be sustained and advanced rather than abandoned. To develop this third proposition further, which is discussed in detail in Chapter 6, additional theoretical insights are drawn from the IR literature on compliance bargaining and international institutions.

Before proceeding to discuss these propositions in the rest of the book, Chapter 2 provides the empirical narrative of AFTA. It describes in detail the unfolding of the AFTA project between 1991 when the initial decision to establish a free trade area in ASEAN was made and 2002, the eve of completion of the project's first stage involving free trade in manufactured goods. It highlights major trends in AFTA, as well as identifies puzzling aspects of the regional project, issues that were first raised in the introductory chapter and which the remaining chapters attempt to explain.

2 The unfolding of a regional economic cooperation project: AFTA, 1991–2002

Despite predictions to the contrary, the AFTA project was substantially advanced since its formal inception in January 1992 through the acceleration of its pace and widening of its liberalisation agenda. Nevertheless, the AFTA story becomes more ambiguous when the project's implementation record is assessed. Notwithstanding the ambitious commitments made in all three of its component programmes, namely the CEPT, AFAS and the AIA, implementation was at times problematic as one or another government attempted to withhold participation in certain AFTA programmes or backtracked on liberalisation commitments already made. This led to a number of disagreements among member governments, of which three disputes – over liberalising trade in agriculture, automobiles and petrochemicals – have been the most notable thus far. Also noteworthy was the initial decision to treat ASEAN and foreign investors differently in the AIA, a decision that was eventually overturned after three years. As already noted in the introductory chapter, this was somewhat puzzling given that member governments were using the carrot of the single regional market to attract foreign investment to the region. This chapter provides a detailed description of these trends and developments in AFTA between 1991 and 2002, before the rest of the book takes up the task of explaining why AFTA evolved in the way it did during this period.

Ambitious commitments

The AFTA project can be divided into three phases for analytical purposes (Table 2.1). Phase 1 from 1991 through 1995 is best described as the initial consolidation phase of AFTA. Although an initial agenda was worked out through a series of inter-governmental consultations, some member governments soon went back on some of their initial commitments as a result of domestic political changes and growing domestic business opposition to AFTA. This caused considerable confusion over the project's future. Nevertheless, by the end of 1995, the ASEAN governments had not only reaffirmed the free trade goals of AFTA, they also agreed to hasten its implementation and expand its scope by committing

Table 2.1 Three phases of the AFTA project, 1991–2002

PHASE 1 (1991–95) Initial consolidation phase	*PHASE 2 (1996–97) Expansion phase*	*PHASE 3 (1998–2002) Financial crisis & post-crisis consolidation phase*
Initial agenda (January 1992): free trade area by 2008 Tariffs on manufactured products targeted at 0–5%; Excludes unprocessed agricultural products and services; Staggered start date for implementation later allowed. **Consolidation of AFTA (December 1995): project acceleration and detailed programmes adopted** New deadline is 2003, with a 0–5% tariff target; Implementation start date fixed for 1 January 1994; Rules for elimination of Temporary Exclusion List adopted; Programmes to reduce/remove non-tariff barriers and in trade facilitation. **Consolidation of AFTA (December 1995): agenda expansion** Unprocessed agricultural products; Services; Industrial cooperation; Investment; Intellectual property rights; Dispute resolution.	**Services** Based on ASEAN Framework Agreement on Services (AFAS); First round of services negotiations begun in seven priority sectors; 1st package of commitments: December 1997; 2nd package: December 1998. **ASEAN Industrial Cooperation (AICO) scheme formally launched (1996)** Requires minimum 30% national equity; Minimum of 2 firms from 2 ASEAN countries required to participate; Firms must be involved in joint industrial production or the pooling/sharing of raw and intermediate materials. **The ASEAN Investment Area (AIA) initiative** Initial negotiations. **Unprocessed agricultural products** Negotiations to iron out differences among members and to develop suitable modalities for liberalisation. **Agreement on Dispute Settlement Mechanism adopted (1996)** **Trade facilitation programmes** Customs surcharges eliminated by 1996.	**Amendments to the CEPT scheme** New flexible deadline for 0–5% tariff rate set at 2002 (1998 decision), although formal deadline remains 2003; Zero tariff AFTA set for 2010 (initially 2015) for original members (1999 decision); Notification procedures for CEPT changes adopted in October 1998; Protocol for modification of original CEPT concessions adopted in November 2000. **Short-term incentives to enhance the investment climate*** National offers coordinated in an ASEAN package. **Investment: AIA framework agreement signed (October 1998)** Initially, full national treatment and market access by 2010 in manufacturing for ASEAN investors; For non-ASEAN or foreign investors, full investment privileges to be accorded by 2020. **Revisions to the AIA: 1999** Full market access and national treatment by 2003 in manufacturing, for ASEAN investors, and by 2010 in other selected sectors; Foreign investors accorded these privileges in 2020.

Table 2.1 (Continued)

PHASE 1 (1991–95) Initial consolidation phase	*PHASE 2 (1996–97) Expansion phase*	*PHASE 3 (1998–2002) Financial crisis & post-crisis consolidation phase*
		Revisions to the AIA: 2001 Foreign investors to receive full market access and national treatment in non-manufacturing sectors by 2010, in line with ASEAN investors.
		Agriculture Protocol adopted in 1999 on liberalising sensitive agricultural products.
		Services Second round of negotiations completed (1999–2001); Third round (2002–04) launched.
		Other framework agreements and programmes adopted to support AFTA: On goods in transit (December 1998); Mutual recognition arrangements (December 1998); On electronic commerce (November 2000); Trade facilitation programmes.
		Industrial cooperation Certain AICO criteria relaxed.

Note
* Not directly a part of the AFTA project but, nevertheless, impinge on AFTA.

unprocessed agricultural products, services and investment to joint liberalisation. Phase 2, the expansion phase of AFTA covers the years 1996 and 1997 and is the period when detailed negotiations on agriculture, services and investment liberalisation, as well as on industrial cooperation got underway. Phase 3 from 1998 through 2002 represents the financial crisis and post-crisis consolidation period when new initiatives were undertaken in response to the crisis and existing initiatives were further consolidated.

The initial consolidation phase (1991–95)

In June 1991, the then Thai Prime Minister, Anand Panyarachun, publicly advocated the idea of an ASEAN free trade area. Two months earlier, in April 1991, Anand had first broached the idea with the Singapore Prime Minister, Mr Goh Chok Thong, and later pressed the idea on his other ASEAN counterparts over the next few months (Stubbs 2000: 304). The idea was then endorsed as an ASEAN project by the ASEAN foreign ministers in July 1991 and later at the twenty-third ASEAN Economic Ministers' meeting (AEM)[1] in October, the same year. The economic ministers agreed that all member countries should subscribe to the establishment of AFTA simultaneously, so that within fifteen years a single regional market where internal tariffs were between 0 and 5 per cent would become a reality. The instrument that would operationalise AFTA was the Common Effective Preferential Tariff (CEPT) scheme. The twenty-third AEM agreed that a framework agreement should be drafted under which specific areas of cooperation could eventually be negotiated. The economic ministers then tasked the Senior Economic Officials Meeting (SEOM) of ASEAN to work out the form and substance of the framework agreement to be signed at the forthcoming Fourth ASEAN Summit in Singapore in January 1992.[2]

In each country, discussions about AFTA were confined to a small group, as leaders, ministers and officials tried to gauge the minimum level of commitments they could credibly make (Stubbs 2000: 304). By the time of the Fourth Summit, senior officials from the economics ministries in the various ASEAN governments had together worked out preliminary details of the two agreements that would launch AFTA and provide its operational workings. The official summit declaration, namely the *Singapore Declaration* set out the broad areas for ASEAN cooperation in the security, political and economic fields (ASEAN 1992a). The *Framework Agreement on Enhancing Economic Cooperation* (ASEAN 1992b) and the *Agreement on the Common Effective Preferential Tariff Scheme for the ASEAN Free Trade Area* (the CEPT Agreement) (ASEAN 1992c) focused specifically on the principles and procedures for establishing AFTA within fifteen years. The last two agreements, both signed in January 1992, collectively constitute what may be regarded as the foundational agreements of AFTA.

Considerable ambiguity in the CEPT scheme

The foundational agreements stipulated that tariffs on intra-ASEAN trade in manufactured goods including capital goods and processed agricultural products would be lowered to between 0 and 5 per cent within fifteen years starting from January 1993. Raw materials, unprocessed agricultural products and services were not covered in the original agreements. An ASEAN content of at least 40 per cent was required for products to qualify for preferential tariffs. While Anand's original proposal had suggested a ten-year time frame for the realisation of AFTA, which Singapore and Malaysia supported, the time frame was extended to fifteen years to take account of objections from Indonesia and the Philippines. The Indonesian and Philippine governments had been concerned that some of their domestic industries were too weak and had requested for special and differential treatment under AFTA.[3]

Although the CEPT was the primary instrument to implement AFTA, its ten articles provided only general guidelines on tariff reduction schedules while also allowing substantial flexibility in the tariff reduction exercise (ASEAN 1992c). For instance, while Article 2 specified that products to be included in the CEPT were to be identified on a sectoral or product group basis at the Harmonised System (HS) 6-digit level, exclusions at the HS 8- or 9-digit level for specific products were permitted. No limits were placed on the number of products that might be excluded in this manner. Despite allowing for a review of products excluded from tariff liberalisation after eight years, no further details were provided on what should happen after the review.

Article 4 of the CEPT agreement outlining the tariff reduction schedule reveals the considerable flexibility built into AFTA. For products with tariff rates above 20 per cent, ASEAN members were called to initially harmonise internal tariffs to 20 per cent or less within a five- to eight-year time frame beginning from 1 January 1993, with each country working out its own schedule of reduction. Although the CEPT agreement advised members to adopt an annual rate of reduction, this was ultimately left to individual members. Subsequent tariff reductions from 20 per cent to 0–5 per cent were to be undertaken within a seven-year time frame, making a total fifteen-year implementation period. In this instance, a minimum annual rate of reduction of 5 per cent was specified in the CEPT Agreement. The tariff reduction schedule for products whose prevailing tariff rates were already below 20 per cent on 1 January 1993 was left to individual governments to determine. These schedules were not to be binding on governments, but were merely indicative. The CEPT scheme thus displayed enormous flexibility including a very long implementation phase, especially for products whose initial tariffs were below 20 per cent. Although the CEPT did offer some guide to liberalising tariffs, the few details that it provided were somewhat hazy. No clear guidelines were provided for the elimination of quantitative restrictions and non-tariff barriers (NTBs) either. Article 5A of the CEPT merely stipulates that NTBs on products should be eliminated gradually within five years of the first CEPT tariff concession on those products.

It was only during the course of 1992 that additional implementation details were worked out, which were finalised at the third AFTA Council[4] meeting in December 1992, just one month before the 1 January 1993 start date for tariff liberalisation.[5] These details were contained in three documents published by the ASEAN Secretariat, namely the *Operational Procedures for CEPT*, *Rules of Origin for CEPT*, and *Interpretative Notes to the Agreement on the CEPT Scheme for AFTA* (ASEAN Secretariat 1993). The most important of these details were the fast track schedule for fifteen product groups, the normal track schedule for remaining manufactured goods, as well as the nature of exclusions allowed (Table 2.2). These schedules were, however, deemed to be indicative only, with member governments allowing a faster or slower rate of tariff reduction provided the targeted tariff rates were reached by the stipulated end dates (ASEAN Secretariat 1993: 4–5).

Despite the details of the CEPT scheme being firmed up during the course of 1992, the AFTA project remained a very flexible programme of trade liberalisation. For instance, while temporary exclusions were allowed

Table 2.2 Implementation details (1992) of the CEPT scheme

CEPT implementation (start date 1 January 1993 or 1 January 1996)[a]	*Target date for achieving 0–5% tariff rate*		*Exclusions allowed*
	Fast track[b]	*Normal track*	
Initial tariff rates above 20%	1 January 2003 (within 10 years)	Initially to 20% by 1 January 2001 or 1 January 1998 (within 5–8 years) Then to 0–5% by 1 January 2008 (within 7–10 years)	General exemptions[c] Temporary exclusions Permanent exemptions[d]
Initial tariff rates at or below 20%	1 January 2000 (within 7 years)	1 January 2003 (within 10 years)	

Source: Compiled from information in ASEAN Secretariat (1993: 3–4).

Notes

a Target dates to be reached on schedule, irrespective of start date.

b Covers 15 product items, namely vegetable oils, chemicals, fertiliser, rubber products, pulp and paper, wooden and rattan furniture, gems and jewellery products, cement, pharmaceuticals, plastics, leather products, textiles, ceramics and glass products, copper cathodes, electronics.

c To protect national security, public morals, human, animal or plant life/health; and to preserve articles of artistic, historic or archaeological value.

d Essentially for unprocessed agricultural products.

subject to a review after eight years, permanent exemptions were also possible. The idea behind the rather long eight-year period of temporary protection was to allow individual governments sufficient time to prepare their respective domestic industries for AFTA tariff reductions. There was, however, nothing to prevent member governments from continuing to exclude products after the eight-year temporary exclusion period, for instance by transferring products to the Permanent Exemption List (also called the Sensitive List). This extremely flexible arrangement added to the uncertainty inherent in the AFTA project.

Although tariff reductions were initially scheduled to begin on 1 January 1993, member countries were later allowed a grace period until January 1995 to begin their respective CEPT liberalisation programmes. The staggered approach had been adopted to assuage both Thailand and Indonesia whose governments had chosen to opt out of AFTA altogether for several of the fifteen categories of products designated for fast track tariff cuts.[6] These two governments thus planned to begin accelerated tariff reductions only from 1995, and to delay beginning normal track tariff reductions until between 1996 and 1999 (Table 2.3).[7] On the other hand, Malaysia and Singapore pledged to begin tariff reductions as scheduled on 1 January 1993. The Philippines was already committed to a unilateral programme of tariff reductions under Executive Order 470 that was to end in 1995, after which it would continue to reduce tariffs under the CEPT programme.

The AFTA project ground to a halt in 1993 despite the allowances made to ensure cooperation of all AFTA founding members. Malaysia and Singapore were unhappy with the staggered approach since that placed their domestic industries at a disadvantage.[8] Malaysia, in fact, considered delaying its AFTA tariff cuts until 1995, when all ASEAN

Table 2.3 AFTA tariff reduction start dates (adopted December 1992)

	Fast track		*Normal track*	
	Initial tariffs above 20%	*Initial tariffs at or below 20%*	*Initial tariffs above 20%*	*Initial tariffs at or below 20%*
Brunei	NA[a]	1995	1994	1996
Indonesia	1995	1995	1998	1996
Malaysia	1993	1993	1993	1993
Philippines	Unilateral[b]	Unilateral[b]	Unilateral[b]	Unilateral[b]
Singapore	1993	1993	NA[a]	1993
Thailand	1995	1995	1998	1999

Source: Compiled from information in ASEAN Secretariat (1993: 17–20).

Notes

a Not applicable, since there were no tariffs above 20 per cent.

b Until 1995.

countries were obliged to begin CEPT tariff reductions to ensure that Malaysian industries were not at an unfair disadvantage in AFTA.[9] The new Thai government of Prime Minister Chuan Leekpai elected in mid-1992 called for a 'transition period' for AFTA as Thai businesses began pressing the newly elected government to delay its AFTA commitments.[10] In Indonesia too, the commitment to AFTA began waning as ministers less committed to trade liberalisation were selected to the new cabinet announced by President Suharto in mid-March 1993 while protected businesses, especially the state-enterprise sector, also began pressing policymakers to rethink AFTA.

Nevertheless, by October 1993, senior officials in ASEAN had worked out a proposal to re-launch AFTA, with five of the six ASEAN countries now pledging to begin AFTA tariff cuts by 1 January 1994.[11] Thus, the staggered implementation programme was replaced in favour of a common start date, although a year later than originally scheduled. Member governments also agreed to include 41,147 tariff lines for liberalisation through a revised CEPT package for 1994, accounting for 88.3 per cent of their total tariff lines (ASEAN Secretariat 1993: 24).

Other serious problems remained despite the advances made in 1993 to kick-start the project. These included the lack of clear guidelines on how NTBs were to be reduced. NTBs were potentially a considerable stumbling block to forming a regional free trade area in ASEAN (Ravenhill 1995: 859). The most common NTBs in ASEAN were customs surcharges, technical measures, and domestic monopoly and licensing arrangements (Table 2.4). Many of the NTBs deriving from import licensing rules and state monopolies were found in the agricultural sector, which explains why the majority of business complaints about NTBs in ASEAN was directed at the agricultural rather than the manufacturing sector. In addition, non-harmonised customs classification and valuation systems also created

Table 2.4 Most prevalent non-tariff barriers in ASEAN

Non-tariff barriers (NTBs)[a]	*Number of tariff lines affected*
Customs surcharges	2,683
Additional charges	126
Single channel for imports (monopolistic practice)	65
State-trading administration (monopolistic practice)	10
Technical standards (technical measure)	568
Product characteristic requirements (technical measure)	407
Marketing requirements (technical measure)	3
Technical regulations (technical measure)	3

Source: ASEAN Secretariat (1995: 15).

Note

a Definitions of the various NTBs are found in ASEAN Secretariat (1995: 10–15).

opportunities for discrimination against imports (Chia 1998: 226). The institutional arrangements for the AFTA project were also inadequate in rule interpretation and dispute settlement, which, given the lack of detail in the foundational AFTA agreements were particularly necessary.[12] The preference in ASEAN for political rather than administrative or juridical arrangements for dispute settlement and problem resolution was seen as placing a substantial burden on ministerial agendas in AFTA, with the possibility that AFTA could become stalled in the process (Ravenhill 1995: 861).

Consolidating the AFTA project

In 1994 and 1995, economic ministers meeting at both Council and Ministerial levels substantially modified the AFTA programme. The leaders of ASEAN formally accepted these amendments at their fifth summit in Bangkok in December 1995 (ASEAN 1995a,b,c). Five improvements to AFTA were adopted.

First, the 0–5 per cent CEPT tariff target for manufactured goods was re-scheduled, to be reached within ten years instead of the original fifteen years with concomitant changes to the fast and normal track schedules (Table 2.5).[13] Member governments also agreed to begin implementing fast track tariff reductions from 1 January 1996.[14] Moreover, a total of 44,752 tariff lines were included in the revised 1996 CEPT

Table 2.5 Revised (1994/95) implementation details of the CEPT scheme

Revised CEPT implementation (start date 1/1/94)	*Target date for achieving 0–5% tariff rate*		*Exclusions allowed*
	Fast track	*Normal track*	
Initial tariff rates above 20%	1 January 2000 (within 7 years)	Initially to 20% by 1 January 1998 (within 5 years) Then to 0–5% by 1 January 2003 (within 5 years)	General exemptions[a] Temporary exclusions[b] Permanent exemptions[c]
Initial tariff rates at or below 20%	1 January 1998 (within 5 years)	1 January 2000 (within 7 years)	

Source: ASEAN Secretariat (1995: 1–2).

Notes

a Unchanged. See Table 2.2 for definition.

b To be eliminated in 2000. Also, 20 per cent of items in this list to be transferred automatically to CEPT Inclusion List annually over five years beginning January 1996 and ending January 2000.

c A few unprocessed agricultural products only. Also termed the 'Sensitive List'.

package, representing over 90 per cent of all tariff lines in ASEAN, a slight improvement over the previous package.[15]

Second, AFTA's scope was expanded as unprocessed agricultural products were brought under the CEPT mechanism though with a number of, as yet undecided, exclusions. This was a notable advance in AFTA, given that all the ASEAN countries except Singapore and Brunei had sizeable agricultural communities that member governments usually tried to protect from competing imports. These governments had initially been adamant that unprocessed agricultural products would be excluded from AFTA. A working group was set up to explore ways to include into the CEPT framework those agricultural products member governments still insisted on excluding.

Third, procedures governing the Temporary Exclusion List were tightened. The revised rules stipulated that member governments would have to transfer, on an annual basis, 20 per cent of the current 3,141 items currently in the Temporary Exclusion List to the CEPT Inclusion List between 1996 and 2000. The first instalment of 682 products was to be transferred to the Inclusion List on 1 January 1996.[16] While previously the Temporary Exclusion List was only to be reviewed in 2000, the amendments meant that the list would effectively cease to exist after this date, with the final transfer to the Inclusion List made on 1 January 2000.

Fourth, senior officials from member countries developed trade facilitation programmes and adopted measures to reduce NTBs (ASEAN Secretariat 1995: 9–25). The former included measures to harmonise tariff nomenclature, customs valuation systems and customs procedures, as well as the introduction of a Green-Lane system to expedite customs clearance of CEPT products. Work on the elimination of NTBs included measures to align product standards to international standards and to facilitate mutual recognition of product testing and standards. Some aspects of trade facilitation, notably harmonising customs nomenclature and valuation systems among the ASEAN countries were also expected to contribute to reducing NTBs.

Finally, apart from including unprocessed agricultural products, AFTA's scope was further expanded as new issue areas like services, investment and industrial production were brought under its ambit for regional cooperation, although further details were left for the future to be worked out. These were collectively known as the 'AFTA-Plus' programmes and involved coordinating border and non-border arrangements in these new issue areas to complement the reduction of tariffs and non-tariff barriers to form a single regional market (ASEAN Secretariat 1998a: vii). In addition, member governments agreed to develop a regional mechanism to protect intellectual property (ASEAN 1995e). The ASEAN leaders also agreed to develop a mechanism for dispute settlement in AFTA (ASEAN 1995a).

The expansion phase (1996–97)

As noted above, the formal commitment to expand AFTA's scope was made at the Fifth ASEAN Summit in Bangkok in December 1995. Details on how cooperation was to be achieved in services and investment liberalisation as well as in industrial production were later worked out by the senior officials of ASEAN through a series of consultations throughout 1996 and 1997, some of which are ongoing at the time of writing. In addition, negotiations over the specifics of agricultural trade liberalisation continued during this period to overcome the impasse that had emerged in 1995 as a number of countries retracted earlier liberalisation offers. A formal *Protocol on Dispute Settlement Mechanism* (DSM) was also adopted in November 1996 (ASEAN 1996b).

Cooperation in services

The *ASEAN Framework Agreement on Services* (AFAS), signed in December 1995, aimed at liberalising trade in services within ASEAN, while its goal was to eventually establish an ASEAN free trade area in services by 2020 (ASEAN 1995d; ASEAN Secretariat 1995: 31). The AFAS committed member governments to further negotiations to liberalise seven key service industries, namely finance and banking, tourism, telecommunications, shipping, air transport, construction and business services (ASEAN 1995d). More specifically, member governments were committed to eliminating substantially all existing discriminatory measures and market access limitations among ASEAN member countries within a reasonable timeframe that was, however, not clearly specified. Article IV of the AFAS pledged member governments to make commitments that went beyond their offers in the General Agreement on Trade in Services (GATS) at the multilateral track. Also, Article VI explicitly denied the benefits of the Agreement to service providers from non-ASEAN member countries unless these service providers had established substantive operations in an ASEAN member country. Thus far, two rounds of negotiations to obtain specific commitments have been completed. The first round of negotiations between 1996 and 1998 produced two packages of broad commitments, while the second round (1999–2001) produced one package of commitments. A third round of services negotiations was launched on 1 January 2002 and is scheduled to end on 31 December 2004.[17]

The ASEAN Industrial Cooperation Scheme (AICO)

The ASEAN Industrial Cooperation (AICO) Scheme was launched in April 1996, when economic ministers signed the *Basic Agreement on AICO* to promote joint industrial production in ASEAN (ASEAN 1996a). Under the AICO scheme, the participating companies must be involved in some form of joint industrial production, either through producing component parts for the other company or through the sharing of raw and/or intermediate resources. Products of an AICO arrangement were set to immediately enjoy tariff rates of 0–5 per cent among the two countries concerned without having to wait for either the fast or normal track programmes under the CEPT. A 30 per cent national equity requirement was imposed on companies wishing to be considered for AICO privileges, although a waiver provision was later included to allow firms already operating in the region but unable to meet the national equity criterion to participate in AICO.[18] The AICO scheme effectively allowed firms to enjoy the benefits of a regional free trade area for particular approved products well before the 2003 deadline for tariffs to reach the 0–5 per cent target. In fact, the AICO was instituted as a way to accelerate trade liberalisation for specific products traded between particular firms engaged in transnational production in ASEAN without the need to alter the general liberalisation schedule outlined in the CEPT.

The AICO replaced two previous programmes of industrial cooperation in ASEAN, namely the ASEAN Industrial Joint Ventures (AIJV) and the Brand-to-Brand Complementation Scheme (BBC). Both these earlier schemes had attempted to facilitate joint industrial production within ASEAN although the BBC was specifically targeted at the production of automobile parts and components. The AICO scheme, initially limited to manufacturing industries, was far more flexible than the schemes it replaced, particularly the AIJV. For instance, the AICO scheme required the participation of a minimum of only two member countries agreeing to grant the specified tariff privileges to participating companies, with at least one company to be located in each participating country. Previously, at least four firms from four member countries were required to participate in the AIJV.[19]

The ASEAN Investment Area (AIA)

At the December 1995 Bangkok Summit, the ASEAN leaders also agreed to establish an ASEAN Investment Area (AIA), a long-term project that would seek to gradually eliminate national investment restrictions in favour of more liberal rules for investors. Throughout 1996, 1997 and in the first nine months of 1998, senior officials worked out the details of the programme. By October 1998, a *Framework Agreement on the ASEAN Investment Area* was ready to be signed by ASEAN economic ministers (ASEAN 1998d). The details of the AIA programme are discussed below.

The financial crisis and post-crisis consolidation phase (1998–2002)

Just as the core ASEAN member governments agreed to hasten the implementation of AFTA and expand its scope in 1994–95, a further set of advances to AFTA commitments occurred after the Asian financial crisis began in July 1997. Decisions were made to further accelerate the completion of the free trade area and expand its scope while the AIA programme was also improved. Programmes begun earlier were consolidated, among which the most notable was the completion of a second round of services negotiations in 2001, while a third round was launched in January 2002. In addition, a number of short-term liberalisation measures to enhance the investment climate in ASEAN were adopted. Although these were not formally part of AFTA, they are best regarded as supplementing the AFTA project. These new initiatives were outlined in detail in a *Statement on Bold Measures* adopted by member governments at the Sixth ASEAN Summit in Hanoi in December 1998 (ASEAN 1998c).

Advancing the CEPT

The ASEAN leaders had, at their Second Informal Summit in Kuala Lumpur in December 1997, recommended the acceleration of both the CEPT and the AIA although they left details for their ministers to work out.[20] In October 1998, the twelfth AFTA Council agreed to accelerate the implementation of AFTA by calling on member governments to reduce as many tariff lines as possible to zero per cent by 2003. At this time, individual governments also made significant offers to accelerate AFTA, especially by submitting previously excluded products for liberalisation.[21] This was noteworthy, since there had been some previous discussion among the ASEAN member governments in 1998 on whether to delay CEPT implementation because of the regional financial crisis.[22] By the time of their Sixth Summit, the leaders of ASEAN decided that member countries should bring forward to 2002, the date by which tariffs in the core ASEAN countries would reach the 0–5 per cent target. The official completion date remained 2003, however (ASEAN 1998c).[23]

A year later in September 1999, the thirteenth AFTA Council meeting decided to set the target date for complete elimination of all tariffs at 2015, for the original six signatories.[24] Later, at their Third Informal Summit in Manila in November 1999, the ASEAN leaders committed themselves to eliminating all tariffs and import duties by 2010, five years earlier than the 2015 deadline initially agreed to by their economic ministers only two months previously.[25]

Short-term measures to enhance the investment climate

As part of the *Statement on Bold Measures* adopted at the Hanoi Summit in 1998, the ASEAN governments adopted a set of short-term measures to enhance the ASEAN investment climate (ASEAN 1998c,e). Each ASEAN government agreed to extend special privileges to qualified ASEAN and non-ASEAN investors in the manufacturing sector, provided applications

Table 2.6 Short-term investment incentives offered in December 1998

Country	*Domestic market access*	*Equity offers*
Brunei	Not applicable.	100% foreign equity in high-tech and all export-oriented industries.
Indonesia	For all industries except those in Negative List and those operating in bonded zones.	100% foreign equity in wholesale/ retail trade, all manufacturing and in listed banks. After 15 years, some local equity ownership is necessary.
Malaysia	For all industries except those in Negative List.	100% foreign equity in all manufacturing except seven specific activities/products. No export conditions.
Philippines	For all industries except those in Negative List.	In the process of opening wholesale/ retail trade to foreign ownership. Foreign companies allowed into domestic construction sector.
Singapore	For all industries except those in Negative List.	Extension of 30% corporate income tax allowance to selected manufacturing and service industries.
Thailand	For all industries except those in Negative List.	100% foreign equity in all manufacturing projects.

Source: ASEAN (1998c,e).

were received between January 1999 and December 2000. These special incentives covered seven areas, among the most significant being 100 per cent foreign equity ownership in selected sectors and domestic market access (Table 2.6). In addition, the ASEAN governments also agreed to waive the 30 per cent national equity requirement for AICO projects, but only for projects approved during the 1999–2000 period. The waiver period was later extended by a year until 31 December 2001.[26]

Advancing the ASEAN Investment Area

Under the terms of the 1998 AIA Agreement, member governments were committed to gradually according national treatment and allowing market access in the manufacturing sector to ASEAN investors beginning immediately, where possible. Members were, however, allowed to maintain exemptions from the privileges granted to ASEAN investors, until 2010 through a Temporary Exclusion List and indefinitely through a Sensitive List. The latter was only to be periodically reviewed with no firm timetable provided for its elimination. Any restrictions on foreign investors were to be removed by 2020.[27] Amendments were subsequently made to the AIA programme, first in 1999 and later in 2001.

A 1999 amendment to the original AIA Agreement extended its coverage to include agriculture, forestry, fisheries, mining, as well as services incidental to all these sectors.[28] A decision later in the year stipulated that all temporary exclusions for ASEAN investors in manufacturing were to end by January 2003 instead of 2010, seven years earlier than initially envisaged.[29] All other sectors would be open to ASEAN investors by January 2010. No conditions were imposed on the Sensitive List.[30] Foreign investors would realise these benefits only in 2020.

The AIA was again amended in September 2001. The AIA Council[31] decided to bring forward the deadline when all restrictions against foreign investors would be removed. All foreign investors were to be accorded full national treatment and market access privileges by 2010 in all sectors covered by the AIA Agreement rather than the original 2020 deadline.[32] In short, ASEAN investors ceased to enjoy privileged status in the AIA, except in the manufacturing sector where they were accorded full market access and national treatment privileges by 2003. In other sectors covered in the AIA, ASEAN investors would receive full market access and national treatment privileges at the same time as foreign investors.

Further consolidation of AFTA

During this period, existing programmes in AFTA were consolidated, particularly in services and agriculture. As already noted, a second round of services negotiations was completed in 2001, and a third round begun in January 2002. Agreement was finally reached on agricultural trade liberalisation and a protocol signed in 1999, after four years of wrangling over a number of sensitive items. A series of additional framework agreements were adopted, notably to facilitate the movement of goods through the ASEAN countries, for mutual recognition of testing and standards in ASEAN, as well as to facilitate electronic commerce. These programmes were supportive of the primary AFTA agenda to create a single regional market within ASEAN. To that end, work was also underway during this period on additional trade facilitation programmes, notably to harmonise and standardise customs procedures and arrangements.

The status of implementation

The previous section described the extensive range of programmes and commitments made by ASEAN governments under the AFTA project. Contrary to earlier predictions that it would not advance beyond its initially limited agenda, the AFTA project was not only sustained, its pace was accelerated and its scope widened. Commitments to advance tariff liberalisation were forthcoming throughout the decade, while programmes were developed to address non-tariff barriers as well as to facilitate free trade in the region through a range of supporting programmes. Yet, as the following discussion shows, the implementation record in AFTA was mixed. Delays and setbacks were experienced in a range of sectors, notably in agriculture, services and investment, although the CEPT scheme was, by and large, on schedule, notwithstanding the temporary withdrawal of automobiles from CEPT liberalisation.

Implementation of CEPT tariff liberalisation

Tariff liberalisation on goods trade within AFTA was essentially on schedule. Since its re-launch in 1994 after a disastrous start, or non-start, member governments have each year lowered tariffs on a range of products under the CEPT framework, with these reductions gazetted in national annual legal customs enactments.[33] By 2001, 98.3 per cent of total tariff lines in the core six ASEAN countries were included in the CEPT framework, up from 98 per cent in 1999 (Table 2.7). This was a substantial improvement over 1996 and 1998 when respectively 90 per cent and 94 per cent of these countries' total tariff lines were subject to AFTA disciplines.[34] Moreover, on 1 January 2002, tariffs on 96 per cent of tariff lines in the Inclusion List of the core ASEAN countries had already reached the 0–5 per cent end tariff range compared to a figure of 90 per cent of tariff lines in 2001, well on schedule for the 2003 deadline for AFTA.[35] Moreover, by 2003, 48 per cent of total tariff lines of the six core members will be at the zero per cent tariff level, based on current liberalisation rates (Table 2.8).

Table 2.7 CEPT implementation package for 2001 (submitted in 2000)

Country	*Number of tariff lines*				
	Inclusion List[a]	*Temporary Exclusion List*	*General Exemption List*	*Sensitive List*[b]	*Total tariff lines (ASEAN-6)*
Brunei	6,284	0	202	6	6,492
Indonesia	7,190	21	68	4	7,283
Malaysia	9,654	218	53	83	10,008
Philippines	5,622	6	16	50	5,694
Singapore	5,821	0	38	0	5,859
Thailand	9,104	0	0	7	9,111
ASEAN-6 Total	43,675	245	377	150	44,447
	(98.3%)	(0.6%)	(0.9%)	(0.3%)	(100%)

Source: Joint Press Statement, *Fourteenth AFTA Council Meeting*, October 2000.

Notes
a Includes both fast and normal track products.
b Essentially unprocessed agricultural products, which follow a delayed implementation schedule.

Table 2.8 Number of tariff lines at 0 per cent by 2003 (based on 2001 CEPT package)

Country	*Number of tariff lines in Inclusion List*				*Percentage*			
	0%	*>0%*	*Other*	*Total*	*0%*	*>0%*	*Other*	*Total*
Brunei Darussalam	5,071	1,205	0	6,276	80.8	19.2	0	100
Indonesia	3,929	3,263	0	7,192	54.6	45.4	0	100
Malaysia	6,048	3,991	0	10,039	60.3	39.8	0	100
Philippines	4	5,572	0	5,576	0.1	99.9	0	100
Singapore	5,859	0	0	5,859	100.0	0	0	100
Thailand	171	8,933	0	9,104	1.9	98.1	0	100
ASEAN-6 Total	21,082	22,964	0	44,046	47.9	52.1	0	100

Source: ASEAN Secretariat website (www.aseansec.org).

Temporary Exclusion List (almost) eliminated as scheduled

Since January 1996, the core ASEAN member governments have transferred at least 20 per cent of products in their Temporary Exclusion List to the Inclusion List in accordance with the commitment made in 1994–95. The final instalment of products in the Temporary Exclusion List was moved to the Inclusion List at the start of 2000 as scheduled, and tariffs on these products brought down to 20 per cent, after which the rates will be reduced to 0–5 per cent by 2002/2003. Only the Temporary Exclusion Lists of Malaysia, Indonesia and the Philippines remained, and these comprised 0.6 per cent of the total tariff lines of these countries (Table 2.7). The products excluded were petrochemicals, agricultural products and automobiles. Agricultural products now follow a delayed liberalisation schedule, while Malaysia formally withdrew automobiles from CEPT disciplines until 2005, both developments causing considerable tension within ASEAN. Why these disputes arose and how they were dealt with will be discussed in detail in Chapters 5 and 6. A further blow to AFTA's credibility was the Philippines' intention to defer liberalisation of its petrochemicals industry, conveyed to the September 2002 AFTA Council meeting by Trade Secretary, Manuel Roxas.[36]

Average CEPT tariff rates have fallen

The average CEPT tariff rate for the six core ASEAN members has fallen from 12.76 per cent in 1993 to 2.89 per cent in 2002.[37] Based on tariff implementation packages already committed to by the different countries, the average regional rate for all ten members is projected to fall to 2.63 per cent by 2003 (Table 2.9).

Averages can, and often do, mask substantial variation in tariff rates for individual products, however. In 1996 for instance, Malaysia, Indonesia and Thailand maintained tariffs in excess of 100 per cent on 29, 58 and 11 per cent of their tariff lines, respectively (Azarcon 1997: 107–8), compared to a regional average CEPT rate of 8.2 per cent (ASEAN Secretariat 1996: 26). Yet in the same year, Malaysia also maintained a zero per cent tariff rate on a substantial 53 per cent of its total tariff lines, compared to figures of 19 per cent and 4 per cent for Indonesia and Thailand respectively (Azarcon 1997: 108). On the other hand, tariffs on products still excluded remain high. Malaysia, for instance, continues to maintain tariffs ranging from 25 to 300 per cent on imports of automobiles, which remain on the Temporary Exclusion List.[38] Nevertheless, it is also important to keep in mind that about 93 per cent of all products in the combined ASEAN Inclusion List now display tariff rates of 0–5 per cent (Table 2.10).

Table 2.9 Average CEPT tariff rates (per cent)

Country	*2000*	*2001*	*2002*	*2003*
Brunei	1.26	1.17	0.97	0.96
Indonesia	4.77	4.36	3.73	2.16
Malaysia	2.85	2.59	2.45	2.07
Philippines	4.97	4.17	4.07	3.77
Singapore	0	0	0	0
Thailand	6.07	5.59	5.17	4.63
ASEAN-10[a]	3.74	3.54	3.17	2.63

Source: ASEAN Annual Report 1999–2000.

Note

a Regional CEPT tariff rates are weighted averages, with the number of tariff lines in the Inclusion List for 1999 used as weights. Average regional tariffs for all ten members (ASEAN-10) will tend to be higher than the average for the core ASEAN-6, as new members reach the 0–5 per cent target rate at a later date.

Table 2.10 Number of tariff lines with rates of 0–5 per cent at 2001

Country	*Number of tariff lines at 0–5% tariff rate*	*Proportion of the Inclusion List at 0–5% tariff rate (%)*
Brunei	6,107	97.3
Indonesia	6,483	90.1
Malaysia	9,117	90.8
Philippines	5,017	90.0
Singapore	5,859	100.0
Thailand	8,193	90.0
Total	40,776	92.6

Source: ASEAN Secretariat website (www.aseansec.org).

Analysis of progress on tariff liberalisation in AFTA is complicated by the fact that shifts in tariff policy in the ASEAN countries during the 1990s were the outcome of developments on three fronts: unilateral tariff reforms, tariff reductions agreed to under the GATT/WTO multilateral framework, and CEPT-based tariff reductions under AFTA. Thus, it will be useful to compare the CEPT rates in the ASEAN countries with the MFN or generalised tariff rates applicable to products from all sources, which would help us assess the often made claim that AFTA was, in reality, a redundant exercise in tariff liberalisation as the CEPT merely repeated the MFN tariff reductions instituted by national governments.

It is true that until 2000, MFN and CEPT tariff rates were fairly close. The core ASEAN governments had unilaterally reduced the MFN rates for their countries, particularly between 1994 and 1996 (ASEAN Secretariat 1996: 43). Moreover, the Malaysian and Singaporean governments had extended their respective CEPT tariff concessions to non-ASEAN traders on an MFN basis during this period. Similarly in Thailand, Indonesia and the Philippines, unilateral tariff reductions closely followed AFTA tariff reduction schedules (Pangestu 1996: 9; Gochoco-Bautista 1998: 210).[39] As a result, it was unsurprising to find MFN and CEPT tariff rates at similar levels. What is important, however, is that the ASEAN governments generally multilateralised their CEPT tariff concessions rather than merely re-designating their MFN tariff concessions as CEPT ones. This suggests a certain commitment on their part to AFTA *per se*.

Nevertheless, the question of whether the CEPT/AFTA was redundant is a salient one. After all, only about 1.5 per cent of intra-ASEAN trade in the mid-1990s utilised CEPT rules of origin certification, suggesting that CEPT-driven regional trade was very low (Teh Jr. 1999). This was attributed to the small difference between CEPT and MFN tariff rates, which probably did not make it worth the while for manufacturers to apply for CEPT concessions.[40]

This picture is, however, expected to change as the completion date for AFTA approaches when CEPT and MFN rates are expected to increasingly diverge.[41] Azarcon (1997: 122) projected a substantial difference of almost 13 percentage points between MFN and CEPT rates in 2000 in Thailand, based on 1996 Thai MFN tariffs. Although MFN rates have fallen further in the country since 1996, the difference between MFN and CEPT rates is expected to remain substantial, according to Thai finance ministry officials.[42] Under Thailand's new tariff structure unveiled in 1999, the MFN tariff exceeds the CEPT rate by between 2 and 15 percentage points on average.[43] In selected sectors like petrochemicals, steel, automobiles and unprocessed agricultural products, MFN rates are far higher than these averages, with the CEPT–MFN differential consequently even higher on these products. In Indonesia, the average MFN rate is scheduled to fall to a maximum 10 per cent by 2003, a significant five percentage points higher than the CEPT rate, although many individual

Table 2.11 MFN–CEPT tariff differentials, 2001

Country	*Total tariff lines (at HS 9-level)*	*MFN rate exceeds CEPT tariff rate (% of total tariff lines)*	*MFN rate exceeds CEPT tariff rate by more than 5 percentage points (% of total tariff lines)*
Malaysia	11,729	31.4	25.8
Thailand	10,998	61.2	43.0
Philippines	5,915	36.8	28.8
Indonesia	10,078	26.8	8.75

Source: Author's calculations using 2001 CEPT database from the ASEAN Secretariat (www.aseansec.org).

MFN rates are also set to fall to a maximum 5 per cent by 2000 (Nallappan *et al.* 1998: 50).[44]

Nevertheless, 27 per cent of the total 10,078 tariff lines (HS 9-level) in Indonesia displayed MFN rates that were higher than CEPT rates in 2001, with about 9 per cent of products registering CEPT rates that were more than five percentage points above MFN rates. In contrast, 37 per cent of a total 5,915 product tariff lines in the Philippines displayed MFN rates higher than CEPT rates, while 29 per cent displayed an MFN–CEPT differential of more than five percentage points. Malaysia similarly maintained MFN rates that were higher than CEPT rates on 31 per cent of the country's total 11,729 individual product categories, with the MFN rate on a quarter of all products in the Inclusion List exceeding the CEPT rate by more than five percentage points. MFN rates in Thailand exceeded CEPT rates on almost 62 per cent of the total 10,998 individual product tariff lines in the country's Inclusion List submitted in its CEPT package for 2001, with 43 per cent of individual items displaying tariff differences of more than five percentage points (Table 2.11).[45] AFTA, in short, was no mere window dressing.

Unprocessed agricultural products

Despite members agreeing to their inclusion in AFTA, the liberalisation of unprocessed agricultural products under CEPT disciplines was not expected to advance substantially due to the politically sensitive nature of the agriculture sector in most of the core ASEAN countries. It was, thus, encouraging that a significant 68.5 per cent of the total 2,025 tariff lines in agriculture were placed in the Inclusion List when the initial commitment was made in 1994 to expand the scope of AFTA. Only 18.6 per cent of the tariff lines were temporarily excluded while 12.9 per cent were deemed sensitive (Table 2.12). Unfortunately, the latter category included significant crops grown in the region, especially rice and sugar. Unlike the case of manufactured products, the unprocessed agricultural items

Table 2.12 Status of unprocessed agricultural products in AFTA, 1994

List type	*Tariff lines*		*Intra-ASEAN import value*	
	Number	*Proportion (%)*	*US$ million*	*Proportion (%)*
Inclusion List	1,387	68.5	125.68	31.6
Temporary Exclusion List	377	18.6	130.70	32.9
Sensitive List	261	12.9	141.15	35.5
Total	2,025	100.0	397.53	100.0

Source: ASEAN Secretariat (1996: 29).

included within the CEPT in 1994 accounted for less than a third of the value of intra-ASEAN agricultural imports.[46] A substantial 68 per cent of the value of intra-ASEAN imports of unprocessed agricultural products traded in ASEAN were excluded, with more than one third deemed too sensitive and thus exempted from CEPT/AFTA disciplines (Table 2.12).

Moreover, a dispute emerged between Indonesia and Thailand when the former backtracked on its earlier commitment to reduce tariffs on fifteen specific agricultural items from four product categories, notably rice, sugar, cloves and wheat flour. Negotiations to overcome the impasse were protracted, although it eventually led to the adoption of new categories and schedules for agricultural trade liberalisation formalised in a *Protocol on Sensitive and Highly Sensitive Agricultural Products*, which was signed by the economic ministers of ASEAN in September 1999 (ASEAN 1999). The dispute over agriculture will be discussed in detail in Chapters 5 and 6.

Reduction of non-tariff barriers and trade facilitation

A great deal of effort was put into reducing the incidence of NTBs to trade in ASEAN both jointly under AFTA and unilaterally (Feridhanusetyawan 1998: 5). Member governments were aware that NTBs constituted a significant barrier to creating a regional market, even if full tariff liberalisation were achieved. The private business sector had, moreover, long expressed its view that NTBs constitute a serious obstacle to business in the ASEAN region (Baldwin 1997: 58–60).

Customs surcharges, the main source of NTBs identified in ASEAN were completely eliminated by the end of 1996.[47] As already outlined in the previous section, technical NTBs, the next largest source of NTBs after customs surcharges, were to be addressed through programmes promoting transparency and harmonisation as well as through mutual recognition arrangements. These programmes have already commenced, with most of them ongoing while a few have been completed. In 2000, a draft text of a harmonised customs classification system for ASEAN, namely the *ASEAN Harmonised System of Tariff Nomenclature*, was reviewed to iron out remaining inconsistencies (Pricewaterhouse Coopers 2000). Member governments plan to implement this system by 1 January 2003.[48] They also began implementing the WTO Customs Valuation Agreement in 1997, well ahead of the WTO deadline of 2000 for developing countries. These programmes will complement the Green Lane scheme for CEPT products that had been launched in January 1996 to accelerate customs clearance for CEPT products. Other cooperative projects among customs authorities in the different ASEAN countries were also initiated with the aim of increasing the transparency of customs operations to facilitate regional trade.[49]

A programme was also launched in 1996 to harmonise standards in twenty priority product groups that are significantly traded in ASEAN, using international standards where available. To this end, an *ASEAN Framework Agreement on Mutual Recognition Arrangements* was adopted in December 1998 (ASEAN 1998f). This agreement provides the general principles and conditions for developing sectoral mutual recognition arrangements beginning with the twenty priority product groups, essentially electrical and electronic items, telecommunications equipment and rubber products.[50] In April 2002, the economic ministers of ASEAN adopted the mutual recognition arrangement for electrical and electronic equipment, which will allow testing and certification conducted in the country of origin of a product to be accepted by the importing country without the need for further testing and certification in the latter.[51] This move is expected to facilitate regional free trade in these items, which currently account for 40 per cent of intra-ASEAN trade. Other mutual recognition arrangements are forthcoming in cosmetics, pharmaceuticals, telecommunications equipment and prepared foodstuff.

Despite these efforts, NTBs continue to persist, particularly those arising from domestic regulations. Although Indonesia was a major offender during the 1990s, particularly with regard to NTBs involving domestic monopoly arrangements, most of these were removed in 1999–2000 when the government implemented the economic reform packages negotiated with the IMF (Fane 2000: 27). Still, Indonesia has resorted to anti-dumping duties, as have other ASEAN countries such as Malaysia, while manufacturers continue to complain about NTBs in the form of complex inspection procedures and excessively stringent quality/performance efficiency product standards that deviate from international norms.[52]

ASEAN member governments have attempted to deal with NTBs by assigning a greater role to the private sector in identifying these barriers to trade. Firms were encouraged to lodge complaints over any difficulties they faced when exporting to another ASEAN country, either directly to the AFTA Unit established in the respective national economic/trade ministries or to the AFTA Unit in the ASEAN Secretariat. This seems to be a reasonable step, given that NTBs are often invisible and become apparent only when traders are confronted by problems with exporting/importing. What happens once complaints are lodged, particularly if an NTB is identified, rests on inter-governmental negotiations rather than juridical or administrative mechanisms, which may well prevent a speedy resolution of the problem and introduce further uncertainty into the exercise.

The AFTA-Plus programmes

As already noted, the AFTA-Plus programmes were more difficult to implement. Negotiations over the specific terms and conditions of these programmes were often protracted, especially in services. Nevertheless, it is significant that the ASEAN member governments committed potentially contentious sectors like services and investment to joint decision-making.

Industrial cooperation and the AICO scheme

One of the selling points about the AICO scheme was its supposed administrative simplicity, with the entire process for the approval and granting of AICO privileges not taking more than 140 days (Baldwin 1997: 64). Unfortunately, the reality was quite different, with considerable delays experienced by many private firms submitting applications.[53] Moreover, only fourteen AICO applications were approved over two years between November 1996, when the scheme officially began, and October 1998.[54] This was not for lack of private sector interest in the scheme. Many foreign business leaders complained about delays in processing applications and lack of transparency in approvals.[55]

Foreign firms, including those already operating in ASEAN, were often disadvantaged by the restrictive 30 per cent equity criterion, which prevented firms with less than the requisite national equity share from being accorded AICO privileges. This meant that few approvals were given.[56] Member governments later agreed to waive the 30 per cent national equity requirement and allow greater flexibility into the AICO (ASEAN Secretariat 1997b: 40). Unfortunately, individual governments had considerable leeway to decide on when they would grant these waivers, which meant that applications were often stuck at the approval stage if one of the host countries involved was unwilling to consider waiving the national equity condition (Baldwin 1997: 64).

Since the financial crisis, the 30 per cent national equity requirement was unconditionally waived for firms submitting applications between 1 January 1999 and 31 December 2000. The deadline was later extended, initially by a year to the end of 2001 and then to the end of 2002. Member governments also relaxed other AICO criteria. New investors without any ongoing operations in ASEAN were allowed to submit applications for AICO. Previously, only firms already operating in the region could submit applications to be considered for AICO privileges. These changes, which made it easier to obtain AICO approvals by foreign firms, were probably responsible for the rise in approvals to 36 by September 1999, 63 by October 2000 and 98 by September 2002. These 98 AICO projects are expected to generate a total of US$1.15 billion in intra-ASEAN trade transactions per year.[57] More than 90 per cent of the participating companies are from the automotive sector, with a handful in electronics production.

At their most recent ministerial meeting in September 2002, the economic ministers agreed to set the AICO tariff rate at zero per cent by 1 January 2003 for Brunei, Indonesia, Malaysia, Singapore, Cambodia and Laos. This was designed to maintain the relevance of AICO beyond 2003 when internal tariffs under the CEPT scheme are scheduled to be at the 0–5 per cent level. It effectively fast-tracks the zero-tariff AFTA for approved AICO products.[58] Ministers also agreed to extend the waiver period for the 30 per cent national equity condition by another year to the end of 2003.

Cooperation in services

The framework agreement adopted in 1995 set the stage for a series of further negotiations to obtain more specific commitments in market access, national treatment and other areas of services cooperation. A first round of negotiations commenced in 1996 and ended in December 1998. The negotiating process proved, however, to be rather difficult. Part of the problem was due to the modality of negotiations that was adopted. ASEAN officials submitted voluntary offer and request lists within specific service sectors to the Coordinating Committee on Services,[59] but these very often did not match. It was difficult to obtain a set of balanced concessions that all members were happy with, in sector-based negotiations. Some quarters believe that they might have been easier to obtain if negotiations covering all service sectors had been conducted, which would have facilitated the trading of concessions across sectors.[60] The approach presently adopted in ASEAN services negotiations is to initially obtain ministerial level commitments in different service sectors, and then to coordinate these further at a second stage.[61]

The first round of negotiations produced two packages of commitments, although these essentially outlined broad parameters for cooperation and did not detail substantive commitments.[62] Neither were offers forthcoming in all the seven service sub-sectors. An initial package of commitments in tourism, maritime transport, air transport, business services and telecommunications, as well as a protocol of implementation was adopted in

December 1997 (ASEAN 1997). The arrangements were very flexible. Cooperation in these sectors did not involve all the ASEAN members. The AFAS allows two or more ASEAN members to proceed if the other members are not yet ready to participate in these cooperative arrangements. Thus, in the first package, only tourism cooperation involved all ASEAN members. Cooperation in maritime transport was confined to Brunei, Indonesia, Malaysia and Thailand; air transport cooperation involved Brunei, Malaysia and Singapore; and the Philippines offered concessions in business services.[63] A second package of commitments together with its protocol of implementation was signed in December 1998 (ASEAN 1998a). This second package went further than the initial package adopted in December 1997, with each government making offers in all seven service sectors.[64]

A second round of negotiations began in 1999 and was completed in 2001, resulting in a third package of commitments covering all seven service sectors. This second round of negotiations was targeted at all four modes of service supply, namely cross-border supply (Mode 1), consumption abroad (Mode 2), commercial presence (Mode 3) and the presence of natural persons (Mode 4). Initial commitments were made in Modes 1 and 2, which would allow service suppliers operating in ASEAN to provide services to users from another member country without establishing a commercial presence in that country. Negotiations to obtain offers for Modes 3 and 4 were protracted.[65] It was very difficult to reach an agreement on commitments that would allow non-national service firms to establish a market presence in an ASEAN country, particularly in very sensitive sectors like financial services and telecommunications.[66] A third round of services negotiations (2002–04) is ongoing, and officials are aiming for concessions in all the four modes of supply in all seven service sectors, although the prospects for success seem limited given the sentiments of particular governments.

The removal of foreign equity restrictions in the service industry in Thailand and Indonesia and the result of their respective crisis-induced economic restructuring programmes made these countries ready to commit to services liberalisation in ASEAN. This, however, also added to the difficulties already present in ASEAN in negotiating liberalisation commitments in services. Other governments had to contend with the prospect that services liberalisation would lead to even greater foreign competition since foreign firms would find it easier to establish a commercial presence in these liberalised markets, and then sell their services to other, more closed service markets, like Malaysia for instance. This was permitted under the terms of the AFAS.[67] It prompted a Malaysian government official to remark that such a development did not allow preferential concessions for ASEAN service firms, since foreign service firms with domestic operations in ASEAN were just as likely to benefit from AFTA-based concessions.[68]

Investment liberalisation

The ASEAN governments are scheduled to grant full national treatment and market access privileges to ASEAN investors in the manufacturing sector by 2003, except in sectors placed on the Sensitive List. The other sectors included within the AIA framework – agriculture, forestry, fisheries, mining and services incidental to all these sectors including manufacturing – are to be opened to ASEAN and non-ASEAN or foreign investors from 2010. Despite these laudable aims, the ASEAN governments have placed most of the sectors they wish to exclude from the AIA in the Sensitive List rather than the Temporary Exclusion List (Table 2.13).[69] The former enjoys indefinite protection from foreign, including ASEAN, participation, at least under present rules unlike the Temporary Exclusion List, which has clearly defined end-dates. Most of the Sensitive List exclusions take the form of partial restrictions or additional conditions imposed on foreign investment, usually regarding land ownership, eligibility for government procurement privileges and investment incentives, corporate equity conditions, employment of foreign employees, and other market access and export conditions.

While the ASEAN governments' commitment to liberalise investment flows in ASEAN is laudable, implementation is unlikely to be smooth, as many governments seem prepared to retain investment restrictions for domestic political reasons. Although the Sensitive List, where most of the excluded or restricted sectors were placed, was originally meant to be reviewed on a regular basis, it was only in September 2002 that the AIA Council introduced a timetable for this process, with the first review

Table 2.13 Temporary Exclusion List and Sensitive List, manufacturing sector

Country	*Industry category*							
	Temporary Exclusion List				*Sensitive List*			
	1	*2*	*3*	*4*	*1*	*2*	*3*	*4*
Brunei	Nil	Nil	X	Nil	X	X	X	Nil
Indonesia	Nil	Nil	X	Nil	X	Nil	X	Nil
Malaysia	Nil	Nil	Nil	Nil	X	Nil	X	Nil
Philippines	Nil	Nil	Nil	Nil	Nil	X	X	X
Singapore	Nil	Nil	Nil	Nil	X	Nil	X	Nil
Thailand	Nil	Nil	Nil	Nil	X	Nil	X	Nil

Source: ASEAN Secretariat (1999b: 1).

Notes
X indicates the presence of restrictions.
Industry categories
1 Industries closed to both foreign and national investment.
2 Industries closed only to foreign investment.
3 Industries open, but with restrictions on foreign investment.
4 Others (not specified).

scheduled for 2003.[70] A two-year ASEAN Investment Initiative was also launched at the fifth meeting of the AIA Council in September 2002, which provided for greater consultation with the private sector on the AIA and outlined joint promotion events to sell ASEAN to foreign investors as a single investment destination.[71] Nevertheless, these new measures do not invalidate the ASEAN Secretary General's concern, expressed in early 2002, with the slow pace of implementation of the AIA and the long delay before full national treatment and market access would be accorded to all investors, scheduled for 2010.[72]

AFTA in perspective

The preceding discussion describes how AFTA evolved between 1991 and 2002 from a project that initially focused on tariff liberalisation in manufacturing, to include other, more politically sensitive issue areas like agriculture, investment and services. While an impressive range of commitments was made, the project's implementation record during the period under review was mixed. Tariff liberalisation in manufacturing was the most advanced, although Malaysia decided to temporarily exclude automobiles from AFTA disciplines. Malaysia's move led to considerable tensions with Thailand, especially. The Philippines' recent move in September 2002 to consider temporarily withdrawing petrochemicals from AFTA raised similar concerns in ASEAN. On the other hand, agricultural trade liberalisation suffered significant setbacks. Progress was also more limited in obtaining commitments in services and investment liberalisation, while businesses continued to face numerous NTBs despite the adoption of an extensive range of programmes to address them. Yet, this should not detract attention from the considerable advances made in AFTA over the decade, particularly when compared to the experience of APEC, which a number of scholars initially suggested would overtake AFTA.[73]

The distinctiveness of AFTA is clearly evident when it is compared to the previous phase of economic cooperation in ASEAN that began in 1976–77 and which effectively ended with the decision to establish AFTA.[74] During this early period of economic cooperation, practically everything of interest to regional cooperation seemed to be excluded (Mansfield and Milner 1999: 603). Although a variety of specific cooperative projects had been adopted since 1976, these became bogged down in either inconsequential concessions that made a mockery of the commitment to cooperate or because intransigent governments were unwilling to accord tariff and other concessions to firms and products from their regional partners.[75]

ASEAN's experience with regional economic cooperation during the 1970s and 1980s is clearly different from its experience in AFTA during the 1990s. Does this mean that the ASEAN governments were finally able to place regional interests above national ones when undertaking economic cooperation through the AFTA project? Or is it the case that it was precisely because domestic interests were threatened in some way that AFTA has been advanced? As the discussion in the following two chapters suggests, globalisation presented significant challenges to domestic political economies in ASEAN, or was perceived as doing so, in turn prompting these governments to try to manage these external pressures through regional collective action. In short, domestic and regional interests became closely inter-linked in ASEAN in an era of globalisation. Precisely how systemic, domestic and regional dynamics interacted in the AFTA process is a major focus in the rest of the book.

3 Foreign capital and open regionalism

The growth imperative

How did globalisation influence the ASEAN member governments to embrace AFTA as a regional project? What specific dynamics associated with globalisation account for the particular manner in which AFTA unfolded during the decade? Were domestic political economic dynamics also involved in shaping regional responses to globalisation? These questions are addressed in this chapter and the next, which explain how domestic and therefore regional responses to globalisation were mediated by the political salience of *both* foreign- and domestic-owned capital in the ASEAN countries. This consequently led to two distinct types of regional projects within AFTA – open regionalism, to be discussed in this chapter, and developmental regionalism, which will be examined in Chapter 4. There is already a large literature that explains AFTA as a project of open regionalism aimed at countering the threat of FDI diversion away from the ASEAN economies amidst intense international competition for globally mobile investment capital. Accurate to a degree, this book demonstrates that the concern with FDI was only part of the AFTA story, albeit an important one.

The FDI explanation has been discussed at length in the literature and will not be repeated here, except to re-iterate its main points. Instead, the chapter emphasises how the structural power of foreign investment capital, reinforced by its key role in the domestic political economy of the ASEAN countries, made AFTA vital as a means of defining a distinctive space of production for global capital in the wider Asia-Pacific region, particularly in competition with China. The chapter also emphasises three additional points. First, it explains why the ASEAN countries, already fairly well integrated with global trade and investment flows and already embarking on economic liberalisation programmes domestically, decided to engage in *regionalism* as a response to concerns about FDI diversion. Why not continue with and hasten domestic economic restructuring, which had proved eminently successful in drawing FDI to these countries from the late 1980s? Second, the chapter shows that although AFTA was a project of open regionalism aimed at engagement with the global economy, it displayed only limited neoliberal characteristics. Third, the discussion reveals that there was also a clear departure from open regionalism when member governments agreed to privilege domestic investors over foreign investors in investment liberalisation, albeit for a temporary period of time. This puzzle, yet to be accounted for in the literature, forms the point of departure for Chapter 4, which discusses ASEAN's attempts at developmental regionalism through the AIA component programme of AFTA.

The structural power of foreign capital

The pressure to establish a regional free trade area in ASEAN did not come from investors engaged in some form of direct lobbying of ASEAN governments. Instead, it was exercised through the structural power of foreign capital given by its vastly growing potential to relocate to alternative investment sites and its value as a source of key productive assets for governments wishing to integrate their respective economies with an increasingly competitive world economy. While globalisation shaped these two elements, the dynamics of the domestic political economy reinforced these structural pressures through the key role assigned to foreign investment capital in national economic growth.

Foreign investors had not been active in the deliberations that led to the 1991 decision to establish AFTA (Lim 1994: 132). In fact, many foreign investors, including Japanese investors who were key investors in ASEAN were surprised by the ASEAN decision, with some decidedly pessimistic about the project's viability.[1] Although Japanese firms, particularly automobile firms, had already begun to engage in a regional division of labour in ASEAN by the early 1990s, the Japanese did not push for a region-wide free trade area (Lim 1994: 133). This was because Japan's 'private, public-private and state-level arrangements' helped to coordinate and support the regional activities of Japanese firms that would have otherwise required a formal regionalist scheme (Doner 1997). As such, a generalised free trade area had been somewhat unnecessary to Japanese investors, and might have even eroded Japan's comparative advantage in the region over other foreign investors who were not backed by the kinds of informal institutions that supported the regional activities of Japanese firms. Despite some initial doubts in Japanese business and policy circles, the Japanese government and the powerful Japanese peak business organisation, the *Keidanren* or Japan Federation of Economic Organisations, quickly registered their support for AFTA. A senior official of the Japanese Ministry of International Trade and Industry lauded the 'positive move on ASEAN's part... [in] taking the initiative without having been asked by the major foreign investors'.[2]

Rather than direct pressure by investors, it was the structural power of foreign capital that was significant in influencing the AFTA decision, and later, its consolidation and expansion. Officials preparing for the 1992

Singapore Summit, at which the decision to establish AFTA was formally adopted, admitted that one of the most compelling arguments advanced for AFTA, and which convinced the leaders of its necessity, was its capacity to attract FDI to the region (Akrasanee and Stifel 1992: 36). Most observers of ASEAN had not expected such a decision to be adopted, given the difficulties the grouping had experienced in pursuing economic cooperation in the past, and its rejection of the idea of a free trade area as recently as 1987 at the Third ASEAN Summit in Manila.

It is worth emphasising this point as it shows that the ASEAN leaders were convinced of the utility of AFTA only when it was expressed in terms of the project's economic benefits for their respective economies. It weakens the argument advanced in the literature that AFTA was primarily adopted as an economic instrument to achieve strategic purposes – to keep ASEAN relevant as a regional organisation in the changing strategic environment. At most, the strategic motivation driving AFTA was an initial objective that was soon overtaken by the FDI imperative. A senior Malaysian trade official acknowledged, 'since 1992, the picture got clearer with regard to the economic motivations behind AFTA'.[3]

As discussed in the introductory chapter, it is inconceivable that the ASEAN leaders would have embraced a project that had the potential to introduce real changes to domestic economies if AFTA had not also promised economic benefits. These economic benefits came in the form of the potential to attract the necessary FDI to support high growth strategies in the core ASEAN economies and to ensure their engagement with the world economy. Thus, the initial idea mooted by the Thai Prime Minister Anand Panyarachun in 1991 quickly found support in all the ASEAN capitals. In the early 1990s, economic growth in the ASEAN countries was believed to be under threat as FDI inflows, a crucial source of growth, showed a declining growth trend in terms of relative shares (Table 3.1).

The lure of regional and/or large markets

These pressures alone do not explain what prompted the *regional* response, since ASEAN governments could well have adopted further unilateral reforms or used incentives at the national level to make individual economies more attractive to FDI without engaging in regionalism. It was, however, the awareness, or at least perceptions on the part of ASEAN leaders and policymakers that FDI was attracted to large and/or regional markets – NAFTA, the Single European Market (SEM) and especially China – that convinced the ASEAN leaders of the potential utility of a similar project in ASEAN. It was, in short, the contagion effect at work. Policymakers from the core ASEAN countries, seeing regionalist projects established elsewhere potentially threatening to their respective economies, opted for a similar project in ASEAN. They had become aware that foreign investors were becoming increasingly drawn to these regional

Table 3.1 Flows of FDI to host region/economy, 1983–98 (US$ million)

	Total FDI flows	*Industrial countries*	*All developing countries*	*ASEAN countries*[a]	*(%)*	*China*	*(%)*
1983–88	91,554	71,779	19,757	3,708	*5.2*	1,823	*2.5*
1988	159,101	131,313	27,772	6,991	*25.2*	3,194	*11.5*
1989	200,612	171,722	28,622	7,591	*26.5*	3,393	*11.9*
1990	211,425	176,436	34,689	12,158	*35.0*	3,487	*10.1*
1991	158,936	114,792	41,696	13,400	*32.1*	4,366	*10.5*
1992	173,761	119,692	49,625	12,074	*24.3*	11,156	*22.5*
1993	219,421	133,850	78,813	15,994	*20.3*	27,515	*34.9*
1994	253,506	146,379	101,196	19,681	*19.4*	33,787	*33.4*
1995	328,862	208,372	106,224	21,643	*20.4*	35,849	*33.7*
1996	358,869	211,120	135,343	25,980	*19.2*	40,180	*29.7*
1997	464,341	273,276	172,533	27,813	*16.1*	44,236	*25.6*
1998	643,879	460,431	165,936	21,400	*12.9*	45,460	*27.4*

Sources: UNCTAD, World Investment Report, 1999; ASEAN Investment Database as reported in ASEAN Secretariat (1999a: 131–32).

Notes

Percentage figures (in italics) refer to investment flows as a proportion of total flows to developing countries.

a Includes all ten ASEAN member economies.

schemes, which thus posed a threat to the ASEAN countries for which FDI had become a crucial source of economic growth.

Two developments in the world economy during the early 1990s dominated the concern with FDI diversion, and helped shape the ASEAN response. The ASEAN governments had come to realise that the formation of regionalist projects in the developed world, notably NAFTA and the SEM, was not so much a threat to free trade as much as a potential source of competition for global production capital. Here, the analyses and views of European and North American economists and policy analysts on the implications of NAFTA and the SEM for other countries and regions, including ASEAN, were keenly followed by ASEAN policymakers, and were, no doubt persuasive (Means 1995: 149). While many of these studies reached diverse conclusions, most agreed that the largest impact would be on FDI inflows to ASEAN rather than on trade diversion. In addition, the ASEAN governments saw the emergence of China as an alternative, and potentially more attractive location for foreign investors, compared to the far smaller individual ASEAN economies due to China's vast market.

The important point to note is that the interest shown by foreign firms in investing in NAFTA, the SEM and China demonstrated to ASEAN policymakers the potential of large and/or regional markets in attracting FDI inflows. It made the idea of a single regional market in ASEAN more compelling. The views of the ASEAN leaders can be summed up in the words of Thailand's Prime Minister in 1993, Chuan Leekpai, who cautioned, 'the possible diversion of direct foreign investment to emerging groupings such as the SEM and NAFTA is a perpetual reminder that smaller countries have to unite'.[4] The Head of the Indonesian Board of Investment acknowledged that ASEAN investment officials had, in 1993, 'agreed to work together to invite foreign investors to invest in ASEAN'.[5] The idea was for the ASEAN countries to cooperate in presenting AFTA as a single regional site for FDI. Trade officials from Malaysia confirmed that selling AFTA as an attractive investment location was a key objective of ASEAN.[6]

By 1993, China had become far more threatening as a competing investment location to ASEAN despite initial fears centred on NAFTA and the SEM. The call in January 1992 by Chinese leader Deng Xiaoping for faster and deeper economic reforms in China had sparked off an investment boom in that country (Tan 1993: 11). The sharp rise in FDI flows to China since then was seen as being increasingly at the expense of the ASEAN countries (Table 3.1). Since 1992, the surge of FDI from the Asian newly industrialising economies (NIEs) to ASEAN had moderated, with an increasing proportion of Japanese, Taiwanese and Hong Kong investment flowing to China instead (Parker 1993: 61). Investments from OECD sources, including North American and European sources, to ASEAN similarly weakened (Thomsen 1999: 16). Thus, by the end of 1992, the FDI situation in the core ASEAN countries had become extremely worrying to policymakers and political leaders.

FDI in the domestic political economy: reinforcing the structural power of foreign capital

ASEAN policymakers, and in particular the leaders, recognised the threat to economic growth, and thus to regime legitimacy to which any diversion of FDI from the ASEAN region would contribute. FDI had, by the end of the 1980s, become a crucial source of economic growth in the core ASEAN economies. Between 1987 and 1992, inward FDI flows accounted for a large 11.3 per cent of gross fixed capital formation in ASEAN, compared to 3.9 per cent for developing countries as a whole, 3.3 per cent for Asian developing countries and 4.2 per cent for industrial countries (ASEAN Secretariat 1999a: 129). By 1990, total FDI stock in ASEAN accounted for 18.2 per cent of their gross domestic product (GDP) compared to between 10.3–10.5 per cent for Asian and all developing countries and 8.4 per cent for the industrial countries (ASEAN Secretariat 1999a: 129). For Malaysia, Indonesia and Singapore, the role of FDI in the national economy was even higher than the ASEAN average. Total FDI stock in these three countries represented respectively 24, 37 and 74 per cent of GDP by 1990, up from 21 per cent, 14 per cent and 53 per cent a decade earlier (ASEAN Secretariat 1999a: 129).

It was through FDI that the core ASEAN countries had emerged from the recession of the mid-1980s to engage in outward-oriented industrialisation and become significant exporters of manufactured goods. FDI also introduced the necessary technology and management/organisational skills that enabled the ASEAN economies to plug into international production networks. Foreign investment was, thus, 'aggressively encouraged' by these governments (Parker 1993: 54). These economic concerns with FDI and growth were, moreover, underpinned by political imperatives as well, thereby reinforcing quite substantially at the domestic level the structural power of global capital.

Thailand

The initial idea for AFTA, which came from the Thai government of Anand Panyarachun in 1991, can be traced to concerns of the new, post-coup governing elite with the fall in FDI that followed the February 1991 military coup. While the military justified the coup as a means of ousting the corrupt government of Chatichai Choonhavan that was in place between 1988 and 1991, urban big businesses welcomed the fall of the Chatichai government under which the political influence and power of provincial business had grown at their expense (Case 2002: 157).

Urban businesses aligned themselves with the military soon after the 1991 coup for two reasons. These Bangkok-based conglomerates were highly supportive of the military's appointment of Anand, a widely respected corporate figure and former career diplomat, as caretaker Prime Minister before democratic elections could be held (Phongpaichit and Baker 1995: 355–6). They also seized the opportunity provided by the military coup to constrain provincial businesses that had emerged and thrived during the 1980s under the previous administration. The rivalry between metropolitan conglomerates and provincial businesses had emerged during the 1980s, and continues to date. It was the latter's rapid rise in Thai politics that led to the ouster of urban business elites from the lower house of the Thai parliament in the 1980s, the rivalry later fuelled by the encroachment of provincial businesses into the markets of urban businesses (Case 2002: 157).

Whatever the internal political dynamics and motivations behind the coup, one result was a fall in foreign investor interest in Thailand as expectations of rising political instability in the country grew (Tan 1993: 13; Phongpaichit and Baker 1995: 356). This worried not only the caretaker government of Prime Minister Anand, who in June 1991 had initially broached the idea of AFTA to the other ASEAN leaders, it was also of concern to the Bangkok business elite, which benefited from FDI through extensive joint-venture arrangements (Phongpaichit and Baker 1995: 156). At a more general level, the Thai economy had become increasingly reliant on exports and FDI since the late 1980s (Hewison 2000). In 1992, the number of investment applications fell by 31 per cent, with the biggest decline – 45 per cent – registered in Japanese investment applications (Tan 1993: 13). Worried Thai investment officials, thus, planned 'offensive' strategies to promote FDI into Thailand (Tan 1993: 14).

In addition to these purely economic concerns, there was also the ever-present fear that the military would re-assert its influence should economic growth falter. The military had played a substantial role in Thai politics and economics in the past, but its power and influence had waned significantly since the late 1980s, notwithstanding the military coup in February 1991. The 1992 transfer of power from the military to the democratically elected civilian government of Chuan Leekpai of the Democrat party was expected to remove completely the armed forces from the political arena. The military, however, continued to assert itself behind the scenes during 1993 and 1994, demanding a large military budget, a role in development, and the rehabilitation of the army's political role in the interests of national security (Phongpaichit and Baker 1995: 364). This was worrying the new elite coalition in Thailand made up of reforming bureaucrats, ruling politicians, and the Bangkok-based big business elite. Although urban business had initially aligned itself with the military, the alliance was shaky from the start and these corporate leaders soon distanced themselves from the military (Phongpaichit and Baker 1995: 356). Their concern over FDI and growth took on added significance in this context, particularly since Thailand has had a long history of military coups during domestic economic upheavals, beginning with the first in 1932 that saw the overthrow of the monarchy during the economically troubled times of the Great Depression (Alagappa 1987; Hewison 2000: 199).

Malaysia

Although overall FDI inflows to Malaysia rose until about 1992, the country's policymakers were, nevertheless, worried. Approved investment inflows from Japan, a major investor, fell 30.6 per cent in 1991, while that from Taiwan, a growing investor, fell by 58.3 per cent. If petroleum projects are excluded from investment figures, manufacturing sector FDI in Malaysia registered a staggering decline of 60 per cent in 1992. Policymakers were especially anxious because of a fall in domestic investments in Malaysia coupled with a 42 per cent decline in foreign investment applications in 1992 over the previous year (Tan 1993: 12–13). Although part of the decline in FDI approvals was due to officials becoming more selective in their approvals, preferring projects involving higher levels of technology, skills and capital, policymakers were nonetheless worried by the unfolding FDI picture.

By this time, Malaysian policymakers had come to recognise that China was the country's prime competitor for FDI (Means 1995: 163). They were conscious of the fact that foreign capital remained a critical source of economic growth as well as a means to technological and industrial upgrading, the latter a vital element of Prime Minister Mahathir's Vision 2020 programme to transform Malaysia into a developed country by 2020 (Khoo 1995: 327). This prompted the Malaysian Ministry of International Trade and Industry to step up its international investment promotions in order to 'pre-empt any slowdown (in FDI)'.[7]

As in Thailand, ensuring the inflow of FDI also had important political implications in Malaysia through its role in ensuring growth, a crucial means to political stability. High levels of economic growth brought significant benefits to much of the Malaysian society while also enabling the government to maintain its affirmative action programme for the country's ethnic Malay majority without excessively eating into the wealth shares of other ethnic groups. It also provided the resources needed for the government's patronage machinery, which helped to maintain elite cohesion and thus, the stability of the government and regime (Crouch 1996: 246).[8]

Malaysia had embarked on FDI-led growth as a way out of the mid-1980s recession, during which time latent cleavages among the political elite had become extremely pronounced, threatening the ruling government, Prime Minister Mahathir's personal authority, and the Malay/UMNO-dominated political regime (Crouch 1996: 106–13).[9] The rift was especially deep within UMNO, and between the ruling Malay party and its ethnic Chinese coalition partner, the Malaysian Chinese Association. At the same time, rising unemployment and an increase in private bankruptcies led to a generalised public discontent with the government and regime, which inevitably led to communal tensions as each ethnic group in multiethnic Malaysia saw the other groups as the cause of its own difficulties. These ethnic tensions within Malaysian society were exploited, and thus, exacerbated, by incumbent elites and their challengers struggling for a platform to win votes, leading to expectations of a repeat of the May 1969 ethnic riots in the country. The deteriorating political situation was, however, arrested through political manoeuvring and coercive action by the ruling government in the short-term (Crouch 1996: 106–13). The resumption in economic growth, the result of domestic economic reforms and the fortuitous inflow of FDI from the Asian NIEs during the late 1980s helped to restore growth and consequently, political stability. It is, thus, unsurprising that the FDI situation in the early 1990s caused concern among Malaysian policymakers, given the economic and political implications of a slowdown in growth in the light of the recent unsettling events in the country.

Indonesia

Although FDI increased in Indonesia in 1992, this was due to several large petroleum and mining projects. If these projects were excluded from the figures, FDI actually fell by 54 per cent in 1992, compounded by the sharp 34 per cent decline in domestic investments (Tan 1993: 13). These developments prompted considerable concern in Indonesia (Van der Eng 1993: 20–1). Since the start of the country's economic reform programmes in the 1980s, Indonesia had received significant amounts of FDI, especially from the Asian NIEs.

While the relative share of FDI in the Indonesian economy was less than that of domestic investments, its importance for the Indonesian economy and for growth rests on its high export propensity and its use of more sophisticated technology compared to domestic investors (Lindblad 1997: 29; Djidin 1997: 32). Moreover, the government's plan to attain an average annual growth rate of 6 per cent during the Sixth Development Plan (*Repelita VI*) (1993–98) rested on an investment target of 60 trillion rupiah (US$28 million) over the Plan's five-year period (Surbakti 1999: 75). Domestic private and state investments were not expected to be able to sustain the needed capital investment, especially in the light of the downturn in domestic investments during the early 1990s (MacIntyre and Sjahrir 1993: 12). The critical role of FDI was, thus, underscored.

Foreign capital was vital to maintaining economic growth in the country. Growth was a crucial regime-legitimating device for President Suharto, which allowed him to consolidate his political rule over an essentially fractious nation by steadily improving living standards for Indonesians in general and enabling large numbers of ordinary Indonesians to engage in economic activity (Surbakti 1999: 62). The President also used the material benefits generated by that growth to win friends and co-opt potential adversaries within the state and more broadly in society (Liddle 1999a: 48). In short, economic growth provided the ruling elite, notably the President, with the resources necessary to accomplish economic and political goals through patronage politics (Surbakti 1999: 62–5). The flow of FDI from the NIEs to China rather than to Indonesia from 1993 was, therefore, viewed with alarm by the Indonesian authorities, which was made worse by indications that some firms already established in Indonesia were considering a move to China (Means 1995: 169). A senior Indonesian investment official acknowledged China to be Indonesia's main competitor for FDI.[10]

Singapore

The fall in FDI flows to Singapore during the early 1990s, as in the rest of ASEAN, gave its policymakers much cause for concern. China loomed as a significant magnet for FDI, particularly in view of its discussions with the US on China's possible entry into the WTO (Tan 1993: 15). Moreover, for Singapore, the situation was compounded by the potential indirect effects on its economy, should economic growth in Malaysia and Indonesia falter as a result of a slowdown in FDI to these regional partners. Singapore had, by the early 1990s, embarked on a services-led growth strategy as a way to reduce the island republic's dependence on traditional manufacturing-led growth. One key element of the new approach was to emphasise the city-state as the operational and business headquarters for the regional production operations of TNCs. The 'regional service strategy' was, thus, premised on the growth of manufacturing production, not so much in Singapore but in the other regional economies of Southeast Asia, which Singapore-based TNCs would help coordinate and service (Rodan 1993). Any fall in investment to the rest of ASEAN would, therefore, threaten Singapore's services-led growth programme.

This explains why Singapore's political elite constantly played on the issue of FDI diversion to China, even though Singapore was, at that time, not expected to suffer too much from the China factor due to the complementary rather than competitive relationship of the Singapore economy to the Chinese economy (Tan 1993: 14). Moreover, the political legitimacy of the Peoples' Action Party (PAP) that had ruled Singapore since independence in 1965 was derived from its capacity to preside over improved material conditions, making growth a political imperative as well as an economic one (Rodan 1989: 202).

The Philippines

In the Philippines, the Ramos government elected in 1992, having inherited an economy in severe crisis, proposed an ambitious development plan – Philippines 2000 – that aimed to take the country to NIE status by century's end, a mere eight years away. This required a minimum eight per cent average annual growth rate to be achieved by, among other means, economic liberalisation and FDI (Vos and Yap 1996: 163). The recourse to FDI took on added significance with the decision by the government to close the US air and naval bases in the Philippines in 1992, which led to the withdrawal of foreign assistance from Washington (Hutchison 1997: 85). This, coupled with the continuing high foreign debt burden, led to increased reliance on FDI for growth. In fact, the foreign sector assumed a dominant part in Ramos' 'Philippines 2000' programme (McFarlane 1998: 173).

Thus, the threat of FDI diversion was a serious one for the Philippines government, which had, like other states in the region, come to regard China as one of its main competitors in the FDI game (Gochoco-Bautista 1998: 211). The economic liberalisation programme initiated by Ramos included a political dimension as well. It was designed to challenge the power of the old landed, agricultural oligarchy, which had re-emerged with post-Marcos democratisation as key players in the new Philippine 'elite democracy', this time in new areas of the economy like industry, banking and services rather than in agriculture (Hutchison 1997: 83).

Creating an alternative regional space in the Asia-Pacific for investment and production

Concern in the region over the potential possibility of losing FDI to China was, therefore, quite pronounced. ASEAN policymakers were correct in identifying China as their biggest competitor for FDI. Although other markets, particularly regionalist schemes elsewhere, did have the potential to attract FDI away from ASEAN, China was especially significant because it was part of the Asia-Pacific region. Global capital had, by the late 1980s, adopted a regional focus to its investment and production strategies (Ng and Sudo 1991). The TNCs were increasingly practising a regional as opposed to global division of labour, and establishing production in different regions – Europe, North America, and the Asia-Pacific. This was discussed in some detail in Chapter 1. While the aim of TNCs was to operate business globally, that goal was being increasingly achieved through the development of 'complete and integrated production and management systems within definable regions' (Rodan 1993: 234).

China by itself offered investors a potentially competing 'regional' investment site in the Asia-Pacific region, particularly in view of its (potential) market size (Baldwin 1997: 3). What the ASEAN governments attempted to offer to foreign investors through AFTA, specifically through its CEPT tariff liberalisation component programme, was an alternate single regional space of investment and production, in effect exploiting the 'regional' logic of global capital. AFTA, thus, helped to define a distinctive functional space of production in the wider East-Asian/Asia-Pacific region. Only through AFTA did the ASEAN leaders and policymakers believe that they could meet the FDI challenge from China, particularly as they had reached a limit in terms of the individual investment incentives they were willing to offer potential investors. As an Indonesian investment official explained, 'they (the Chinese) give everything . . . they give all the incentives which we could not give.'[11]

Thus, most scholars agree that fear over the diversion of FDI to China was a major reason why the ASEAN leaders agreed to consolidate the regional project and begin tariff reductions by January 1994 despite the emergence of domestic business resistance to AFTA in a number of member countries. Political leaders also found the potential threat to economic growth from slowing FDI inflows sufficiently overwhelming to advance AFTA further in 1994–95 (Hay 1996). ASEAN leaders consequently shortened, by five years, the time frame when tariffs in AFTA would reach the 0–5 per cent target, introduced new rules to govern the Temporary Exclusion List scheme, and agreed to adopt both a dispute settlement mechanism and an agreement to protect intellectual property rights in ASEAN. By doing so, they were signalling to foreign investors that they were committed to the development of AFTA as a single regional space of production. Moreover, the AICO scheme was adopted as a compromise between the need to attract foreign investors through forming a single market and giving domestic industries sufficient time to adjust to AFTA tariff liberalisation. Notwithstanding the problems investors encountered in getting AICO approvals, the scheme effectively fast-tracked AFTA for selected products on application by investors.

The new issue areas

The FDI explanation was used also to account for the inclusion of agriculture, services and investment within AFTA in 1994–95 (Hay 1996: 266–8). The ASEAN governments, it is argued, wished to keep AFTA relevant to FDI, given the advances made in the GATT, NAFTA and APEC during the mid-1990s in addressing new issue areas such as agriculture, services and investment. The additional commitments in AFTA were necessary in order to maintain ASEAN as a distinctive regional space of investment and production. This explanation is incomplete, however. It is unable to explain why ASEAN investors were treated more favourably than foreign investors in the AIA component of AFTA. While a case may be made that concern with FDI diversion was a factor prompting the inclusion of services and investment within AFTA, Chapter 4 argues that the design of the AIA component programme also revealed a concern on the part of a few governments with nurturing domestic capital. The latter led to deviations in AFTA from open regionalism.

In the case of agriculture, its incorporation into world trade disciplines as a result of the Uruguay Round agreements was largely responsible for its subsequent insertion into AFTA. The incorporation of agriculture into the GATT/WTO helped the Thai government, which had originally wanted AFTA to cover agriculture, a key export sector for the country, to successfully lobby for its inclusion in the CEPT, despite the reservations of other governments, notably Indonesia.[12] The Malaysian, Philippine and Indonesian governments, however, insisted on having a separate arrangement to govern trade liberalisation of the more sensitive agricultural items. Despite making this request, the Indonesian government unilaterally withdrew 15 agricultural products that it had earlier included within the CEPT, which led to a dispute with Thailand. Why this happened and how it was addressed is discussed in Chapters 5 and 6. It is sufficient, at this point, to note that it would have been difficult for the Thai government to advocate including agriculture in AFTA if it had not already been incorporated within the WTO, given the significant reservations in the region on the issue.[13] Nevertheless, the other governments agreed to its inclusion, despite these reservations, in order to reinforce AFTA as a project of open regionalism. As Malaysia's Minister of Primary Industries said in 1994, 'it is a logical and natural action wanting to include agricultural products into CEPT since the world community is committed to free trade liberalisation.'[14]

The financial crisis period

The decision by member governments to further accelerate AFTA as well as introduce additional investment incentives in the region in 1998–99 was also driven by concern with FDI and growth (Bowles 2000: 444). The core ASEAN governments had to make sure that their respective economies remained attractive to FDI amidst the economic turmoil of the regional financial crisis, and they attempted to partly accomplish this through regionalism. As huge amounts of portfolio capital began flowing out of these economies, the imperative of maintaining direct investment became paramount, especially since domestic investments had also suffered a sharp contraction in the region (OECD 1999: 120). AFTA became a tool in the process of maintaining foreign investor interest in the region, particularly as China still loomed as an alternative investment site.

Thus, Bowles (2000: 444) points to the joint adoption of a temporary incentive package in 1998 (Table 2.6) that gave foreign investors additional incentives in each ASEAN country over a two-year period as evidence that the ASEAN governments were using regionalism to attract FDI. As already noted in Chapter 2, the most significant of these incentives was the temporary offer of 100 per cent foreign equity and market access, mostly in manufacturing. The acceleration of the CEPT and the temporary relaxation of the 30 per cent national equity requirement in AICO were the other measures jointly adopted by the ASEAN governments in order to maintain investor confidence during a time of economic distress. The recognition by ASEAN policymakers of the need for joint measures in ensuring foreign investor interest in the region was also reflected in their decision to embark on joint investment promotion missions in 1999–2000 to the major investor countries/regions, the US, Europe, and Japan – a first in ASEAN's history.[15]

Beneath the level of official discourse on open regionalism, however, protectionist elements emerged to strain intra-ASEAN relations as both tariff and non-tariff barriers were employed to shield domestic industries during the financial crisis (Bowles 2000: 445). Some observers of ASEAN point to this development as evidence of AFTA's failure.[16] This is too stark a position. While the adoption of tariff and non-tariff barriers was a setback for AFTA and did strain regional relations, its significance for evaluating progress in AFTA should not be exaggerated.

Many of the import restrictions were announced as temporary for a one to two year period, and were generally part of a set of short-term fiscal measures designed to reduce immediate pressure on countries' external accounts. Thus, a large proportion of tariffs were used to restrict big-ticket items, including luxury imports, transport equipment, and capital goods like steel and heavy machinery (Shimizu 2000: 83). The Philippine government raised tariffs on textile, steel and petrochemical products in response to business demands, but only for one year, although it contemplated temporarily withdrawing petrochemicals from CEPT disciplines.[17] The Philippine government rejected other business demands for protection, because as Trade Secretary, Jose Pardo pointed out, protection 'sends the wrong signal (to investors)'.[18] The point to note is that these particular 'protectionist' moves were brought on by the pressures of recession, and should be assessed in that context. Despite these temporary deviations from the CEPT, tariff liberalisation was on target and the majority of CEPT undertakings fulfilled as Chapter 2 shows. The notable exceptions were Malaysia's 1999 request for a delay in liberalising tariffs on automobiles, and the Philippines' announcement in September 2002 that it may temporarily exclude petrochemicals from AFTA. No formal request on the latter has been submitted at the time of writing.

While Bowles (2000: 444) sees the temporary incentive package as an indication of ASEAN's continued use of regionalism to sustain the FDI-led growth strategy in member countries, this chapter interprets the incentive package somewhat differently. While not denying Bowles' point, this chapter suggests that its significance lies in its temporary nature. The offer to remove restrictions on foreign equity and market access when it was announced was limited to investment applications made between January 1999 and December 2000 only, subject to further review. Moreover, the 30 per cent national equity requirement in AICO was waived for only two years until 2000, later extended by two years to the end of 2002. A number of scholars questioned the significance of these short-term measures when they were announced, and asked whether they would prove sufficiently attractive to investors during a period of economic turmoil (Soesastro 1999: 9). That these incentives were offered on a temporary basis is curious, given the overwhelming pressure in ASEAN during this period to maintain investor confidence and interest in the region. They raised some doubts about the commitment of the ASEAN governments to neoliberal economic reforms.

The short-term nature of these measures suggests that equity ownership and market access remained a sensitive issue in the ASEAN countries. Although Malaysia extended the incentive period until the end of 2003, its temporary nature remains unchanged at the time of writing. While many of Thailand's and Indonesia's temporary liberalisation offers were eventually incorporated into these countries' unilateral and IMF-led reform programmes, this does not alter the main thrust of the argument – that national governments were sensitive, for various reasons, about equity and market access issues.

These sensitivities were also reflected in the AIA programme. Although the AIA was accelerated in 1999 in direct response to the crisis, only ASEAN investors were scheduled to receive in 2003 full market access and national treatment privileges in the manufacturing sector, and in other sectors by 2010, while foreign investors were scheduled to receive full privileges in these areas only by 2020. This rather contradictory move, which did not appear to be helpful to the FDI cause, has still to be explained. It suggests that there were other dynamics apart from the FDI threat that shaped the development of AFTA, particularly its AIA programme. As the next chapter reveals, domestic political priorities centred on the need to nurture domestic capital influenced the design of the AIA.

AFTA: a neoliberal regionalist project?

Despite the anomaly in the AIA, the open regionalist credentials of AFTA in general and the CEPT component in particular cannot be doubted given the project's primary purpose to engage with global capital. One key feature of open regionalist projects is that the exchange of preferences among regional partners is not accompanied by the imposition of new barriers to non-partners. AFTA, having no common external tariff, clearly met this condition. Apart from its broadly open regionalist character, is AFTA also a project of neoliberal regionalism? Scholars like Bowles (2000) believe that it is, despite instances of protectionism during the financial crisis period. This section evaluates this claim using insights from Chapter 1 on neoliberal and embedded neoliberal regionalism as a guide. The analysis focuses on three key indicators, namely the formal design of regional trade liberalisation, the dominant discourse underpinning AFTA and the type of state–market relationship embedded in the AFTA project.

The formal design of regional trade liberalisation

Apart from the absence of a common external tariff, AFTA's neoliberal credentials were reflected in the way members were allowed to unilaterally and voluntarily extend CEPT tariff preferences to non-members on an MFN basis. It meant that the ASEAN member governments were not denied the chance to adopt unilateral economic reforms that went faster or beyond the CEPT in order to meet the unique competitive needs of the domestic economy, provided CEPT commitments were met at the very minimum. Although member governments availed themselves of this privilege on a number of occasions, the extension of CEPT preferences to non-members was not always practised, however. This is reflected in the fairly significant divergence in CEPT and MFN tariff rates in 2001, particularly in Thailand (see Table 2.11). Although member governments did not always multilateralise their CEPT tariff concessions, the mere presence of the option to extend CEPT tariff reductions to non-ASEAN members on an MFN basis reinforces the neoliberal credentials of AFTA.

Whether governments multilateralised their CEPT commitments was influenced by two factors, namely the presence of unilateral economic reform programmes and the need to reduce CEPT-induced tariff distortions. Malaysia, Indonesia, Thailand and the Philippines were engaged in an ongoing process of unilateral economic reforms from the mid-1980s. These economic reforms had initially been undertaken to overcome the economic recession of 1985–86, or, in the case of the Philippines, the economic crisis unleashed by the Marcos regime. They were designed to create the conditions for export-oriented, FDI-led growth. In that context, it made sense to extend AFTA tariff offers to all parties. Tariff reductions under the CEPT framework in AFTA thus dovetailed with unilateral tariff reforms.

In many cases, AFTA tariff reduction commitments drove or preceded unilateral (MFN) reform packages. Thus, the Indonesian deregulation package of May 1995 extended CEPT tariff reduction commitments, outlined the previous year, to all parties (Fane and Condon 1996: 53–4; James 1995: 32). In the Philippines, AFTA forced a change in the pace of economic reforms, with AFTA used to push unilateral trade liberalisation (Gochoco-Bautista 1998: 210). AFTA, more fundamentally, also altered the economic policy agenda in that country. Jesus Estanislao, Chairman of the Philippine AFTA Commission, admitted in 1993 that AFTA would lead to 'a radical departure of the policy orientation' of the Philippine government.[19] In Thailand, general tariff reform was undertaken as part of the country's preparation for AFTA (Krongkaew 1997: 24). A senior Thai Finance Ministry official noted that 'CEPT actually pushes Thailand's MFN tariff reforms'.[20]

A second reason why governments chose to multilateralise their CEPT tariff concessions was to restore the economic competitiveness of those sectors where divergent CEPT and MFN rates would worsen already existing tariff distortions. In Thailand and the Philippines especially, distortions in tariff structures required that the existing high import duties on raw materials and intermediate inputs be reduced on an MFN basis before or at the same time that CEPT commitments came into force. Because inputs that went into manufactured products like textiles were largely imported from outside ASEAN, high MFN tariffs on these inputs in Thailand and the Philippines made final goods less competitive compared with products made in Malaysia and Singapore where MFN input tariffs had been reduced much earlier. Once tariffs on final goods had been reduced to a uniform 0–5 per cent under AFTA, manufacturers in Thailand and the Philippines would have been at a disadvantage if MFN tariffs on relevant inputs had not reduced correspondingly. Final goods manufacturers in Thailand and the Philippines thus lobbied their governments to streamline tariff structures, and particularly to lower duties on imported inputs on an MFN basis to maintain the competitiveness of their products relative to those produced in the other ASEAN countries with less distorted tariff structures.

The textile industry in Thailand was among the worst affected. Thai textile firms urged the government to hasten tariff reform in Thailand before tariffs on final textile products fell to 0–5 per cent under the country's AFTA commitments.[21] Thai textile producers were levied MFN import duties of between 20 and 40 per cent on raw materials and inputs, which were largely imported from non-ASEAN sources, thus placing them at an enormous disadvantage compared to producers from Malaysia. These concerns led to a review of Thailand's tariff structure in 1999 when the import duty on raw materials and primary goods was set at between 0 and 5 per cent on an MFN basis, in line with the CEPT rate and those of the other ASEAN countries.[22]

Trends such as these confirm the neoliberal characteristics of AFTA. The competitiveness of domestic industry was clearly not to be compromised by any desire to maintain preferential tariffs among AFTA member countries to privilege product sourcing only from within ASEAN. The aim, after all, was to use AFTA to create a regional space of production through removing internal barriers to the free movement of economic resources. It was not primarily designed to increase intra-ASEAN trade, although regional trade would be expected to eventually rise if investors established transnational production in ASEAN.

The dominant discourse: globalisation, competitiveness and efficiency

While the specific design of the CEPT reflected its neoliberal credentials, the discourse associated with AFTA was also revealing of the kind of regionalist project that was being constructed in AFTA. Actors construct and use discourses to tell particular stories about the world. Discourses help in creating a cognitive structure that in turn helps shape the expectations of other actors about the world. They are the key elements in the 'mobilisation of bias', shaping the way society 'conceptualises the world or a particular problem', which also shapes the policy agenda by restricting the range of policy possibilities (Stone 2000: 252).

The discourse associated with AFTA was centred on the neoliberal tenets of competitiveness and efficiency. It thus reflected the dominant discourse in the core ASEAN countries that also stressed the importance of competitiveness and efficiency for firms and the economy in meeting the challenges of globalisation (Soesastro 1998). In these countries, national governments used the notion of 'globalisation' to justify and push through domestic economic reforms through deregulation, liberalisation and privatisation.[23] Moreover, competitiveness and efficiency were seen as vital for these economies in the competition to attract FDI and to ensure their integration with the world economy. While these countries cooperated in attracting FDI through regionalism, they also competed with each other to some extent, using individual investment incentive programmes to direct FDI that had been attracted in the first instance by the prospect of the AFTA market to their respective national economies (Rinakit and Soesastro

1998: 198). The option to multilateralise the CEPT and the absence of a common external tariff in AFTA facilitated competitive dynamics within ASEAN amidst the broad commitment to cooperate.

The neoliberal or globalisation discourse in the ASEAN countries was constructed and dominated by policymakers, and directed largely at private business. Its goal was to shape business expectations about economic reforms in general, and tariff liberalisation in particular, to make private business aware that it would no longer enjoy tariff protection as in the past. Substantial domestic business opposition to AFTA had emerged since the project was initially announced, and governments attempted to use discourse as one means of shaping expectations about the direction of economic reforms, including unilateral and CEPT trade liberalisation.[24]

Thus, the Thai Deputy Prime Minister in 1993, Dr Supachai Panitchpakdi pointed to 'competitiveness' as the main challenge for Thailand, and acknowledged, 'we are using AFTA to force competitiveness on local businesses, so you work with low protection.'[25] This was a message repeated by successive Thai governments since then.[26] Malaysian companies were continuously warned to brace themselves for international competition with the implementation of AFTA. Trade Minister Rafidah Aziz explained that liberalisation of the domestic market would 'enable local industries to build up the resilience required to face competition'.[27] The Philippine Foreign Secretary urged domestic firms to shape up for AFTA, which would 'force ASEAN industries to be globally competitive'.[28] In Indonesia, responses to globalisation were framed in terms of enhancing the international competitiveness of firms (Rinakit and Soesastro 1998: 199). Coordinating Minister for National Development Planning in 1996, Ginandjar Kartasasmita, re-affirmed the Indonesian government's commitments to AFTA during discussions with the business sector, warning businesses that the era of government protection of Indonesian firms was over.[29]

Other groups apart from policymakers, notably pro-reform business leaders and liberal economists, were often active participants in the dominant neoliberal discourse as well. This is not to deny the presence of alternative discourses. These did exist, and were focused on the negative aspects of globalisation, including its environmental, social and cultural effects. Nevertheless, during the high growth period of much of the 1990s, the neoliberal discourse of adjusting to globalisation through promoting competitiveness and efficiency was dominant in these countries and spearheaded by policymakers.[30] This was also the discourse associated with AFTA.

In Thailand, during the 1990s, despite an ongoing debate between the globalisers and the localists, the globalisers were predominant. Thai policymakers, notably the powerful technocrats in the civil service, interpreted globalisation as a force compelling neoliberal economic policies, and responded accordingly in policy formulation. Other advocates of the competitiveness discourse included the newly emergent commercial interests and the long established Bangkok business elite, in addition to the technocrats with liberal economic leanings in the Ministry of Finance, the central bank and the planning agency (Hamilton-Hart 1999: 293). Various policy documents were issued since 1994 that emphasise competitiveness as the primary strategy to respond to the pressures of globalisation (Chantana 1998: 266).

Unsurprisingly, these policies were fully supported by elite business interests – essentially the Bangkok-based conglomerates – who favoured a liberal economic environment with an eye on the benefits that foreign capital brought to their own ventures as joint partners, in addition to boosting the stock market. For instance, large Thai corporations like Siam Cement, Charoen Pokphand, the Saha Union, and the leading banks were favoured partners for foreign investors (Phongpaichit and Baker 1995: 156). Other business players outside the group of Bangkok-based conglomerates were less embracing of liberalisation. The globalisers, however, dominated public policy and were able to implement their agenda of liberalisation, while the far less coherent localists were marginal in policy terms (Hamilton-Hart 1999: 287–94). The Thai discourse of competitiveness and efficiency surrounding AFTA was derived from this broader globalisation discourse. Despite the crisis, the predominant discourse in Thailand remained the neoliberal one (Hamilton-Hart 1999: 301–2), at least until the election of Prime Minister Thaksin Shinawatra in January 2001 whose government appears to be less embracing of the neoliberal discourse and the liberal economic policies of previous governments.[31]

Unlike the discourse on globalisation in Singapore, which unambiguously emphasised competitiveness and market efficiency (Yeung 1999), the thrust of the globalisation discourse in countries like Indonesia and Malaysia was not unequivocal. Despite a preoccupation with competitiveness, alternative perceptions and responses to globalisation and its attendant neoliberalism were present in Indonesia and Malaysia even before the financial crisis, although the latter brought these alternative discourses into sharper relief (Murphy 1999; Welsh 1999). Far from being the discourses of non-state actors or civil society groups as in the case of Thailand, these alternative interpretations of globalisation were, in fact, articulated by Malaysian and Indonesian policymakers and political leaders. Reflecting mixed concerns about the purpose of economic development, they led to the adoption of particular policy responses in AFTA that contradicted the project's open regionalist/neoliberal character.

The attitudes and responses of both Malaysian and Indonesian policymakers were largely shaped by the ideas and responses of their respective leaders. As Welsh notes, a large portion of the Malaysian Prime Minister's Vision 2020 document outlining the strategies by which Malaysia would attain developed country status by 2020 emphasises neoliberal market reforms (Welsh 1999: 266). Yet, Dr Mahathir did not fully embrace the western notion of globalisation and its associated neoliberal policies in all areas of policy. As Chapter 4 shows, he also interpreted globalisation to emphasise its negative implications for developing countries and their firms. This particular view of globalisation was reflected in the Malaysian position on AFTA's investment liberalisation programme.

In Indonesia, President Suharto's broad response to globalisation was not to oppose it but to adjust to it (Rinakit and Soesastro 1998: 193–4). Although Indonesian economic policy during the 1990s moved in a broadly neoliberal direction, well-connected big business and powerful political groups were able to influence policy away from the neoliberal agenda in specific cases that were of direct interest to them. This is discussed in Chapter 5. Nevertheless, the ideal of competitiveness was a strong one in Indonesian policy circles, reflected in the extensive neoliberal reforms undertaken, although it did not go unchallenged in both ideational and policy terms as the discussion in Chapter 4 shows. As in the Malaysian case, these alternative discourses were also reflected in Indonesia's response to the AIA.

Contrary to the European experience, the competitiveness discourse in the ASEAN countries with regard to AFTA was initiated and constructed by public policymakers rather than corporate actors, as already noted. It was aimed at legitimising the withdrawal of protection that could disadvantage private businesses. It was also to create a set of expectations among businesses that the government was fully committed to regional tariff liberalisation and that business demands for protectionism would not be entertained. In the EU, on the other hand, it was the transnational business elite and their allies who had successfully defined the discourse surrounding European integration in terms of competitiveness and efficiency, which required a reduction in the scale and scope of state involvement in national economies (Van Apeldoorn 2000: 241). The experience of ASEAN was different as far as the state–market relationship was concerned.

The state–market relationship

If neoliberalism includes the notion of limited government involvement in or direction of the economy, then the competitiveness discourse associated with AFTA, and the nature of the AFTA project itself, reflected only a limited or partial form of neoliberalism. Although it incorporated the notion of business or private sector-led growth, this did not include the associated neoliberal idea of more market and less state at all levels of governance. Even in Singapore, the state retained a substantial role in the economy through the government-linked corporations.

In practice, neoliberalism was largely confined to the international trade regime, while at the domestic level, governments continued to regulate and impose restrictions on business activity, including that of foreign investors, despite domestic economic reforms in the core ASEAN countries. Moreover, all the core ASEAN governments were actively engaged in supplying the necessary public goods like education, skills and infrastructure to support business activity and attract FDI rather than leaving them to the free market to supply. As such, while AFTA, particularly through the CEPT, encompassed neoliberal features, the neoliberalism inherent in AFTA more broadly was only partial or limited.

Conclusion: contradictions and inconsistencies

One of the most notable contradictions in AFTA, and where its departure from the open regionalism of the CEPT is clearest, is found in the investment liberalisation programme. As already noted, the privileging of ASEAN investors over foreign investors in the AIA is curious, given the significant concern among the ASEAN member governments that the region remain attractive to FDI. Paradoxically, when the AIA was accelerated in 1999 in response to the financial crisis, the decision to bring forward the dates for removal of all exemptions from full market access and national treatment privileges was directed at ASEAN investors only, while the deadline for foreign (non-ASEAN) investors remained at the original 2020. It is puzzling that member governments did not remove the discrimination against foreign investors in the AIA during the crucial period of the financial crisis when it would have seemed logical not to jeopardise the already precarious economic climate. The ASEAN Secretary General, in fact, sought to play down this distinction between ASEAN and non-ASEAN investors in the AIA scheme in a bid to reassure foreign investors.[32]

How do we explain this particular anomaly in AFTA? Although the ASEAN governments removed the discrimination against foreign investors in September 2001, the fact that a distinction between foreign and ASEAN investors was adopted and maintained for a three-year period is puzzling given AFTA's acknowledged role as an instrument to attract FDI. It is insufficient to merely cite the emergence of protectionism in one or more of the ASEAN countries or of policy inconsistency as explanation. We need to delve deeper and ask what could have accounted for this departure from open regionalism even though the growth and FDI imperative remained strong during the 1990s, and particularly after the onset of the regional financial crisis in 1997. Clearly, other dynamics were at work in regional economies in addition to the growth and FDI dynamics. In essence, these dynamics revolved around the political economic role of domestic capital in elite governance political systems. The next chapter examines these dynamics in greater detail.

4 Domestic capital and developmental regionalism

Domestic distributive concerns temper the growth imperative

The particular design of the AIA component programme suggests that there is another dimension to the AFTA story apart from open regionalism and the concern with FDI that remains unexplored. It is clear that the approach to investment liberalisation adopted in the AIA sought to privilege ASEAN domestic capital in the AFTA market, at least temporarily for up to a ten-year period. The decision to offer full market access and national treatment privileges to ASEAN investors ahead of foreign investors in the AIA is certainly puzzling given AFTA's acknowledged role as an instrument to maintain the region's attractiveness as a site for FDI. This chapter explains this as a move by ASEAN member governments spearheaded by the Malaysian authorities to use the investment liberalisation programme of AFTA as a developmental tool to build up domestic firms, in addition to employing AFTA's tariff liberalisation CEPT programme to attract FDI to the single regional market. It is a perspective on AFTA that has so far been missed in the literature.

Specifically, the idea was to nurture domestic capital in the face of globalisation pressures by using both the expanded regional market and the offer of temporary investment privileges to domestic-owned capital ahead of foreign investors. These temporary investment privileges took the form of earlier market access and national treatment for ASEAN national investors in the ASEAN regional market, particularly in non-manufacturing sectors. It represents an attempt at developmental regionalism. In other words, AFTA displayed the features of *both* open and developmental regionalism due to the political significance of foreign- and domestic-owned capital in ASEAN. While both forms of regionalism were driven by the imperative of growth, distributive concerns tempered the concern with growth in developmental regionalism.

Although developmental regionalism was not about disengaging from globalisation, policymakers and leaders in at least two countries, namely Indonesia and especially Malaysia, were not prepared to accept the hegemony of foreign TNCs that was a growing feature of globalisation. Fearing that politically important domestic-owned businesses, especially emerging firms, would be adversely affected by unfettered market competition, these governments attempted to nurture firms such as these ahead of what they saw as the inevitability of global market competition by inscribing a developmental approach to AFTA.

Before elaborating on this argument, it is necessary to consider alternative explanations for the AIA puzzle. One possibility would be to view the investment liberalisation programme as an additional tool adopted by member governments to reinforce AFTA as a project of open regionalism and a means to sustain foreign investor interest in regional economies. In this account, the temporary discrimination of non-ASEAN/foreign investors is simply a way of offering domestic capital in the different ASEAN countries sufficient time to prepare for full investment liberalisation in 2020. This explanation appears to have some merit if we consider the way the AIA Agreement was framed. The original agreement, in fact, specified that full market access and national treatment privileges were to be accorded to *all* investors immediately where possible, but allowed governments to maintain temporary exemptions in a variety of sectors and policy areas as they saw fit (ASEAN 1998d). If the exemptions were indeed aimed at offering domestic capital sufficient time to prepare for full investment liberalisation, then why were the exemptions from full market access and national treatment privileges scheduled to be removed for *ASEAN* investors at least ten years earlier than for foreign investors? The exemptions, which were fairly extensive, were to be removed by 2003 and 2010 for ASEAN investors and by 2020 for all other foreign investors (ASEAN Secretariat 1999b). This would not have protected domestic investors from all external investors, since other ASEAN investors were to be treated as domestic investors from 2003/2010. Any explanation of the AIA puzzle must be able to account for this point.

A second possibility is simply that the AIA distinction between ASEAN and non-ASEAN or foreign investors was irrelevant or redundant in the first place due to essentially liberal FDI regimes in ASEAN.[1] This interpretation can be challenged in two ways. First, if the distinction is indeed irrelevant, the question of why policymakers would choose to make it in the first place needs to be answered. It is insufficient to assume that policymakers were acting irrationally or were misinformed, since the implications of instituting such a distinction were actively debated during the three years of discussions leading up to the formal adoption of the AIA Agreement in 1998, and continued to be debated until September 2001 when this particular clause was dropped. Clearly, there were some quarters for which the distinction was salient. In fact, when member governments revised the terms of the AIA Agreement in 1999, a year after its initial adoption, they chose to continue privileging ASEAN investors over foreign investors.

Second, the argument that the foreign-ASEAN distinction is irrelevant or redundant is easily challenged on empirical grounds. Foreign investors continued to face investment restrictions in many of the original ASEAN countries during the 1990s in selected sectors and in particular policy areas despite liberalisation of national FDI regimes, thus making the AIA distinction between domestic and foreign investors significant. This was especially true for the non-manufacturing sectors where fairly restrictive FDI conditions prevailed. These restrictions ranged from equity ownership conditions, market access to certain sectors, land ownership regulations, and access to domestic sources of funds. They are outlined in detail in the first part of this chapter.

Following this, the rest of the discussion elaborates on the chapter's central argument – that globalisation, manifested through changes, or expected changes in multilateral investment rules, raised concerns in some ASEAN countries with regard to the future of politically important domestic firms in global competition, which in turn led to the adoption of a developmental component in AFTA through the AIA.

National FDI regimes in ASEAN

Investment regimes in the core ASEAN countries comprise at least seven categories in which restrictions or differential treatment of foreign over national investors can be maintained. These seven categories cover (a) sectors open to investment, (b) equity ownership, (c) fiscal incentives, (d) taxation, (e) banking and financial regulations, (f) employment conditions and (g) land ownership.[2] While the first category relates to the market access issue in the AIA, the rest of the six categories are relevant to the national treatment issue. If significant conditions or restrictions were imposed on foreign investors compared to national investors in one or more of these categories, then the AIA proposal to accord full national treatment and market access privileges to ASEAN investors ahead of foreign investors would indeed be meaningful.

Thailand

During the 1990s, Thailand's investment regime was governed by two pieces of legislation. The Investment Promotion Act of 1977 (revised in 1992) outlined all incentives available to both Thai national and foreign investors in priority investment sectors while the 1972 Alien Business Law (ABL-72) provided guidelines on foreign equity participation. The latter was especially restrictive, and long subject to demands from foreign business for its review or repeal.[3] ABL-72 protected sixty-three business categories across a range of sectors in manufacturing, services, commerce, agriculture, transportation and construction from full and/or majority foreign participation, unless export conditions and/or promoted status were fulfilled.[4] Under the Thai Land Code, foreign investors were not permitted to purchase land unless operating in a priority sector, although limited 30-year leases were allowed. Investors generally prefer longer periods of lease for security of tenure, with 99-year leases being the norm in industrial countries, while owned land is useful as collateral for local borrowing provided it is permitted (Thomsen 1999: 21). When the AIA was initially adopted, these restrictions on foreign investments were in force under ABL-72, making the AIA distinction between a national investor and a foreign investor significant.

In March 2000, ABL-72 was replaced by the Foreign Business Act of 1999, which liberalised conditions for foreign investment in Thailand.[5] It reduced the number of business sectors restricted to foreign participation from 63 to 42, allowed greater access to foreign majority ownership in Thai industries, and offered liberal land leases of fifty years, renewable for a further fifty years. On the other hand, restrictions on foreign participation remained in many sectors including agriculture and services, particularly computer and electronics services while new, more restrictive investment rules were introduced to tighten the conditions under which foreign businesses operate in Thailand.[6] For instance, the 1999 Act expanded the definition of 'foreign' business to include ventures in which foreigners exercised virtual management control despite owning less than 50 per cent equity. In contrast, ABL-72 had only considered businesses in which foreigners held more than 50 per cent equity to be alien or foreign businesses.

The terms of the 1999 Foreign Business Act, thus, continued to make the AIA distinction between foreign and ASEAN investors a significant one indeed, particularly in the non-manufacturing sectors. Many of the restricted activities under the new Thai law fell under the AIA categories of forestry, fisheries, mining, agricultural activities and in services 'incidental' to manufacturing. While the Thai government, under the terms of the AIA, was only obliged to accord full investment privileges in these sectors by 2010, the point to note is that the AIA distinction between ASEAN and non-ASEAN investors had not become irrelevant under Thailand's new investment law.

In fact, the then Thai Deputy Prime Minister, Dr Supachai Panitchpakdi, had insisted in 1997 that any new law replacing ABL-72 would not accord national treatment to foreign investors despite the latter's strong preference for it.[7] Moreover, the new, populist government of Prime Minister Thaksin Shinawatra elected in January 2001 began to show signs that it was considering tightening the conditions of foreign participation in the economy, especially in still protected sectors like insurance, finance, and even in heavy industries like steel. Thaksin's promise to the Federation of Thai Industries in February 2001 to amend laws that 'work against Thai interests' and for Thailand to cease being a 'slave to the world' won the new government much political support.[8] It reflected the anti-western and anti-globalisation mood in the country, which was a response to the extensive liberalisation undertaken by the previous Chuan government both unilaterally as well as under the conditions imposed by the IMF in its bailout package for Thailand during the financial crisis.

Malaysia

Malaysia has maintained a liberal FDI regime in manufacturing since the mid-1980s, the only significant restriction being that on foreign equity ownership. Nevertheless, majority and full foreign ownership is permitted, but only if certain export conditions are fulfilled.[9] The Promotion of Investments Act (1986) that liberalised the FDI regime after the 1985 recession allows full foreign ownership in manufacturing provided more than 80 per cent of production is exported, while majority foreign ownership is allowed if more than half the produced output is exported. As in Thailand, the presence of these restrictions on foreign ownership made the AIA clause offering earlier national treatment to ASEAN investors potentially significant.

During the financial crisis, the Malaysian government temporarily relaxed foreign investment rules, as did the other ASEAN countries (see Table 2.6). While the more relaxed FDI regime initially applied to investments made between 31 July 1998 and 31 December 2000, it was later extended until the end of 2003, subject to further review.[10] Despite these changes to FDI rules, equity restrictions remained in several categories of manufacturing activities[11] to protect the operations of small- and medium-scale Malaysian-owned enterprises that dominated these activities and that had the potential to act as suppliers to the larger MNCs. Many were, in fact, already doing so. These activities were also likely to be attractive to national investors from the other ASEAN countries. In any case, official Malaysian government policy on equity encourages joint ventures between foreign and domestic partners as a means to increasing Malaysian participation in manufacturing.

The other significant restriction that Malaysia maintained was on the amount that foreign investors could borrow from domestic banking sources (ASEAN Secretariat 1998b: 78). This particular policy on domestic borrowing was especially likely to hinder investment from medium-scale enterprises from the ASEAN countries. National treatment of ASEAN investors in this area removes at least one key obstacle preventing such firms from expanding their operations in the ASEAN region. All things considered, the AIA commitment to offer earlier market access and national treatment to ASEAN investors was a significant policy move for Malaysia, particularly if the temporary relaxation in equity and market access restrictions on foreign investors is not extended after 2003.

The Philippines

The 1987 Omnibus Investment Code substantially liberalised the FDI regime in the Philippines, allowing up to 100 per cent foreign equity in priority sectors. Although the 1991 Foreign Investment Act further liberalised investment rules (McFarlane 1998: 163; Austria 1998: 80), the government continued to maintain equity limits and other conditions on foreign investors as part of the 'Filipino First' clause of the Constitution (Thomsen 1999: 21). Importantly, a negative list of manufacturing activities either closed to foreign participation or in which only limited foreign participation is permitted was maintained, although this list was progressively shortened throughout the 1990s.[12] Apart from this negative list, full foreign equity ownership was permitted in all manufacturing activities open to foreign investors provided at least 60 per cent of output was exported. Otherwise a 40 per cent foreign equity limit was imposed, or 65 per cent in the iron and steel sector (ASEAN Secretariat 1998b: 49–51). The provision of investment incentives was also dependent on equity conditions (ASEAN Secretariat 1998b: 50). Non-Filipino companies were required to become Filipino companies within thirty years by reducing the foreign ownership ratio to less than 40 per cent. Companies that exported all their output were exempted from the divestment requirement, however (ASEAN Secretariat 1998b: 35).

As for land ownership, only Filipino companies, and/or companies with at least 60 per cent domestic equity were allowed to own land (ASEAN Secretariat 1998b: 101).[13] Otherwise, foreign investors were permitted to lease land for fifty years. Although former President Joseph Estrada (1998–2001) proposed to remove all restrictions on foreign ownership of land and utilities, substantial domestic opposition prevented such a move. Even Estrada's predecessor, Fidel Ramos (1992–98) who had presided over extensive neoliberal reform of the Philippine economy, opposed offering parity of equity rights to foreign nationals (Bolongaita Jr 2000: 69). Thus, the Philippine FDI regime maintained significant restrictions on foreign investment ownership and participation in the economy. This meant that the AIA distinction between national, and thus ASEAN, investors on the one hand, and foreign investors on the other was significant, provided Philippine nationalistic sentiments were not also directed at investors from the other ASEAN countries.

Indonesia

The FDI regime in Indonesia was liberalised from 1985, albeit gradually to avoid arousing nationalistic sentiments over control by foreign interests of national economic resources. As in the Philippines, the Indonesian Constitution, specifically Article 33, mandates state control over key economic sectors (Borsuk 1999: 144–7). Extensive liberalisation was introduced in 1994 in which the divestment clause requiring foreign equity to be reduced to below 50 per cent within fifteen years was eliminated, although with certain conditions attached. Also, nine previously closed strategic sectors in services, industry and utilities were opened to foreign investment through joint venture operations (Pangestu and Azis 1994: 21). Full foreign ownership was permitted with few conditions attached while the minimum Indonesian national equity required for joint ventures was reduced to 5 per cent from 20 per cent (Negara 1998: 12).

Furthermore, the IMF restructuring programme adopted, as a result of the financial crisis, removed all foreign investment restrictions in the wholesale and retail trade sectors from March 1998, both of which had remained untouched by earlier deregulation packages (Soesastro and Basri 1998: 24). Nevertheless, significant restrictions on land ownership remained, which restricted foreign corporations to own only the buildings for a maximum period of fifty years (ASEAN Secretariat 1998b: 100–1). Apart from this, the FDI regime in Indonesia was fairly liberal, making the foreign-ASEAN distinction in the AIA somewhat irrelevant in Indonesia, although Indonesian investors could potentially gain from preferential investment treatment elsewhere in ASEAN.

Singapore and the other ASEAN countries

Singapore maintained a liberal FDI regime, with virtually no restrictions on foreign ownership or market access except for national security reasons and in certain industries like banking, shipping, airlines and the utilities. Brunei also maintained a relatively liberal FDI regime. The new members of ASEAN – Vietnam, Myanmar, Laos and Cambodia – generally treated foreign investors better than national investors when offering incentives and in taxation (ASEAN Secretariat 1998b: 48, 64). While their foreign equity policies were often far more liberal than those in the core ASEAN countries, these governments maintained fairly stringent restrictions on land ownership and leasing, while domestic borrowing was generally not permitted (ASEAN Secretariat 1998b: 100–1). In these areas, the AIA clause with regard to foreign versus ASEAN investors was, therefore, significant.

National FDI regimes and the foreign-ASEAN distinction in the AIA

The above survey of FDI regimes in the core ASEAN countries reveals that foreign investors faced particular restrictions when investing in these countries despite the overall liberal FDI climate. These restrictions ranged from equity ownership conditions, market access to certain sectors, land ownership regulations and access to domestic sources of finance, although the restrictions were not identical across the different countries. These restrictions meant that the AIA offer of earlier national treatment and market access privileges to ASEAN investors was meaningful, particularly if one considers the AFTA market as a whole. Although the further liberalisation of FDI regimes in the manufacturing sector, particularly in Thailand and Indonesia as a result of the financial crisis somewhat weakened the distinction between foreign and national/ASEAN investors in individual countries, this did not make the distinction redundant as far as the AFTA market was concerned. Malaysia's crisis-driven liberalisation was undertaken on a temporary basis, indicating that the foreign-national distinction in investment remained crucial. For the core ASEAN countries, the AIA distinction between ASEAN and foreign investors appears to be most relevant in the categories, services 'incidental' to manufacturing, forestry, agriculture, mining and fisheries. Nevertheless, full market access and national treatment privileges to ASEAN investors in these sectors were only to be accorded by 2010.

The very fact that the ASEAN governments chose to emphasise the distinction between ASEAN and foreign investors in the AIA is itself significant, irrespective of later developments in FDI regimes and in implementation. It is this that requires explanation, given that AFTA had become a key instrument to direct global investment capital to the ASEAN region. This chapter suggests that the answer lies in the way certain governments in ASEAN interpreted particular global developments in terms of their impact on the future of domestic capital, especially those segments of domestic capital that had close ties to the political elite and were important in sustaining elite rule. The rest of the chapter elaborates on these arguments.

Globalisation and multilateral investment rules

Apart from the competitive pressures generated by the increasing mobility and changing patterns of global FDI flows, globalisation also manifested itself during the 1990s through the growing pressure from advanced country governments and their TNCs to negotiate multilateral rules to govern 'beyond the border' barriers to free trade. These new rules had the potential to markedly weaken the discretionary authority of governments on key aspects of domestic policy (Smythe 2000: 75). Industrial country governments and the TNCs were especially keen to develop a global investment regime based on rules ensuring full market access and national treatment for all investors. Their efforts were channelled through forums like APEC, the WTO and most notably, the Organisation for Economic Cooperation and Development (OECD). If adopted, such a regime would effectively allow maximum freedom of operation for foreign investors in as many countries as possible.

Creating a level playing field for global corporations

The Uruguay Round agreements, and since then the WTO, had significant implications for FDI, although no explicit set of rules governing FDI *per se* has so far been adopted in the multilateral trading system. The Trade Related Investment Measures (TRIMS) Agreement was limited to regulating investment rules that had trade effects, notably local content requirements. It was the General Agreement on Trade in Services (GATS) negotiated under the Uruguay Round that first brought the specific issue of market access and national treatment for foreign investors to the forefront of global trade negotiations (Gibbs 1997: 189). Although the national treatment principle was watered down substantially in the GATS due to strong objections from developing country governments, WTO members were expected to reconsider the issue during the new round of trade negotiations scheduled for 1999–2000. They were also expected to debate the possibility of including investment under the WTO framework (WTO Secretariat 1999).

While the TRIMS did not sanction the right for foreign firms to market access and national treatment, it was clear that global firms were interested in just such guarantees (Sell 2000: 179–80). TNCs from the industrial world were increasingly keen on developing global rules that would maximise their freedom of operation globally (Smythe 2000: 72). Industrial country governments led by the US backed these demands, and in 1991 instructed the OECD to begin discussions on a more comprehensive investment regime that also included the national treatment principle. The US had turned to the OECD because of the difficulties Washington had encountered in negotiating the TRIMS agreement at the GATT (Smythe 2000: 78–9). The goal, nevertheless, was to develop a new global regime in which non-OECD members would participate, since it was in the non-OECD world that TNCs faced the most restrictions, when investing.

The OECD began formal negotiations on a Multilateral Agreement on Investment (MAI) in 1995, which was to be open to accession by non-OECD countries. The MAI advocated national treatment, the right of entry and establishment of foreign investment, the right to full equity ownership, as well as national treatment rights in privatisation (Khor 2001: 86–7). The EU countries, in particular, wanted the MAI to eventually migrate to the WTO to enable trade leverage to be used in disciplining governments and resolving disputes over the free movement of investment (Smythe 2000: 80). Although the MAI was eventually shelved in 1998 due to disagreements among OECD members as well as strong opposition from non-governmental groups representing labour and the environment, it generated enormous controversy in the developing world, including in ASEAN. The MAI episode revealed to ASEAN policymakers the rising interest among industrial country governments and global corporations in introducing global rules to guarantee the free movement of investment in the world economy.[14]

The investment issue was also pursued in APEC, though with only partial success. Although the grouping's developing country members were opposed to adopting a binding trade and investment liberalisation agreement, the United States, backed by Canada, Australia and New Zealand, succeeded in getting APEC members to adopt a set of investment principles that included national treatment. Developing country member governments, however, ensured that the investment code was non-binding on members (APEC 1994). Importantly for the argument developed in this chapter, this episode signalled to the ASEAN countries the keen interest of industrial country governments and the TNCs in negotiating global investment rules.

Although investment was kept firmly off the negotiating agenda in the WTO by a group of developing countries led by India and Brazil and including Malaysia and Indonesia, it was not certain that this state of affairs would continue. WTO members had agreed as a compromise to study the issue further and had set up a working group on investment in 1996. Its brief was not only to study the trade-investment nexus more carefully but also to assess the feasibility of incorporating investment into the WTO. Many governments regarded the reprieve as only temporary, particularly since the WTO was scheduled to review and re-negotiate the TRIMS in 2000 (Sell 2000: 182). The expectation was that it was only a matter of time before such guarantees to foreign investors were written into the WTO regime (Khor 2001: 86).

These expectations were not misplaced. In 1998, the WTO General Council decided that the Working Group on Investment should continue its work until the Seattle ministerial meeting in 1999 when members would decide on whether to incorporate investment within the WTO.[15] The European Commission was particularly interested in ensuring that the national treatment principle formed a key part of any future WTO regime on investment (Khor 2001: 87). The issue of investment rules was clearly a lasting concern for TNCs and their parent governments.[16] The point to note is that the expectations of an impending global investment regime reinforced perceptions in ASEAN of the further intensification of market competition for domestic firms and of the further dominance by foreign corporations of national economies. They led at least two of the five original ASEAN member governments to contemplate providing preferential investment treatment for ASEAN firms in the AFTA regional market as a means to build up domestic firms.

The ASEAN response to multilateral developments

Most of the ASEAN countries rejected the idea of a global regime for investment when it first became clear in the early and mid-1990s that many industrial country governments were considering such a project. Malaysia especially was opposed to the notion of national treatment. Trade minister Rafidah Aziz rejected the demand for

> free movement of investment across national borders and for national treatment,...[which] will remove the right of national governments to implement national level investment policies which may either restrict a foreign presence in certain sectors, or which may provide

> preferential treatment to national firms to enable them to grow and be able to compete with large established foreign firms.
>
> Rafidah Aziz (1996)

Malaysia also convened a special conference of developing countries in July 1996 to explore a common 'south' stand on a number of issues that industrial country governments were expected to raise at the First WTO Ministerial Conference in Singapore in December 1996. It successfully obtained a consensus position amongst those participating at the conference against the investment issue.[17]

Indonesia formally outlined its objections to the inclusion of investment in the WTO by jointly submitting a petition together with Malaysia and six other developing countries on the matter.[18] Thailand initially rejected the idea of a global investment agreement.[19] After the financial crisis, however, the Thai Cabinet agreed to support the adoption of a broad trade and investment agreement at the WTO Ministerial Meeting in Seattle, provided issues like investment incentives, dispute settlement between governments and private business, and national treatment principles were excluded.[20] Although Thai support was for a more limited agreement compared to the more comprehensive MAI, the government was, no doubt, responding to the country's need to remain attractive to FDI in the face of loss of investor confidence in Thailand. Singapore was more sympathetic to the idea of a global investment regime.

Although practically all the core ASEAN countries rejected the idea of a global investment regime that would include the principle of national treatment, the concerns were strongest in Indonesia and especially Malaysia as already noted, and were centred on the future of domestic firms. These concerns were reflected in alternative interpretations of globalisation that deviated somewhat from the dominant competitiveness discourse although the notion of competitiveness was not totally rejected.

Alternative interpretations of globalisation

Although for the most part globalisation was interpreted in a positive manner in ASEAN, as a process through which national economies could participate in global wealth creating activities that would benefit national society, other interpretations and discourses were also evident. The primary discourse, emphasising competitiveness, continued to focus on the importance of adopting neoliberal economic reforms in order to adjust to globalisation (Soesastro 1998). This was discussed in Chapter 3, which also pointed out that in Malaysia and Indonesia, alternative readings of globalisation were also present that deviated from the neoliberal competitiveness discourse. These competing discourses essentially emphasised the possible demise of domestic firms, particularly emerging firms, as a result of having to compete with well-established foreign corporations. These sentiments became especially pronounced during the time of the debates and moves in the OECD, the EU and the WTO to inscribe global investment rules.

While the competing discourses on globalisation in Malaysia and Indonesia did not reject the idea of competitiveness *per se*, they stressed other dimensions of competitiveness that were marginalised in the neoliberal discourse. Notably, these alternate discourses emphasised the importance of nurturing the competitiveness of *domestic-owned* firms and the key role of governments in that process, the aim being to enable their development into firms capable of competing with the TNCs in the global market. These discourses thus reflected developmental ideas.

In Malaysia, Dr Mahathir, the Prime Minister, had largely shaped discourses on globalisation, which by the mid-1990s had become a common part of the Malaysian political and economic scene (Welsh 1999: 272). The centralisation of power in the office of the Prime Minister coupled with the personal authority that he largely enjoyed, at least until the financial crisis, meant that his ideas and interpretations generally prevailed and were translated into official policy. What was most notable about Malaysian discourses on globalisation was the embrace of only parts of the globalisation message associated with the Washington Consensus.[21] Other aspects were redefined or re-interpreted, again largely by the Prime Minister.

In the Vision 2020 document of 1990, which laid the foundation for the Prime Minister's attitudes and responses to globalisation and his strategies to achieve developed country status for Malaysia, the neoliberal message of markets, competition and competitiveness was explicit. Mahathir's aim was to 'secure the establishment of a competitive economy… that is subjected to the full discipline and rigour of market forces' (Mahathir 1990: 3). The Prime Minister also appeared to accept the nature of global market competition when he commented that 'entry into the world market pits our companies against all comers and subjects them to the full force of international competition … a challenge we must accept…' (Mahathir 1990: 9). As already noted in the previous chapter, the adoption of policies of deregulation, privatisation and liberalisation in Malaysia was consistent with these ideas.

Despite the emphasis on competitiveness, other concerns were never ignored, only de-emphasised. By 1996, however, the Prime Minister's long-held concerns about the inequalities in the global economy re-surfaced in the discourses associated with globalisation. The timing of his re-interpretation of globalisation, even before the financial crisis hit Malaysia, was linked to the flurry of activity at the OECD on the MAI, the move to embrace new issues in the WTO, and the pressure on Malaysia to make better market opening offers in the GATS financial services negotiations. At the Sixth G-15 Summit in Harare in November 1996, the Prime Minister pointed out that 'in the name of globalisation, developing countries have been called upon to account for many things, be it the environment, labour standards, investment laws, financial services, or other development issues'.[22] Mahathir also began enunciating the view that globalisation was a threat to developing countries in general, and their firms in particular.[23] This interpretation became increasingly pronounced since the 1997 financial crisis. The competing discourse also drew attention to the emergence of huge corporations and banks that dominated economies everywhere through having acquired or absorbed small companies and banks, particularly in the developing world (Mahathir 1998: 111). The emphasis on growth through embracing neoliberal policies was also confronted by concern with building up domestic firms.

In Indonesia, three competing discourses were evident during the 1990s. All three shared the same perception of globalisation as an inevitable economic force, which Indonesia needed to cope with to 'survive' (Rinakit and Soesastro 1998: 193). These three discourses, nevertheless, viewed competitiveness and the means to achieve it through different lenses. Although neoliberal ideas about competitiveness appeared to be dominant, seemingly reflected in the trade and investment liberalisation undertaken during the mid-1990s, neoliberal policies were essentially limited to the external sector. This was pointed out in the previous chapter. Reforms to deregulate the domestic economy, increase market competition and privatise state enterprises were far more limited, however, reflecting not only the particularistic interests of the politically well-connected but also competing concerns in Indonesia with nurturing domestic capital.

The discourse of the economic nationalists emphasised the importance of economic reform to meet the competitive challenges of globalisation, but advocated state intervention to protect strategic industries and sectors from foreign domination and for governments to help leapfrog technological development (Murphy 1999: 235). Minister of Research and Technology, B.J. Habibie, later Suharto's Vice-President in 1998 and subsequently Indonesian President for a year until late 1999, was the most prominent proponent of these ideas. These ideas resonated with many Indonesians, who regarded a state-controlled economic system to be sacrosanct under the country's Constitution (Rinakit and Soesastro 1998: 196). Moreover, the nationalists were also concerned about the dominance of the Indonesian economy by ethnic Chinese Indonesian business (Borsuk 1999: 142).

The discourse of the economic populists, like that of the liberals and the nationalists also emphasised economic restructuring, but the populists saw a crucial role for the state in nurturing small- and medium-scale, indigenous businesses and the rural economy, rather than large, strategic industries. Like the nationalists, the populists, the most notable of whom was Adi Sasono of the Muslim Intellectuals Association, were also concerned by the dominant position of ethnic Chinese Indonesian capital, which the populists believed had thrived under the liberal economic policies of the government (Murphy 1999: 235). Thus, the populists were in favour of an affirmative action programme similar to that in Malaysia to upgrade the economic position of the majority indigenous population (Murphy 1999: 247).

The once dominant position of the liberal technocrats in the Indonesian bureaucracy and government who had pushed through neoliberal policies since the mid-1980s declined considerably as the 1990s wore on. By 1994, President Suharto had appointed many economic nationalists to his cabinet, until then dominated by liberal technocrats (Borsuk 1999: 140–3). These policymakers increasingly embraced the idea that deregulation and liberalisation could be strategically integrated with state-driven industrial policy to help develop domestic industrial and commercial capabilities (Robison 1997: 53). The concern with nurturing domestic capital was clearly reflected in these discourses in Indonesia, and ultimately in policy preferences.

Although alternative interpretations of globalisation challenging its purported beneficial effects were present in Thailand and the Philippines, constructed largely by non-governmental organisations, the powerful liberal technocrats in these respective governments continued to emphasise a conventional neoliberal policy agenda of growth and international competitiveness (Chantana 1998: 271–4; Gochoco-Bautista 1998: 222). In both countries, the technocrats were supported by outward-oriented big businesses, especially in Thailand. In the Philippines, the neoliberal economic agenda found support in the significant constituency that had emerged by the 1990s advocating economic reform in order to challenge the power of the old-landed oligarchy (Hutchison 1997). Nevertheless, departures from neoliberal policies, including in AFTA, were not uncommon in the Philippines, driven by particularistic business interests with substantial political influence. Departures from liberal economic policies and from AFTA were less evident in Thailand due to the powerful coalition of interests – technocrats and urban-based big business – in favour of the neoliberal agenda (Krongkaew 1997: 33–5).

Using the AIA as a developmental tool

In response to concerns about the future of emerging domestic capital, the Malaysian side advocated a developmental role for the AIA that would help nurture *domestic* capital through the privileging of ASEAN investors in the AFTA market. Thus, Article 3 of the AIA lists as one of its objectives, 'increasing the flow of investments into ASEAN from *both* ASEAN and non-ASEAN sources' (ASEAN 1998d).[24] A senior Malaysian trade official acknowledged that the AIA was designed not only to increase the inflow of FDI into the region but also aimed at 'developing and helping ASEAN investors'.[25] Preferential market access and national treatment privileges for ASEAN investors were aimed at providing domestic (ASEAN) firms space to grow and become internationally competitive before TNCs were allowed full investment privileges in the regional market.[26] With these privileges, the single regional market under AFTA would provide the necessary scale and learning economies for domestic firms, at least theoretically.

The lure of large domestic firms and ASEAN multinationals

The AIA was not only aimed at stimulating the growth of large domestic firms, a crucial part of the project was also to encourage the development of ASEAN conglomerates through joint ventures or other forms of alliances among ASEAN domestic investors as a means of competing with the global corporate giants. A senior official from the ASEAN Secretariat explained, 'the ASEAN countries saw the need to develop regional MNCs using the grace period before foreign investors would be accorded the same privileges'.[27] There was clearly a move to nurture domestic capital, especially emerging capital, through the AIA as well as use the latter to catalyse the formation of ASEAN multinationals.

The AIA essentially introduced a developmental agenda into AFTA without necessarily jeopardising the role of the CEPT component in attracting FDI. The ASEAN governments were sufficiently realistic not to adopt inward-looking policies that restricted or rejected FDI, with governments remaining committed to foreign investment and open regionalism in the CEPT. Whether the idea of using the AIA as a developmental tool was workable is a separate issue that falls beyond the scope of this book. Why such a project was adopted is the more interesting question, to be addressed below.

Although it was the Malaysian government that initiated the idea of using the AIA as a developmental tool, which Indonesia supported, all the respective investment agencies in the core ASEAN countries accepted the need to initially accord investment privileges to ASEAN investors in the AIA and only later to extend these to non-ASEAN investors.[28] This point had, in fact, been extensively debated during the three years of consultations that led up to the formal signing of the AIA Agreement in October 1998. It had been noted at these consultations that privileging ASEAN investors would be difficult to justify on economic grounds, since foreign TNCs possessed the wealth-creating assets that the ASEAN countries required in order to participate in increasingly sophisticated global production.[29] Nevertheless, it was also acknowledged that preferential treatment of ASEAN investors could potentially stimulate intra-ASEAN investments and facilitate the emergence and growth of indigenous ASEAN multinationals, which was a necessary vehicle 'to compete in a world economy increasingly characterised by globalisation and competition' (Chia 1996: 21).

ASEAN leaders and policymakers were broadly united on the importance of domestic firms becoming large and/or multinational as a means of meeting global market competition. The Singapore government's 'Local Enterprises 2000' strategy, first enunciated in the country's 1991 Strategic Economic Plan, proposed to groom a group of promising local enterprises over the next ten years to become the MNCs of the future (Wong and Ng 1997: 136). President Suharto advocated large and medium-sized firms for Indonesia as a means to face competition from TNCs.[30] On the one hand, this may well reflect Suharto's need to justify the regime's preferential treatment of the conglomerates of his ethnic Chinese allies and family members. On the other hand, Suharto was supportive of his Research and Technology Minister, B.J. Habibie's plans to develop large, technologically advanced firms as a means for Indonesia to leapfrog technology development and join the ranks of the advanced industrial economies (Mardjana 1999: 51). The private sector also echoed these sentiments. The President of the ASEAN Business Forum agreed that 'we are too small to go out and fight with the Fortune 500 companies',[31] while the Thai private sector urged its government to support the creation of regional Thai firms.[32]

While investment officials were broadly united on the need to accord investment privileges to ASEAN investors ahead of foreign investors, they differed on how to define an 'ASEAN' investor in terms of its minimum ASEAN equity share (or maximum foreign equity share). This was a critical point in the AIA negotiations, since many domestic investors in the ASEAN countries were also involved in joint ventures with foreign capital. In any case, FDI was an important player in ASEAN and the ASEAN governments were not advocating keeping out FDI; they were only interested in nurturing domestic capital through temporary privileges accorded to the latter, and particularly in non-manufacturing sectors. As already noted, developmental regionalism was to be achieved through the AIA without jeopardising the role of the CEPT in attracting manufacturing sector FDI.

Thus, it was not surprising that a very open economy like Singapore advocated a liberal definition of an ASEAN investor that stipulated only a minimum 30 per cent ASEAN equity share. This meant that any venture up to a maximum foreign equity share of 70 per cent could qualify for national treatment and market access privileges.[33] The Thai Board of Investment, in contrast, advocated a minimum ASEAN equity share of at least 51 per cent in keeping with prevailing Thai investment policy, at least during the initial negotiations on this matter. On the other hand, the Thai Commerce Ministry that has overall charge of AFTA policy and negotiations was more concerned about emphasising the AIA as a tool to attract FDI rather than its developmental role. It was able to pressure the Board to lower the minimum ASEAN equity figure to 30 per cent.[34] The other countries, all with varying degrees of restrictions on foreign participation, preferred a more conservative definition, however. In the end, the ASEAN governments agreed to define an ASEAN investor as a domestic investor according to each prospective host country's local investment laws and policies. Flexibility prevailed for two reasons. First, it allowed individual governments the independence to adopt mixes of domestic/ASEAN and foreign investment that met national needs. Second, it continued to facilitate joint ventures between foreign and domestic firms as a way of building up the domestic partner through technology transfer and learning from the foreign partner.[35]

Malaysia: the main proponent

As already noted, Malaysia was especially vocal in advocating large enterprises as a means of facing global competition, emphasising in particular the idea that ASEAN multinationals or conglomerates would be best able to weather global market competition rather than smaller firms. It was Prime Minister Mahathir's belief that only products from large firms would be able to penetrate the world market. Thus, he advocated using the state to assist 'small and medium industries . . . to grow bigger', for all Malaysian firms to become 'sturdy and strong' and be able to 'take on the world' (Khoo 1995: 330).

Since the early 1990s, senior officials of the Economic Planning Unit, the foremost economic policymaking agency in the country, had begun emphasising, often with great urgency, the need to nurture domestic capital, revealing the extent of official discomfort with the country's overwhelming reliance on FDI. A senior official from the Unit noted that 'FDI cannot be relied upon to build up an indigenous base, which is required for long-term sustainable industrialisation . . . building up indigenous industries, owned and controlled by Malaysians is more complex but is more important in the long run'.[36] The head of the Unit in 1992 explained that the thrust of economic policy over the next few decades would be 'the creation of Malaysia's own multinationals and global companies' (Ali 1992). Thus, it was not surprising to find that Malaysia was the main advocate of a developmental approach to the AIA.[37]

The Malaysian government saw the AIA as an opportunity for national companies to grow and develop their industrial and commercial capabilities by exploiting the investment privileges that the investment agreement would accord them in the regional market compared to foreign investors.[38] Trade minister, Rafidah Aziz advocated regional level mergers and acknowledged that discussions had been held among ASEAN policymakers on how to encourage national firms to form large ASEAN conglomerates to exploit regional market opportunities as well as to compete effectively in the global market, including in service sectors.[39] Rafidah also suggested the possibility of an ASEAN financing mechanism, such as a Pan-ASEAN Export–Import (EXIM) Bank to provide financial backing for ASEAN conglomerates in their regional operations.[40]

Of the other core ASEAN countries, only the Indonesian government explicitly supported the Malaysian position. In October 1998, Coordinating Minister for the Economy, Ginandjar Kartasasmita endorsed the Malaysian suggestion of using the AIA to develop ASEAN multinationals and conglomerates that would be globally competitive.[41] Although officials from the Commerce Ministry in Thailand found the privileging of ASEAN investors in the AIA to be contradictory to AFTA's role as an instrument to attract FDI to ASEAN, neither Thailand nor Singapore rejected the Malaysian suggestion.[42] There were no disputes in ASEAN over the AIA,[43] unlike the very vocal and public disputes over petrochemicals, agriculture and automobiles.

The regional financial crisis, however, drew attention to the contradictions inherent in AFTA between privileging ASEAN investors and attracting foreign investors from outside the ASEAN region. It was noted in the previous chapter that the ASEAN Secretary General was somewhat critical of the distinction the AIA made between ASEAN and non-ASEAN investors in view of the urgent need to boost FDI flows to the region as a result of the financial crisis. A senior Thai investment official also expected the crisis to force the ASEAN governments to play down the intra-ASEAN investment emphasis and focus on strategies to attract FDI from outside the ASEAN region.[44] Although the discriminatory clause in the AIA was finally removed in September 2001, the fact that this form of developmental regionalism was contemplated and maintained for three years requires explanation.

The political importance of domestic capital in ASEAN

The different positions of the ASEAN governments on the AIA reflect the political importance of domestic-owned capital in these societies and the coalitions formed by the latter with the political/ruling elite. Malaysian and Indonesian approaches to the AIA, specifically the privileging of domestic/ASEAN investors, lay in the key role played by domestic capital in these societies, particularly their political role. Although Thailand and Singapore did not actively champion a developmental clause in the AIA, the absence of a challenge from these governments on the issue needs to be explained.[45] As the following discussion shows, the Malaysian move to privilege domestic/ASEAN investors through the AIA was actually helpful to domestic-owned capital in Singapore and Thailand undertaking expansion in the regional market.

Singapore: economic restructuring, domestic capital and regionalisation

The mid-1980s recession led the Singapore government to recognise the vulnerability of the island economy to global economic upheavals as a result of its over-reliance on FDI, manufacturing production, and exports to developed markets as well as the lack of indigenous entrepreneurs (Yeung 1999: 7). This led to the adoption of a new growth strategy that emphasised services as a vital growth sector, the expansion of domestic capital and regionalisation (Rodan 1993: 229). While FDI remained important, the expansion of domestic capital was regarded as crucial for Singapore's competitiveness (Yeung 1999: 8) and as a way to reduce the over-reliance of the economy on external capital (Singapore 1993: 3). Regionalisation was aimed at 'geographically expand[ing] the Singapore economy itself' (Rodan 1993: 225). The regionalisation strategy not only emphasised Singapore's role as a springboard for global TNCs locating in Singapore to operate in the region, it was also regarded as a means of enabling domestic capital to expand beyond the confines of the limited domestic market (Parsonage 1994: 1–4; Yeung 1999: 8).

The novel feature about the new growth strategy was the commitment to facilitate the expansion of domestic private capital, which was a turnaround for the PAP government that had governed Singapore since the early 1960s. Singapore's development strategy in the past had relied heavily on FDI, driven by the PAP government's historical distrust of the predominantly ethnic Chinese domestic capital. The animosity between the PAP and Chinese business stemmed from the latter's perceived support for 'Chinese chauvinism' and left-wing/communist political elements within the PAP during the party's factional struggle during the turbulent 1960s (Turnbull 1989). The bias towards foreign capital in development was compounded by the government's belief that domestic private capital lacked the capability to engage in efficient production (Parsonage 1994: 10). Moreover, state capital had taken on the role of domestic private capital, engaging in a range of activities in services, heavy industry and high technology activities through government-linked corporations (GLCs) (Wong and Ng 1997: 124).

After the 1985 recession, the nurturing of domestic private capital, including the building up of large domestic corporations became a priority for the government, although these goals were not to be achieved through protectionism. Instead, the government's approach was to supply the necessary public goods like human resources, research and development facilities, information, as well as fiscal and financial incentives to support domestic capital in market competition (Singapore 1991). The regionalisation drive – Regionalisation 2000 – was a key element in creating the conditions to enable the expansion of domestic capital. Domestic firms were seen as natural suppliers and joint venture partners to the GLCs, which had already begun diversifying their operations to the ASEAN region (Rodan 1997: 160). The concentration of domestic private firms in the now critical services sector, particularly in finance and commerce, reinforced the role of domestic capital in Singapore's future growth.

Although domestic private capital in finance and manufacturing was already investing abroad since the late 1980s, largely in the ASEAN region (Yeung 1999: 12), 'Regionalisation 2000' was an effort to actively encourage and hasten the process. Singapore Prime Minister Goh Chok Tong emphasised that 'going regional is part of our long-term strategy to stay ahead. It is to make our national economy bigger, our companies stronger and some of them multinationals'.[46]

Moreover, the service sector, emphasised as the new growth sector for the economy, was heavily reliant on the regional market, which made services inextricably linked to the regionalisation strategy. The competitive advantage of Singapore service firms also lay in the regional market (Dicken and Yeung 1999: 119). Lacking the necessary ownership-specific advantages to compete with global TNCs in global markets, local service firms were not keen to venture further afield. This explains why Singapore was keenest among the ASEAN countries to negotiate services liberalisation within AFTA.[47] The government's recognition of the trend towards the unbundling and outsourcing of previously in-house services such as logistics and information technology services for manufacturing industry (Singapore 1998: 38) also explains its desire to include services 'incidental' to manufacturing and other economic sectors in the AIA.[48] The regionalisation drive required an active regional diplomacy to negotiate the institutional framework necessary to facilitate the expansion of domestic capital. The Singapore government's support and championing of AFTA, thus, needs also to be seen in this light, and not solely in terms of AFTA's role in attracting FDI.

The regionalisation drive also brought political benefits to the ruling government. As already noted in Chapter 3, economic growth was a key component of political legitimacy for the PAP government. The regionalisation strategy allowed the PAP government to regenerate the bases of its domestic legitimacy by incorporating domestic capital as a source of growth. Not only was this move aimed at diversifying the sources of economic growth for Singapore, it allowed the PAP government to co-opt domestic Chinese business as part of the ruling elite, albeit as the junior partner in the ruling coalition of political/bureaucratic elites and state capital.

The discussion suggests that the privileging of ASEAN investors in the AIA did not contradict the interests of the Singapore government. In fact, it benefited Singapore's economic restructuring strategy based on the expansion of domestic capital through regionalisation. The regional financial crisis prompted a re-think of the regionalisation strategy, however, with Singapore opting for a more global strategy to diversify risk and avoid 'putting all its eggs into the regional basket' (Yeung 1999: 9). Regionalisation, nevertheless, remains a key plank in Singapore's growth strategy for the future, although it is unlikely to be premised solely on ASEAN alone but will extend to other regional configurations.

Thailand: domestic capital and overseas expansion

Domestic capital has played a key role in the Thai economy from the 1950s. Although Thailand experienced an FDI boom since 1985, foreign capital did not overwhelm domestic capital, which also expanded considerably after 1985, often in joint ventures with FDI (Phongpaichit and Baker 1995: 156). Most importantly, domestic capital, particularly urban (Bangkok-based) big businesses had also begun to expand overseas. Unlike Singapore, Thailand did not have a formal policy to develop domestic capital or a formal regionalisation policy to support the overseas expansion of Thai private capital. Nevertheless, the government's commitment to AFTA served the interests of the Bangkok-based business elite, which was in close alliance during the 1990s with both elected politicians and liberal technocrats in the bureaucracy who advocated open economic policies for Thailand, including regional trade liberalisation (Krongkaew 1997).

Overseas expansion in the 1990s by outward-focussed elements of Thai domestic capital was especially evident outside manufacturing industry where large family-based Thai conglomerates dominated (Phongpaichit and Baker 1998: 28). The Shinawatra group, the Samart group, the Charoen Pokphand group and the Ucom group, for instance, ventured overseas to Southeast Asian markets in a variety of activities related to their core domestic business in telecommunications and information technology. As in the case of Singapore, the decision to privilege ASEAN investors in the AIA did not necessarily contradict the interests of the political and state elites nor that of its business allies since it clearly benefited internationally oriented Thai domestic businesses seeking to venture abroad.

That was, however, the state-of-play in 1998 when the AIA was initially adopted and the effects of the 1997–98 financial crisis were still unfolding in the country. Since then, the collapse of significant elements of Thai big businesses lent new emphasis to the role of FDI in spearheading growth in Thailand as the Democrat Party under then Prime Minister Chuan Leekpai sought to restructure the Thai economy towards greater market openness and competitiveness. Hence, there was an attempt by Thailand to de-emphasise the foreign-ASEAN distinction in the AIA through attempts to bring forward the deadline for full foreign equity ownership in investment. The Deputy Secretary General of the Thai Board of Investment, Chakramon Phasukvanich, in fact, suggested that the crisis might force ASEAN to play down its intra-ASEAN investment area in favour of attracting FDI from outside ASEAN.[49] In the end, ASEAN member governments chose to maintain the foreign-ASEAN distinction in the AIA.

For the Thai government, the most important reason for establishing AFTA was to attract FDI.[50] Despite this, the privileging of ASEAN investors in the AIA did not necessarily contradict the interests of the political and bureaucratic elite and their business allies since the AIA did not jeopardise the workings of the CEPT, which was the primary instrument used to attract FDI to the region. More importantly, the AIA benefited Thai capital seeking to venture abroad. The importance of AFTA to Thailand should, therefore, also be seen in this light, as a mechanism that also benefited the growth of domestic, especially the Bangkok-based, business elite.

Indonesia: domestic capital, patronage networks and economic nationalism

The support given by Ginandjar Kartasasmita, Coordinating Minister for the Economy in the Habibie government, for the Malaysian proposal to use the AIA to nurture ASEAN firms and to develop ASEAN multinationals needs to be seen in the light of Ginandjar's credentials as an economic nationalist. It was earlier pointed out that the economic nationalists envisaged a key role for the state in directing markets to achieve particular national goals, particularly technological development and the nurturing of indigenous Indonesian capital. Dr Habibie and Ginandjar were both in favour of reducing Indonesian dependence on foreign technology (Djidin 1997: 26). Habibie also justified his state-driven high-technology strategy in terms of enabling Indonesia to quickly move to higher value-added production in the face of competition from cheap-labour economies like China and Vietnam (Brown 1998: 200). Despite his broad commitment to neoliberal reforms, former President Suharto during his tenure had also been attracted to and generally supported Habibie's vision (Liddle and Mallarangeng 1997: 174; Borsuk 1999: 163). This was unsurprising, as Suharto was rather ambivalent about the value of free markets, seeing them only in instrumental terms as a means to deliver regime-legitimating growth.

Economic nationalist policies thus encompassed an economic imperative, emphasising growth though with a strong infant industry or strategic trade flavour, as well as a political agenda, namely the redistribution of economic wealth from non-indigenous to indigenous hands.[51] Ginandjar's response to the Malaysian proposal to employ the AIA to develop domestic capital, and President Habibie's support of it, need to be seen in this context.

Indonesian domestic capital may be divided into ethnic Chinese capital, indigenous or *pribumi* capital and state capital, all of which were politically significant but for different reasons. The ethnic Chinese entrepreneurs dominated big business in Indonesia, having gained their economic fortunes and pre-eminent position in Indonesian business through connections with politically influential persons, including military elites and especially President Suharto. Because of their Chinese ethnicity, they occupied a very vulnerable position in Indonesian society (Robison 1996: 91). In return for political protection and economic benefits, the ethnic Chinese conglomerates provided funds to the President, which he disbursed to selected organisations and individuals in return for political support (Liddle 1999a: 51). The Chinese were, therefore, a crucial link in Indonesian patronage politics although they were strongly resented by indigenous Indonesian business interests[52] and the indigenous Indonesian public. The President and government were generally sensitive to anti-Chinese sentiment, which indigenous business exploited (Robison 1996: 95). The government's support to both state and indigenous private capital needs to be seen against this background of resentment against Chinese businesses, particularly the conglomerates.

State-owned enterprises, some of which were part of the strategic industries programme initiated by Habibie, constituted a large part of the Indonesian economy during Suharto's rule, which were only partially reformed through privatisation during the 1980s and 1990s, and continue to remain salient in the post-Suharto era. The role of public enterprises as agents of development is legitimised by Article 33 of the Indonesian Constitution, which accords a primary role to state control of 'branches of production essential to the state and governing the life and living of the public' (Mardjana 1999: 41). Moreover, public enterprises were considered to be the 'fortress for the indigenous', a bulwark against ethnic Chinese and foreign domination of the economy (Mardjana 1999: 47). State enterprises were found in virtually all sectors, particularly infrastructure, finance, telecommunications and the high-technology industries within the purview of Habibie. Although strongly criticised by the technocrats, and even by indigenous business interests who feared their potential crowding out by state capital, Suharto generally supported the strategic industries programme as it reflected his vision of a developed Indonesia (Borsuk 1999: 163).

As for private indigenous capital, Suharto also used economic favours like preferential credit and import licenses to encourage the growth of an indigenous business class during much of the 1970s and 1980s (Liddle 1999a: 52). These preferential policies enabled the President to ensure the political support of the indigenous elites[53] who were ultimately beholden to the President as a result of their special treatment (Liddle 1999a: 68). Nevertheless, these preferential policies led to the creation of a second corporate elite group – indigenous big businesses. These policies supporting indigenous businesses continued into the 1990s despite the broad neoliberal reforms undertaken during this period. In fact, the appointment of the economic nationalists to influential positions in the 1993 cabinet reshuffle appeared to herald the further rise of the fortunes of indigenous big businesses, particularly since economic nationalist policy-makers advocated a more interventionist approach to economic policy, one that emphasised the development of domestic, especially indigenous business capabilities (Robison 1997: 53). Indigenous capital soon became concentrated in sectors like power, roads, cement, telecommunications and broadcasting, banking and finance, and retail trade (Nallappan *et al.* 1998: 46). Interestingly, many of the indigenous business elites participated in politics but they did not confine their participation and support to the state party, Golkar and at times worked with opposition parties as well (Robison 1996: 93). Indigenous business was, therefore, a politically salient group that the President and government could not afford to ignore.

The political salience of indigenous and state capital did not, however, end with the fall of Suharto and the financial crisis. Many Indonesians, including economic nationalist policymakers, regarded further neoliberal reforms sanctioned by the IMF as attempts by western interests to impose a form of capitalism on Indonesia that would, once again, 'prevent *pribumi* Indonesians from taking their rightful place at the economic table' (Habir 1999: 202). The redistribution imperative to achieve economic parity between the ethnic Chinese and foreign investors on the one hand and indigenous groups, particularly in business, on the other, remained strong. Both Habibie, Indonesian president in 1998 when the AIA was adopted, and Ginandjar had long been in favour of reducing Indonesian dependence on foreign investors and in weakening the dominant position of the ethnic Chinese business elite by building up state and indigenous businesses (Djidin 1997: 26). While Habibie championed state capital, Ginandjar championed indigenous business interests (Liddle 1999b: 20–1). It is not clear, however, that developmental regionalism through the AIA would have been feasible as a means to help develop indigenous Indonesian capital. It was more likely that the larger, more advanced ethnic Chinese businesses would have been the project's main beneficiaries. Nonetheless, the point to note is that Ginandjar's open support of Malaysia's developmental approach to the AIA emerged out of such ideas and the ascendance of indigenous business interests. AFTA could fulfil twin purposes – as an exercise in open regionalism to attract FDI and as an exercise in developmental regionalism. The financial and political crisis in Indonesia meant, however, that the growth imperative, particularly to attract FDI to the country, became vital while IMF reforms made it difficult to translate economic nationalist ideas to firm policies.

Malaysia: ethnic politics, economic nationalism and domestic capital

The political salience of domestic capital in Malaysia is tied up with the country's ethnic politics and with the broader economic nationalism of Prime Minister Mahathir. The original 'ethnic Malay capitalist project' of the 1970s and 1980s soon became bound up during the late 1980s and 1990s with a broader Malaysian economic nationalism that sought to develop a more encompassing Malaysian capitalist class that would lead towards parity with the developed countries, although the ethnic project was by no means dismantled (Khoo 2000: 214). The Malaysian government's approach to the AIA, as a means to develop domestic capital through stimulating their regional expansion on preferential terms, needs to be viewed against these dynamics in the domestic political economy.

Between 1970 and 1990, a state-directed development programme – the New Economic Policy (NEP) – drove the Malaysian political economy. The NEP was the outcome of ethnic riots following the May 1969 elections. It reflected Malay concerns at the community's economic marginalisation and fears that they would lose their political dominance to the relatively better off ethnic Chinese community as a result. Among the policy's objectives were the creation of a Malay business (and middle) class and the achievement of a target of 30 per cent Malay equity in the corporate sector (Tori 1997: 212). The NEP was vital to the legitimacy and security of the UMNO-dominated regime, since it enabled both a more equitable distribution of wealth for the Malays as well as Malay political dominance through the control of economic resources. The United Malays National Organisation (UMNO) has long been the leading Malay party in Malaysia, regarded as the champion of Malay political rights in multiethnic Malaysia.[54]

Although the NEP was replaced by the National Development Policy in 1991 that scaled back ethnic preferences, the goal of creating a Malay business community continued to be emphasised in the 1990s (Tori 1997: 236). Even the privatisation programme undertaken as part of the economic restructuring package adopted in response to the mid-1980s recession was actively used to create a Malay business class to fulfil the NEP goal (Crouch 1996: 39). Privatisation largely benefited UMNO-linked Malay businesspersons, although a number of ethnic Chinese and Indian businesses gained as well. This group, in turn, became a valuable source of political and material support for UMNO (Gomez 1996). By the late 1990s, therefore, this politically influential rentier domestic business community had become part of the governing elite (Khoo 2000: 221).

The new Malaysian conglomerates that emerged out of privatisation and other preferential policies were also a key component of the wider economic nationalism of the Malaysian Prime Minister. Especially after the mid-1980s recession, policy had moved beyond the NEP's narrow focus on building a *Malay* capitalist class to advocate the growth of large, *Malaysian* firms as a means of meeting the competitive challenges of the global economy, although NEP goals remained salient (Khoo 2000: 216). The policy shift reflected the strategic vision of the Prime Minister, who was no longer content with Malaysia remaining a Third World producer of industrial commodities. Thus, he stressed the building up of Malaysian corporations and conglomerates able to compete with foreign TNCs in what was perceived to be an intensely competitive world economy.

Since foreign firms were dominant in the far more efficient, export-oriented manufacturing sector, it was in the non-manufacturing sectors that emerging domestic capital, including ethnic Malay capital found its niche, using market restrictions as well as access to preferential treatment through political connections as a means to profits (Khoo 2000: 218). As already noted in a previous section, the expectation among policymakers was that global rules would eventually allow foreign corporations unrestricted access to the domestic market. It was clear that Malaysian firms, including the politically privileged ones, would eventually have to compete with global firms, not only in international markets but in the domestic market as well.

A former coordinator of Malaysian participation in OECD workshops, Ong Hong Cheong, notes that foreign interest in 'national treatment [of investment] was seen by both the Malaysian government and the private sector to pose the biggest threat to domestic companies'.[55] Ong further points out that an

> alarming aspect of the MAI was the open-ended definition of investment, because it meant that the MAI would be binding on the host country to allow foreign multinational companies the full right to both establish [a] new presence and to expand their [existing] presence in the manufacturing, services and other sectors of the economy in addition to the right to take part in new privatisation exercises . . . the MAI could also lead to eventual foreign domination of the banking and financial sector, a totally unacceptable political proposition.

The writing on the wall was clear. The expectation that global rules would eventually allow foreign corporations unrestricted access to the domestic market was very strong indeed among policymakers.[56] They expected Malaysian firms, including the politically privileged ones, to eventually have to compete with global firms both in international markets and in the domestic market as well. If politically important domestic firms were not ready for global market competition, their demise would have significant political repercussions for the NEP goal of advancing a Malay business class, for Mahathir's personal authority, and ultimately for the stability of Mahathir's ruling coalition as well as the security of the UMNO-dominated political system. The new business elite nurtured through the state by Mahathir were also important players in Malaysian patronage politics. The developmental role envisaged for the AIA by the Malaysian side was, therefore, intimately related to ensuring the survival of these politically important domestic firms that were key players in the Malaysian political economy.

The growth imperative overwhelms: reviewing the AIA

In September 2001, the ASEAN governments agreed to remove the disparity in the AIA between foreign and domestic/ASEAN investors in the non-manufacturing sectors, thus offering foreign investors full market access and national treatment privileges by 2010 rather than in 2020.[57] How do we explain this policy shift?

Although the AIA had been adopted in October 1998, right in the throes of the financial crisis, it was at that time not expected to adversely affect manufacturing sector FDI since its discriminatory effects were largely, though not solely, confined to the non-manufacturing sectors. It was the flow of FDI to the manufacturing sector that was considered to be crucial during this period, since it had been the main engine of growth and exports in ASEAN from the mid-1980s, and was believed by political leaders to be the main means of recovery from the crisis. Some member country officials as well as the ASEAN Secretary General believed that the AIA as it was then designed would jeopardise the inflow of FDI during such difficult times when the liberal reformist credentials of member governments were at stake.[58] Nevertheless, the latter continued to maintain the AIA in its original form. Instead, member governments accelerated CEPT tariff liberalisation in 1998 as a means of reassuring foreign investors that they were committed to realising the single regional market, the main 'carrot' used to attract FDI flows to ASEAN. Member governments also temporarily relaxed investment restrictions for a one- to two-year period in selected manufacturing sectors in their respective countries as a way of maintaining investor interest in the region, as already noted.

Nevertheless, member governments agreed in August 2000 to a one-year study on the AIA in view of the report presented by the ASEAN Secretary General the previous month that revealed a fall in investment into ASEAN from US$28 billion in 1997 to US$13 billion in 1999.[59] Moreover, the report also showed that the ASEAN economies received only 17 per cent of FDI flows to Asian developing countries in 1999, compared to about 60 per cent in the early 1990s. China, on the other hand, received about 60 per cent in 1999, up from 18 per cent during the early years of the decade. The negative correlation was not lost on ASEAN officials and leaders.[60] China's potential accession to the WTO and the anticipated diversion of FDI to China as a result added to the sense of urgency among the ASEAN leaders with regard to the FDI situation.

Concern about the future of FDI flows to ASEAN became especially pronounced by the middle of 2001, and it was this that finally prompted member governments including Malaysia to review the AIA in September 2001.[61] By this time, it seemed clear that growth in ASEAN was in serious jeopardy as all the main engines of growth in the global economy – the US, Western Europe and Japan – seemed headed into recession. In fact, it had become clear by early 2001 that a global economic slow-down was imminent, threatening the recovery that most member economies had experienced over 1999–2000 (MIER 2001a,b). Falling demand in the US during 2001, still the region's main export market, meant that the ASEAN region appeared to be facing a more severe downturn than the 1997–98 regional financial crisis. Not only were export markets threatened, but foreign investment too was expected to slow further as a result.[62]

In short, growth and FDI had, by the middle of 2001, emerged as the overwhelming priority for the ASEAN governments, including Indonesia and Malaysia. In addition, foreign investors, notably American investors pressed the ASEAN governments to accelerate national treatment under the AIA by citing the need to counter the diversion of FDI to China.[63] It must be emphasised, however, that the relative decline of FDI inflows to ASEAN throughout the 1990s, and especially since the financial crisis, was not the result of the ASEAN-foreign distinction in the AIA. Nevertheless, there was concern in ASEAN that this particular clause could send the wrong signals to foreign investors at a time when ASEAN was under severe scrutiny by foreign investors and was facing a rather precarious foreign investment/growth situation. The ASEAN decision of 14 September 2001 to allow full market access and national treatment for *all* investors by 2010 in the non-manufacturing sectors was, therefore, directed at re-affirming ASEAN's openness to FDI.[64] The attempt at developmental regionalism was halted, and open regionalism (at least, the FDI variant) has re-emerged as the main feature of ASEAN economic regionalism in the quest for growth.

Yet, it is also important to bear in mind that member governments have not agreed to implement complete regional investment liberalisation in non-manufacturing sectors anytime soon. This is targeted for 2010, suggesting that at the national level, full investment liberalisation will proceed cautiously. Domestic capital, in short, remains a key focus in the individual ASEAN economies, but support for it will likely be addressed through national instruments where possible and available rather than concerted regional ones. The regional instrument has been reserved once again to realise the FDI/growth imperative, but this is not to suggest that domestic distributive priorities have been marginalised across ASEAN. In fact, the AFTA experience confirms that the tussle between growth and domestic distribution is a key dynamic driving regional cooperation. As the next chapter shows, the delays in negotiating services liberalisation and Malaysia's temporary withdrawal of automobiles from AFTA disciplines reveal that there are sectors where regional liberalisation will proceed cautiously, driven by domestic distributive priorities despite the overall concern with growth. Thus, the AFTA story shows that while governments in Southeast Asia turned to regionalism as a collective policy response to the pressures associated with globalisation, the tussle between growth and domestic distributive imperatives ultimately shaped the manner in which cooperation unfolded and the forms that regionalism took.

Conclusion

By examining the interaction between globalisation and domestic political economy dynamics, this chapter shows that policymakers and leaders in the ASEAN countries were also concerned with ensuring the growth and viability of domestic firms as with their anxiety over FDI inflows. While both forms of regionalism associated with AFTA – open and developmental regionalism – were driven by the growth imperative, distributive concerns were weaved into the concern with growth in the case of developmental regionalism. The latter paid special attention to nurturing domestic capital in anticipation of new global rules that were seen to be potentially damaging to emerging firms. The developmental dimension to the AFTA story is one that has so far been missed in the literature.[65]

While all the core ASEAN governments used regionalism to facilitate the expansion of domestic capital, governments in Malaysia especially and Indonesia advocated preferential investment treatment of domestic firms in the ASEAN market through the AIA, the idea being to nurture domestic capital to enable them to meet global competition eventually. Governments and leaders of these countries were most concerned about the survival of those segments of domestic capital that were valued for their perceived role in sustaining incumbent elite rule and in helping to underpin the legitimacy and security of the prevailing regime.

Nevertheless, the AIA Agreement was designed in a rather flexible manner since it did not prevent any member from according market access and national treatment privileges to *all* investors at any point before 2020. It was effectively a compromise between those advocating a developmental approach in AFTA through the AIA and those wishing to maintain the project's original interest in attracting foreign investors by using the carrot of the single regional market. As such, it is unclear whether the idea to use the AIA to build up domestic firms would have been workable. That, in any case, is not the main concern of the analysis, which is to account for the anomaly the AIA presents to prevailing FDI-centred explanations of AFTA.

Despite the broad commitment to nurture competitive domestic firms through developmental regionalism, implementation proved to be rather more difficult. As the next chapter illustrates in its discussion of departures from AFTA commitments, the imperative of distribution was so overwhelming in certain instances that governments found it difficult to immediately implement their AFTA commitments, including the AIA. Despite the latter's perceived potential to stimulate the development of larger, more capable domestic/ASEAN firms, some governments feared that immediate regional investment liberalisation and the privileging of ASEAN investors would challenge the dominant position of favoured domestic firms in the domestic market.

5 Re-negotiating AFTA commitments

The domestic distributive imperative overwhelms

The previous two chapters show how both open and developmental regionalism in AFTA were driven by concern with growth as the ASEAN governments responded to the pressures of globalisation, although distributive concerns were weaved into the concern with growth in developmental regionalism as governments also sought to nurture domestic capital. The tension between growth and distribution in the ASEAN countries was, in fact, a constant theme during the 1990s. In some instances, distributive concerns overwhelmed the concern with growth as governments sought to protect certain social groups and selected firms against the competitive effects of regional liberalisation. In these instances, despite initially agreeing to regional liberalisation, governments were prepared to re-negotiate their original AFTA commitments to protect the interests of these politically important groups and of those domestic firms with close ties to the political elite. The first part of this chapter elaborates on this theme by focusing broadly on the implementation of regional liberalisation commitments in manufactured goods, investment and services. Discussion in the rest of the chapter focuses on three specific disputes in AFTA – petrochemicals, agriculture and automobiles – which clearly illustrate how departures from AFTA commitments occurred to protect firms with close ties to the political elite.

Resistance to AFTA: a general survey

Despite the advances made in AFTA, which are described in Chapter 2, the regional project was not without problems. Although member governments often made ambitious commitments for liberalisation, they sometimes attempted to withdraw their initial undertakings, particularly as implementation loomed ahead. This problem virtually occurred in all the component programmes in AFTA, although some issue areas experienced greater setbacks than others.

The CEPT

Chapter 3 explains how external pressures from globalisation drove advances in AFTA, including the renewed commitment in 1993 to implement the CEPT. This occurred despite growing opposition from certain domestic business interests, particularly in Thailand, the Philippines and Indonesia who were in favour of going slow on or even withdrawing from AFTA commitments. These included, for instance, the Philippines Chamber of Commerce and Industry,[1] the Indonesian Automobile Industry Association (GAIKINDO),[2] the Thai petrochemical industry,[3] Thai electronics, plastic products and iron and steel firms, and Philippine apparel, footwear and iron and steel firms.[4] On the other hand, other business actors from these countries supported AFTA. Indonesian businesses with export capabilities like the Salim group wanted AFTA hastened[5] in some issue areas, while export-oriented Philippine and Thai industrialists welcomed the adoption of the AFTA project[6] as did the Federation of Malaysian Manufacturers.[7] The picture, therefore, is one of diversity of domestic business attitudes to AFTA in the ASEAN countries.

The diversity of business demands with regard to tariff liberalisation in goods trade meant that policymakers were, by and large, able to adopt a fairly independent course based on calculations of the broad interest of the country or of certain segments of the ruling elite. As Chapter 3 shows, the overriding concern of the ASEAN governments was on growth, particularly where the CEPT was concerned. These governments were committed to using the CEPT specifically, and AFTA more broadly as a means to create a regional market to which foreign investors would be attracted and, for some governments, to provide the space for the expansion of outward-looking domestic capital. As a result, governments generally resisted demands from firms wishing to delay tariff liberalisation. Governments were, nevertheless, sympathetic to business concerns about regional trade liberalisation and dealt with them in various ways. A range of domestic adjustment measures was adopted to help firms, particularly in Thailand and the Philippines. These included financial and technical assistance, reduced utility charges, as well as fiscal incentives.[8] Moreover, these governments also negotiated a more flexible mode of CEPT implementation that gave domestic firms sufficient time to prepare for regional trade liberalisation.

The ASEAN governments continued since then to resist demands from domestic businesses to delay CEPT implementation, including during the financial crisis period. Although import restrictions were adopted during 1998–99 in a number of ASEAN countries, these were temporary, a direct response to the crisis-induced economic slowdown, and thus not significant instances of protectionism, a point already noted in Chapter 3. Although the head of the National Business Development Centre in Indonesia called for the 2003 target date for the CEPT to be postponed to 2010 in view of the regional economic crisis, the government's economic advisory council rejected the demand.[9] By this time, Indonesia had adopted the IMF bailout package of reforms, and reneging on the CEPT would not have sent the right signals to the international investors that the country was keen to attract. The Federation of Philippine Industries also asked the government to suspend CEPT implementation until 2003,[10] but its demand was not entertained, although the government in September 2002 signalled its intention to temporarily exclude petrochemicals from the CEPT, as Malaysia had done with automobiles.[11] Similarly, the Thai government refused to accede to business demands to delay the CEPT.[12] Although Malaysia excluded automobiles from the CEPT, the government, on the explicit instruction of the Prime Minister, rejected all other business demands to delay tariff liberalisation for other products.[13]

One question that arises is, why out of all other business demands for protection the Malaysian government negotiated to withdraw automobiles from AFTA disciplines, ostensibly for a two-year period. The Malaysian automobile episode is especially interesting because the government came under considerable pressure from the Thai government and from foreign investors to refrain from this move. Apart from automobiles, other cases caused similar consternation in ASEAN. The petrochemicals case is noteworthy because four of the six core ASEAN countries attempted to delay regional liberalisation, although only the Philippines has announced its intention to temporarily withdraw petrochemicals from the CEPT scheme. Indonesia's move during the 1990s to raise tariffs on selected petrochemical products without any prior warning to its AFTA partners best illustrates how the interests of politically well-connected domestic firms were able to challenge the government's commitment to regional cooperation. A similar dynamic accounts for Indonesia's withdrawal of fifteen types of agricultural items from AFTA, backtracking on its initial commitment to subject these items to CEPT liberalisation. In both these instances, Indonesia's move sparked off a row within ASEAN. These three cases – petrochemicals, agriculture and automobiles – will be discussed later in the chapter. They reveal how the ASEAN governments, despite their overall commitment to AFTA were, nevertheless, prepared to re-negotiate their original commitments in particular instances in order to protect the interests of politically important social groups and domestic firms that had close ties to the political elite. The distributive imperative clearly predominated.

Investment and services

Although the ASEAN governments led by Malaysia originally designed the AIA as a developmental tool to nurture the growth of domestic capital, the reality of domestic interests meant that even this project faced some difficulty in implementation. Member governments found it hard to offer national treatment and market access privileges to ASEAN investors initially, since even that was expected to adversely affect domestic firms. These governments managed to negotiate a flexible mode of implementation similar to the CEPT model that incorporated both a Temporary Exclusion List and a Sensitive List that would delay investment privileges to ASEAN firms for different periods of time. Interestingly, member governments chose to place most of the sectors they wished to exclude from the AIA in the Sensitive List rather than the Temporary Exclusion List, thereby maintaining indefinite protection from all, including ASEAN, investors (see Table 2.13). It was only in September 2002 that these governments agreed to begin reviewing the Sensitive List from the following year. Governments were also taking too long to put in place national legislation to allow governments to differentiate ASEAN from foreign investors.[14]

As for services, the ASEAN governments found it especially difficult to advance their negotiations to obtain specific commitments to liberalise trade in services in the financial and telecommunications sectors.[15] Malaysia was especially unwilling to consider liberalising foreign equity and market access conditions for financial services, which Singapore and Thailand favoured. This is unsurprising, since domestic banks were key players in the Malaysian political economy, and liberalisation would have reduced the space for patronage-based manoeuvring to take place (Gomez and Jomo 1997). Similarly, domestic firms with strong ties to the political elite, such as Renong, were prominent players in telecommunications, which made it difficult for the Malaysian government to commit to broad-based liberalisation in this sector that might have jeopardised their dominant position.

It was not always the domestic firm that was the hindrance, however. Regional liberalisation also became a casualty of the business–politics relationship so prevalent in the region, seen in the rejection by the Malaysian government of a proposal by the Renong Group, a prominent Malaysian conglomerate, to form a strategic tie-up with Singapore Telecommunications (SingTel), a corporation linked to the Singapore government.[16] The Malaysian Prime Minister had reportedly been against the idea of a close connection between Renong, which had close ties with the ruling Malay party, UMNO, and the Singapore PAP government.[17] There has been a long history of mutual suspicions between the Malaysian and Singaporean governments in general, and their two respective governing parties, UMNO and the PAP in particular, going back to the days when Singapore, briefly a part of Malaysia from 1963 to 1965, was 'expelled' from the federation due to political differences between the two parties.[18] Their differences were fundamental, with the PAP challenging the 1957 terms of independence negotiated with the British that emphasised Malay political dominance in Malaysia in return for citizenship rights for the ethnic Chinese and Indian immigrant communities (Crouch

1996: 22). The PAP formula endorsed equal political status for all ethnic communities. It was clearly difficult for the Malay/UMNO elite to allow a company with close political connections with the PAP government in Singapore to acquire a stake, even a non-controlling one, in Renong, a showcase of Malay corporate success and a key member of the ruling ethnic Malay elite coalition, at least until very recently.

Other countries were none too happy with Malaysia's hesitant market opening offers in the finance and telecommunications sectors. To governments in Singapore and Thailand, advancing negotiations in these sectors was important since domestic capital was concentrated in finance and telecommunications respectively, and was looking to the regional market for expansion. The slowdown in the pace of services negotiations at the GATS did not help matters; instead, it reduced the pressure on some ASEAN governments to ensure that AFTA kept pace with global developments.[19]

The following three cases – petrochemicals, agriculture and automobiles – illustrate in greater depth the sensitivities involved when sectors in which domestic firms with close political connections were required to liberalise. In these instances, distributive concerns with ensuring that the economic gains or rents went to politically important social groups, and especially to firms and individuals with strong ties to the political elite, led governments to attempt to re-negotiate their original AFTA commitments. This was despite the broad commitment of the same governments to regional trade liberalisation, which they saw as a means to securing a critical source of growth, namely FDI. These moves led to disputes with other member governments that did not share the same distributive concerns and for whom the original commitment to engage in regional liberalisation yielded superior outcomes.

Tariff liberalisation of petrochemicals in AFTA

The tensions that emerged in AFTA over tariff liberalisation in the petrochemicals sector had their roots in the designation of the petrochemical industry as a strategic industry in four ASEAN countries – Malaysia, Thailand, the Philippines and Indonesia. These governments believed that a domestic petrochemical industry was fundamental to industrial development, particularly in view of the industry's substantial linkages with other, downstream industries like textiles, chemicals, plastics and fertilisers. Apart from the Philippines, the other country projects had been initiated even before the decision to form AFTA was made.[20]

Governments were not willing to forgo these national plans, especially since investments had already been committed to the project in the four countries. In all cases, state and private, including foreign, capital was involved. Because huge capital investments and a long gestation period were necessary, state capital was often necessary, which made national governments committed to ensuring the project's viability. This often included tariff protection. Private investors, both domestic and foreign, had also committed to participating in these projects on the understanding that the projects would be accorded protection, at least initially. Moreover, politically connected firms that were involved in this sector often used their political influence to demand tariff protection, in the process overturning official policy, illustrated most clearly in the case of Indonesia.

It is, thus, unsurprising to find that this sector was subject to tensions among the core ASEAN governments as each sought to protect its own strategic industry, often reinforced by demands from the domestic and foreign firms involved. Apart from Thailand and the Philippines, tariffs on petrochemical products in ASEAN were very low at the start of the 1990s, mostly between 5 and 10 per cent. Malaysia, however, raised tariffs on key petrochemical items to 30 per cent in 1992 and introduced an import permit scheme in 1994, while Indonesia imposed customs surcharges and hiked tariffs in 1993, 1996 and 1997. Although Malaysia's move raised some concern in ASEAN, especially with Singapore, it was Indonesia's actions that caused much of the tension among ASEAN members in this issue area. Most recently, in September 2002, the Philippines signalled to its ASEAN partners that it was considering invoking the protocol on modification of CEPT concessions for petrochemicals, which would allow the government to temporarily exclude this sector from regional tariff liberalisation.

Thailand: the influence of big business

The petrochemical industry in Thailand began when the government established an upstream petrochemical plant in 1989 as a joint venture between state and private capital, and accorded the industry promoted/strategic industry status (Lucas 1998: 72). The upstream petrochemical industry soon grew, producing a range of petrochemical resins like polyethylene (PE), polypropylene (PP), and polyvinyl chloride (PVC) that were used in downstream industries like plastics, textiles, and fertilisers. The industry was comprised almost entirely of Thai capital, particularly the Bangkok-based big business groups like Siam Cement, Thai Petrochemical Industries, Vinythai and HMC Polymers (Lucas 1998). Many of these conglomerates had extended their original downstream activities in plastic products and textiles to venture into the upstream sector to produce petrochemical resins.

This move was part of a larger trend in the 1990s of Thai conglomerates moving into heavy industries like cement, steel and power, and petrochemicals (Phongpaichit and Baker 1998: 43). They were encouraged by the government policy to deepen Thailand's industrial structure, which meant substantial investment incentives. Moreover, foreign capital was increasingly dominating export-oriented manufacturing activities, and Thai conglomerates had begun to look elsewhere for market opportunities. They found it in heavy industries, where their local knowledge and political clout provided them with an advantage over foreign investors (Phongpaichit and Baker 1998: 28).

By the mid-1990s, however, excess domestic capacity affected profitability, while export markets were not readily available since most countries in ASEAN and in the other East-Asian countries had their own supplies from domestic firms. The petrochemical industry, thus, lobbied hard to prevent the scheduled reduction in import duties on petrochemical items from 27 to 20 per cent due in 1998 under the CEPT fast-track schedule. Downstream producers of plastics and textiles that used petrochemical inputs, on the other hand, wanted tariffs lowered.[21] These firms, however, did not have the bargaining power of the large firms owned by some of the country's most powerful business families that dominated the upstream sector. The latter, particularly through the Federation of Thai Industries, was successful in influencing the industry ministry and the Board of Investment to back their demands for tariff protection.[22] Both these government agencies argued that the petrochemicals sector was a vital industry that needed to be nurtured. The finance and commerce ministries, on the other hand, opposed the tariff move, citing the need for Thailand to conform to its CEPT commitments.[23]

Big business used the decision by Indonesia to raise tariffs on petrochemicals to press its own case in Thailand, citing the unfair competition in AFTA that would ensue should Thailand press ahead with tariff reductions before its ASEAN counterparts.[24] The finance ministry agreed in May 1999 to allow petrochemical tariffs to remain above 20 per cent for a three-year period to allow affected firms sufficient time to adjust to increased competition. The Plastics Industry Club within the Federation of Thai Industries, however, pressed the government to reconsider its decision to maintain high tariffs on petrochemicals, which would raise the cost of production of downstream Thai industries and reduce their export competitiveness.[25] In the end, Thailand reduced tariffs to 5 per cent on almost all petrochemical items as part of its 2001 CEPT package of offers.[26]

The Philippines: developing a strategic industry

In the early 1990s, the Philippine government initiated moves to develop an integrated petrochemicals industry by establishing an upstream naphtha cracker plant to supply petrochemical monomers to mid-stream domestic petrochemical producers of PP and PE (Lim 1998: 140). The project experienced great difficulties, despite initial interest shown by foreign investors from Taiwan and Thailand. The former later invested in Malaysia. These firms were caught in a domestic controversy aroused by nationalist sentiment against preferential treatment to foreign firms. Although the naphtha plant has yet to be built, state company, Philippine National Oil

Corporation Petrochemical Development Corporation (PNOC-PDC), is spearheading the project with a 30 per cent stake in the cracker plant. The other investors include the Brunei government and Petronas of Malaysia.[27]

Since 1999, the Philippine government has contemplated withdrawing petrochemicals, notably PP and PE, from CEPT disciplines as a way to get the local industry on its feet after the ups and downs experienced by the project since its inception.[28] Since 2001, domestic mid-stream producers of PP and PE have been intensely lobbying the trade secretary to retain the 15 per cent tariff on these items beyond the 2003 CEPT deadline. These firms argued that they needed to be protected now in order to ensure that they would still exist by the time the naphtha cracker plant begins operations in 2004. Should they be put out of business by cheaper imports once tariffs were reduced to 0–5 per cent in 2003 as required under the CEPT, there would be no domestic mid-stream firm to guarantee purchase of the monomers to be produced by the upstream cracker plant once it comes on-stream.[29] Philippine trade secretary, Manuel Roxas' initial rejection of these industry demands placed him on a collision course with the energy secretary, Vincent Perez who had been instrumental in bringing in the foreign partners for the naphtha plant.[30] The chair of the Federation of Philippine Industry, the overarching business association in the country, opposed the protectionist move, which was, however, endorsed by the Association of Petrochemical Manufacturers of the Philippines.[31] In fact, the government had already set tariffs on almost all petrochemical products at 3 per cent in its 2001 CEPT package of offers, indicating its intention to adhere to the CEPT schedule.[32] In the end, however, the industry lobby seemed poised to win the battle. Trade secretary Manuel Roxas announced in September 2002 that his government was considering temporarily excluding petrochemicals from AFTA. This move raised some concern among the other ASEAN governments, particularly Singapore, over its implications for AFTA's credibility.[33]

Malaysia: a strategic industry and politically important firms

Malaysia raised tariffs on petrochemical items, notably PP and PE, to 30 per cent in 1992.[34] Although this hurt downstream producers of plastics, who demanded a review of the tariff, the government maintained the high tariff to protect the fledgling petrochemical industry, dominated then by Titan Polyethylene, a Taiwan–Malaysia joint venture.[35] Moreover, in April 1994, a new policy was instituted that required prior government approval for the import of PP and PE. Malaysian plastics firms criticised this move, since it raised the cost of petrochemical inputs while also reducing the availability of supply. Ostensibly for a two-year period, the 'approved import' scheme benefited Titan, the major producer of PP and PE in Malaysia, which now had the right to reject applications by downstream producers to import these products.[36] While reiterating Malaysia's commitment to CEPT tariff reductions, the Malaysian Trade Minister, nevertheless, justified the import approval scheme as necessary to allow fledgling, strategic industries sufficient time to become profitable.[37]

Titan was favoured because of its importance to Malaysia's heavy industries programme first begun in the early 1980s by Prime Minister Mahathir. Petrochemicals were regarded as a key strategic industry vital for developing an integrated Malaysian industrial sector. To spearhead this process, the Malaysian Trade Minister wooed Titan, which had been considering investing in the Philippines, to Malaysia.[38] Interestingly, Titan's local partner was PNB (*Permodalan Nasional Berhad* or the National Equity Corporation), a company that had been set up in 1978 to increase the Malay share of corporate wealth by purchasing and holding shares on behalf of the community. The political importance of these investors in the domestic political economy coupled with the role envisaged for the sector in national development plans explains why the government chose to take actions that ran counter not only to the CEPT but to Malaysia's WTO obligations. Although Malaysia had informed its AFTA partners of its plan to introduce the import permit scheme, this did not prevent intra-ASEAN tensions, particularly with Singapore, long a major supplier of petrochemical products to Malaysia. Singapore filed a complaint (#95-01) at the WTO, challenging the legality of Malaysia's 'approved import' scheme, although the complaint was later withdrawn when the Malaysian government removed what was clearly a non-tariff barrier (Schott 1996: 8).

Indonesia: policy reversals for the politically connected

When Indonesia agreed in 1992 to include petrochemicals in the CEPT fast-track inclusion list, the country's tariffs on petrochemical imports ranged between 5 and 20 per cent. In 1993, however, the authorities raised the tariff on plastic pellets from 5 to 20 per cent, while also imposing an additional 20 per cent customs surcharge (Van der Eng 1993: 30). In early 1996, the authorities extended the 20 per cent customs surcharge to cover five additional petrochemical items. Interestingly, a year earlier, President Suharto had indicated that he favoured protection of strategic industries such as petrochemicals to enable them to develop successfully (Rosser 2002: 141). When the customs surcharge had to be removed at the end of 1996, as part of AFTA's programme to eliminate NTBs, it was replaced by a 20 per cent tariff on eight petrochemical items under Finance Ministry Decree #94 issued in early 1997. The tariff reduction schedule in this Decree was made consistent with the CEPT schedule of tariff reduction, in that tariff rates for 2003 were set at 0–5 per cent. Nevertheless, this move challenged members' expectation of a standstill on tariff levels under the CEPT.

Two months later in April 1997, an amendment to Decree #94 was issued. Decree #151 transferred these eight items from the CEPT inclusion list to the Temporary Exclusion List as well as raised tariffs on them to between 25 and 40 per cent. No prior notice of these actions had been given to Indonesia's ASEAN partners. According to the new tariff reduction schedule, tariffs on these petrochemical products would remain above 20 per cent in 1998, which contravened the CEPT fast track schedule, only falling gradually to the 0–5 per cent target in 2003. Indonesia's move was not well received in ASEAN.

The close involvement of conglomerates associated with the friends and family of President Suharto in the petrochemical industry explains these specific tariff reversals in 1993, 1996 and especially in 1997, which occurred amidst the broad policy trend in the country towards trade liberalisation (Rosser 2002: 140–1). The 1993 customs surcharge and tariff hike on plastic pellets benefited PT Petrokimia Nusantara Interindo, a joint venture between British Petroleum and Indonesian companies controlled by Suharto's son, Sigit Harjoyundanto that had just begun to produce similar pellets (Van der Eng 1993: 30). The additional tariff hikes of 1996 and 1997 benefited the US$1.6 billion olefin project of the Chandra Asri consortium and the US$600 million Arun Aromatic centre. The Chandra Asri project located in West Java was a joint venture between Japanese investors and three influential Indonesians, including Prajogo Pangestu, a prominent ethnic Chinese business tycoon and a close personal friend of President Suharto as well as Bambang Trihatmodjo, another of Suharto's sons (Hill 1992: 17). A third Suharto son, Tommy Mandala Putra, was involved in the Arun project located in North Sumatra.

The Chandra Asri case is especially interesting because it brings into sharp relief the influence of patronage politics on economic policymaking in Indonesia. Although bureaucrats essentially drive broad policy change in Indonesia, whether they are liberal technocrats or economic nationalists, the Chandra Asri case reveals how individual business actors were able to overturn specific policy decisions through their close connections with the ruling elite, notably with the President himself (Surbakti 1999: 67–8). When in December 1994 Chandra Asri formally petitioned the government to introduce a tariff of 35–40 per cent on competing imports, the finance minister Mar'ie Muhammad, a noted liberal technocrat, rejected the request. The President then intervened, re-assigning the authority to grant tariff requests from the finance minister to the Coordinating Minister for Industry and Trade, Hartarto, who was more supportive of Chandra Asri's petition (Hobohm 1995: 29).

The favouring of Chandra Asri is said to represent the return of a favour by the President to Prajogo Pangestu.[39] As already noted in Chapter 4, ethnic Chinese business groups in Indonesia have often provided funding for other troubled firms and state enterprises when asked by the President, a practice that has safeguarded the operations of Chinese businesses in a country where ethnic Chinese are often regarded with suspicion. In return, these businesses receive benefits that help their activities, such as state concessions and licenses. Prajogo Pangestu had provided US$220 million in 1990 to help cover the US$420 million that Bank Duta, the country's fifth largest private bank, had lost in foreign exchange speculation (Djidin 1997: 28). Information about the bank's losses had been kept away from the thousands of ordinary Indonesians who had purchased shares in the bank. The Bank Duta affair was a potential political minefield for the President since three of the charitable foundations that he chaired held a majority 72 per cent stake in the bank (Borsuk 1999: 145). Suharto turned to his two close ethnic Chinese allies – Prajogo of Chandra Asri and Liem Sioe Liong of the Salim group – who provided the necessary bailout funds.

Liberalisation of unprocessed agricultural products

In a move that was strikingly similar to the petrochemicals episode, the Indonesian government in early 1995 backtracked on its earlier decision to commit 15 unprocessed agricultural products to CEPT liberalisation by 2003. Indonesia had proposed to transfer these products from the Temporary Exclusion List to the Sensitive List that would effectively accord these items indefinite protection. The main product groups withdrawn by Indonesia were rice, sugar, cloves and wheat flour. Thailand then threatened to withdraw 44 agricultural items from AFTA in retaliation.[40] Although a compromise was worked out to extend the original 2003 deadline to 2010 for these particular products to accommodate Indonesia, Indonesia soon backed away from the revised arrangement despite initially endorsing the new deadline.[41] Further negotiations became necessary. The episode raised considerable tensions within ASEAN, notably between Thailand, an agricultural exporter, and Indonesia. How the matter was resolved will be discussed in the next chapter. This section focuses on the domestic political economy dynamics that drove the Indonesian actions.

The Indonesian authorities explained their actions in terms of the need to safeguard the welfare of Indonesia's substantial rural community. Indonesian Minister of Trade and Industry in 1995, Tunky Ariwibowo, pointed out that 'all of these items are sensitive items that have an influence on the welfare of our farmers'.[42] The interesting point is that Indonesian intransigence on the agriculture issue is only partly explained by the government's wish to secure the welfare of farmers. It may be valid only in the case of rice and possibly sugar. While the CEPT could have introduced cheaper rice and sugar imports from other producer countries in ASEAN like Thailand and the Philippines, thereby adversely affecting farmers' incomes, wheat is not grown in any ASEAN country, while only Indonesia grows cloves. It is, therefore, in the case of rice and possibly sugar that the argument about protecting the welfare of domestic farmers is most relevant. In the case of the other agricultural items, their withdrawal from the CEPT was related to their role in the business activities of individuals and firms with close connections to the political elite, notably President Suharto.

Rice and rice farmers in ASEAN

Rice is one of the most regulated agricultural commodities in ASEAN, through both trade policy restrictions and domestic price stabilisation schemes. Both these policy instruments helped governments to maintain adequate supplies of rice, the staple food in the region, as well as to ensure a stable minimum price to farmers and a stable maximum price to consumers (Acosta 1998: 38). The rice stabilisation scheme in Indonesia was under the sole control of a state agency, the National Logistics Agency (BULOG). For Thailand, rice was also a major export, which explains the Thai government's interest in securing market access for rice in ASEAN, long a closed market for rice imports. This was, however, easier said than done.

Indonesia

Rice farmers were a politically important group in Indonesia, given the country's large rice farming, rural community and Indonesia's official policy of self-sufficiency in rice for purposes of national security (Hill 1994: 72–8). The country's rice policy and indeed its actions to re-negotiate tariff liberalisation of the rice sector in AFTA need to be viewed in this context.[43] Although rice self-sufficiency was attained in 1985, rice imports were, nevertheless, allowed whenever domestic output was insufficient to meet domestic demand or to replenish emergency buffer stocks. The authorities, however, preferred to control the quantity and price of rice imports, with BULOG given sole importing authority. Although formal MFN tariffs on rice were fairly low, around 17 per cent in the early 1990s, later reduced to zero in the deregulation package of 27 June 1994, these rates were unbound at the GATT/WTO (Pangestu and Azis 1994: 25; Acosta 1998: 197).[44] This allowed the Indonesian authorities to maintain higher tariff rates whenever necessary in order to stabilise domestic rice prices and insulate the home market from import competition. Nevertheless, the import of rice, even if necessary due to domestic production shortfalls, never became politically acceptable (Manning and Jayasuriya 1996: 28). Subjecting rice to CEPT disciplines would have been difficult, given these political realities.

Malaysia and the Philippines

Rice was a politically sensitive product for Malaysia and the Philippines as well, and these governments joined Indonesia in attempting to re-negotiate the final tariff rate and target date for liberalisation of rice tariffs. For the governments of both these countries, rice farmers were an important political constituency, although the political salience of rice farmers had declined in Malaysia since the 1970s with the fall in the share of agriculture in the economy.[45] Nevertheless, the majority of rice farmers in Malaysia are ethnic Malays concentrated in the Northern states of Kedah, Perlis and Kelantan where the opposition Islamic party, PAS[46] is a strong contender for the Malay vote. This demographic fact continues to give political salience to rice farmers in Malaysia and explains Malaysia's decision to re-negotiate rice tariffs in AFTA.[47] The Philippine government also chose to re-negotiate the tariff liberalisation schedule for rice in order to maintain the livelihood of Philippine rice farmers, much to the disquiet of Thailand. The price of rice in the Philippines had been projected to fall considerably if rice tariffs were liberalised under AFTA (Acosta 1998: 181). To offset the possibility of a slump in rice prices, the Philippines maintained MFN tariffs on rice imports at 30 per cent (Acosta 1998: 197).

The political economy of liberalising trade in wheat, sugar and cloves

The Indonesian decision to withdraw wheat flour, sugar and cloves from Indonesia's CEPT inclusion list was surprising since tariffs on these items were very low at the time the dispute emerged in 1994–95. In fact, prevailing tariffs on wheat flour and sugar were set at zero, although domestic monopoly arrangements constituted a significant NTB on imports (Pangestu and Azis 1994: 25). Although Indonesia undertook fairly extensive economic reforms during the 1990s, these monopolies remained untouched (Borsuk 1999: 144). These arrangements benefited powerful state-owned enterprises, especially BULOG, and politically connected firms and individuals who often worked with BULOG to exploit the rents from these monopolies. BULOG, incidentally, was the sole agency authorised to import sugar and wheat flour into Indonesia (Chung *et al.* 1998: 32).

Indonesia's AFTA commitments had the potential to jeopardise these arrangements, which explains its withdrawal of these items from the CEPT Inclusion List. Under AFTA rules, NTBs on any product included in the CEPT would have to be eliminated within five years (ASEAN Secretariat 1996: 31).[48] If Indonesia agreed to include these particular agricultural items in the CEPT, it would also have been required to dismantle the domestic monopolies associated with them. The authorities chose, instead, to withdraw wheat, sugar and cloves from the CEPT to preserve the monopoly privileges and rents that accrued to these individuals and firms. In doing so, they invoked GATT/WTO rules that exempted products regulated by state trading enterprises.[49]

Wheat flour and the conglomerate connection

In Indonesia, during the Suharto era, the wheat flour milling industry was monopolised by PT Bogasari Flour Mill, part of the Salim Group owned by Liem Sioe Liong, a long-standing Suharto ally. Liem's role in helping the President to bail out Bank Duta was discussed above. Bogasari was a joint venture between Liem and Suharto's adopted brother and cousin, Sudwikatmono (Habir 1999: 183). BULOG sold imported wheat to Bogasari at heavily subsidised prices, which Bogasari processed and allegedly sold back to BULOG at inflated prices that was said to have brought Bogasari substantial monopoly rents (Rosser 2002: 135). Consequently, consumers and downstream industries paid higher prices for wheat flour. The Salim group, however, is said to have gained cheap wheat flour for its instant noodle activity, one of the fastest growing markets in Indonesia and the world. The group's food manufacturing arm was, as a result, reportedly able to corner about 90 per cent of Indonesia's instant noodle market (Rosser 2002: 135). AFTA tariff liberalisation would certainly have challenged BULOG's monopoly on wheat flour imports, and consequently ended the monopoly rents that went to private conglomerates like Bogasari and the Salim group in the process.

Technocrats in government in favour of economic liberalisation had long tried to end the wheat flour monopoly, which reduced the efficiency of downstream producers including the small and medium-scale enterprises (Schwarz 1994: 111). The initial Indonesian decision to agree to regional trade liberalisation in agricultural products reflects the policy preferences of this group. Nevertheless, the technocrats failed to prevail over politically influential business actors. Interestingly, Bogasari's articles of incorporation provided for 20 per cent of its profits to be channelled to two charitable foundations run by the President's wife and the military (Habir 1999: 183). Suharto had established the charitable foundations to dispense funds, often collected through contributions from his friends and business associates in the ethnic Chinese community, to selected organisations and individuals in return for political support (Liddle 1999a: 51–2). It was therefore unsurprising that the government chose to withdraw wheat flour from the CEPT despite having initially agreed to its inclusion in view of the political and bureaucratic connections of affected business actors.[50]

Sugar and the state-owned enterprises

BULOG's monopoly on sugar imports similarly explains Indonesia's withdrawal of sugar from AFTA. The sugar industry in Indonesia is dualistic, comprising a modern, efficient sector that operates in southern Sumatra and is essentially privately owned.[51] An inefficient, state-owned sector operating outdated refineries also exists, concentrated in eastern

Java and survives through protection from import competition. Even in the more liberal policy environment of the 1990s, state-owned enterprises possessed substantial political clout, largely due to their role in fulfilling Article 33 of the Indonesian constitution that emphasises state control over the economy. They were regarded as 'agents of development', and undertook distributive functions (Mardjana 1999: 42). State-owned enterprises in the sugar industry were no different.

The control by BULOG of sugar imports, ostensibly to maintain an adequate price to sugarcane cultivators, also allowed the state-owned refineries to sell their refined sugar output to domestic consumers at high prices, earning rents in the process. These state enterprises channelled part of the rents that accrued to local governments in the provinces.[52] This form of arrangement, common in Indonesia throughout the Suharto regime, was a key mechanism the central government used to redistribute income to the provinces, and thus to try and gain political legitimacy. Consumers, however, paid the price, but the Constitution provided the legal and ideological justification for such actions in the name of national development and preserving the unitary state in Indonesia (Mardjana 1999: 42).

Cloves and Tommy Suharto

Unlike the case of rice, sugar and wheat flour, the sale and marketing of cloves during the 1980s was decentralised. Farmers sold cloves to various traders who resold them to domestic manufacturers of the special Indonesian spice-flavoured cigarettes known locally as *kretek* (Borsuk 1999: 151). Unfortunately, the income of clove farmers was not steady, as it depended on the prevailing market price for cloves. Nevertheless, there was little evidence of collusion among the traders to buy from farmers at low prices. This arrangement changed in December 1990 when the government was directed by President Suharto to set up a Clove Support and Marketing Board (BPPC), its official aim being to increase the incomes of clove farmers that it alleged had been suppressed by cigarette manufacturers and clove traders (Hill 1992: 23). Cloves were thus designated 'an essential commodity' that needed to be regulated by the state. The chair of the new board was Tommy, Suharto's youngest son.

The reality was that in the late 1980s, a group of clove traders, after having failed to corner the domestic clove market, sought out Tommy Suharto to help them set up a government-sanctioned clove monopoly to buy from clove farmers and sell to the cigarette manufacturers (Borsuk 1999: 151). What the traders had not managed to accomplish on their own was now to be achieved through political influence and state assistance. Although the Board initially bought cloves from farmers at prices higher than the prevailing market price, this could not be sustained in the face of the significant market distortions the Board's actions were creating

(Hill 1992: 23). Despite public outcry, the President intervened and set a new, lower price for cloves, although the Board continued to sell at far higher prices to cigarette manufacturers. The Board reaped substantial monopoly profits as a result. One estimate suggested a potential gain for the BPPC of US$100 million per year (Schwarz 1994: 154).

The President's personal interest in maintaining his son's clove monopoly explains why Indonesian policymakers, even if they privately preferred to see the clove trade deregulated, had to insist on withdrawing cloves from the CEPT. The House Speaker and the Secretary-General of the government party, Golkar, were highly critical of the clove board's activities (Hill 1992: 23–4), as were the Association of Cigarette Manufacturers (GAPRI), the World Bank and the liberal technocrats in government (Rosser 2002: 139–40). These individuals and groups, however, wielded little political power in Indonesia's authoritarian, patronage-based political system centred on President Suharto, who clearly supported and protected his son's interests and activities in the clove market.

Post-financial crisis developments

The second IMF bailout package signed in 1998 committed the Indonesian government to eliminate BULOG's monopoly over the import and distribution of all agricultural commodities including wheat flour and sugar by February 1998, although rice continues to be regulated by the agency. The clove marketing board was also to be abolished by June 1998 (Soesastro and Basri 1998: 24). The Habibie government that succeeded Suharto in May 1998 managed to implement these reforms despite resistance from business actors involved in the activities scheduled for deregulation. The ongoing reform process in Indonesia, accompanied by the breakdown of the old patronage coalition centred around Suharto (Robison and Rosser 2000), has made it easier for the government to reach a compromise with its ASEAN counterparts on the agriculture issue in an effort to resolve the impasse in agricultural trade liberalisation in AFTA.

AFTA and automobiles

All the core ASEAN countries maintained high MFN import tariffs on automobiles during the 1990s, which also applied to trade in autos within ASEAN since all the ASEAN governments had placed autos in their respective Temporary Exclusion Lists.[53] Except for Singapore, all the other governments used high tariffs to shield domestic auto producers from import competition. By 2000, all items in these lists, including autos, were scheduled to be brought within the CEPT and their tariffs immediately lowered to 20 per cent, after which tariffs were expected to fall to the 0–5 per cent end tariff range by 2002/2003. Malaysia, however, announced in 1999 that it would seek ASEAN approval for a two-year delay for auto trade liberalisation in AFTA. This raised an outcry from the other ASEAN countries but especially from Thailand, which was poised to emerge as the regional centre for auto production spearheaded by foreign capital.

The Malaysian move came at a highly inopportune time – during the financial crisis period. The ASEAN governments, Malaysia included, were under considerable pressure to attract FDI to restore economic growth, and one of the instruments they employed was the potential single AFTA market. They were also keen to reassure foreign direct investors that they remained committed to open markets. Malaysia, especially, had been subject to considerable criticism over its illiberal policy responses to the financial crisis that had culminated in the imposition of temporary capital controls in September 1998 (Khoo 2000). Malaysia's decision to delay CEPT liberalisation of its auto sector appeared to be ill timed and counter-productive from the regional point of view of remaining attractive to FDI.

Indonesia and the Philippines: late liberalisers

Although the Philippines had started the decade with high auto tariffs, this was gradually lowered and by October 1999, MFN tariffs on passenger car imports ranged from 10 per cent (for completely knocked down units, CKD) to 40 per cent (for completely built up units, CBU) (Legewe 2000: 9). Indonesian tariffs on passenger cars too had fallen from 200 per cent to between 65 and 80 per cent for CBU and from 65 per cent to between 35 and 50 per cent for CKD under the June 1999 tariff reform exercise (Aswicahyono *et al.* 2000: 224).

Before this, the Suharto children had been major players in the industry, protected by the industry's high tariff structure. With the end in 1998 to the controversial national car policy that had allocated preferential benefits solely to Tommy Suharto's Humpuss conglomerate,[54] the Indonesian government adopted a more liberal stance on auto liberalisation in AFTA, rejecting domestic business demands to delay the CEPT for autos.[55] In a bid to help domestic car producers, however, the government decided against according CEPT preferences to the import of second-hand or re-conditioned cars, which were more likely to compete with the domestic industry than new autos.[56]

The Malaysian and Thai auto industries: divergent development paths

Malaysia's move to delay liberalising the auto sector in AFTA and Thailand's vehement response to it reflects the divergent development trajectories of the auto sector in these two countries.[57] Malaysia's industry is essentially state-led, while the private sector has largely driven developments in the Thai automobile sector, although the Thai government had initially attempted to shape the industry's development path using policy instruments such as the tariff and local content regulations. Their dissimilar development paths reflected distinct domestic political economy dynamics. The auto industry in Malaysia was designed to fulfil multiple objectives, economic as well as political, through the country's national car project. The Thai industry, on the other hand, was not beset by such demands.

Automobile production in Thailand: driven by foreign capital

Despite their distinct trajectories, the 1960s saw similar import-substitution strategies adopted in both countries based on domestic assembly of cars using imported CKD kits (Abdulsomad 1998: 275). It was only from the 1980s that the development paths of the auto industries in Thailand and Malaysia began to diverge. The Thai industry continued along the protected, import-substitution path begun in the 1960s and involved private local and foreign capital. In 1991, however, the Thai industry was liberalised substantially, part of the broader liberalising trend initiated by the post-coup government of Anand Panyarachun (Thailand 2000). Some restrictions were maintained, notably local content regulations.[58] Nevertheless, the liberalising trend forced domestic automobile assembly and component firms to improve efficiency and produce higher quality cars and components to meet international standards for export (Abdulsomad 1998: 282). Automotive tariffs under the CEPT were reduced to 0–5 per cent in 2000, well ahead of the CEPT schedule, although MFN rates were set at 33 per cent for CKD and 80 per cent for CBU (Thailand 2000: 11).

Substantial investment from foreign auto-makers and component suppliers flowed into Thailand during the 1990s, partly encouraged by Malaysia's monopolised car sector, which soon led to Thailand emerging as the centre for automobile and auto parts manufacturing in Asia (Abdulsomad 1998: 275–84). Investors who had established or were planning to establish automobile plants in the country included the big names in the industry like Ford, General Motors, BMW and Honda (Thailand 2000: 12). Many of them were looking ahead to liberalisation of the automobile industry under AFTA that was scheduled to begin in 2000 and were positioning their firms to exploit the regional market by using Thailand as a production base.

Thus, Malaysia's move to temporarily withdraw automobiles from AFTA disciplines was a blow to automobile firms located in Thailand. Major foreign automobile players in Thailand began pressing the Thai government to ensure that AFTA remained on track for automobiles.[59] BMW's President, Karsten Engel, warned that the expansion of BMW's Thai plant hinged on the completion of the single AFTA market in automobiles.[60] The Malaysian automobile market accounted for a substantial portion of the regional market, about a quarter of total vehicle sales in 1996 in the so-called 'Big Four' ASEAN automobile market (Malaysia, Thailand, Indonesia and the Philippines) targeted by motor vehicle producers. The value of the Malaysian market to automobile manufacturers paradoxically increased as a result of the financial crisis since large declines in vehicle sales in the other three countries meant that Malaysia's share of the ASEAN market rose to about 42 per cent.[61] In 2001, Malaysia accounted for 34 per cent of the 'Big Four' ASEAN motor vehicle market, up from its share in 1996.[62] The significance of the Malaysian market explains why global automobile producers who had set up in Thailand with an eye to the regional market were dismayed at Malaysia's move to exempt cars from regional trade liberalisation.

The Malaysian auto industry: driven by domestic capital and multiple goals

Although Malaysia has long had a domestic car industry based on the assembly of foreign vehicles, the Malaysian Prime Minister Mahathir opted to develop an indigenous automobile manufacturing capability in the country through a national car project. Introduced in the early 1980s, it was part of Mahathir's heavy industries programme. Proton, the national car company, involved state capital while a minority equity stake was awarded to Mitsubishi of Japan, which provided the technical input. In the 1990s, a second national car project was adopted called the Perodua, involving a mix of state capital, domestic private capital and foreign capital, the last through Daihatsu of Japan. The Perodua catered to the small passenger car segment, and thus did not directly compete with the Proton. Other national car projects involving Proton, ethnic Malay private capital and foreign investors such as Citroen of France were also encouraged. The national car industry developed through extensive state support that ranged from high import tariffs on competing products, direct and indirect financial assistance as well as government procurement (Tyndall 1999: 4).

Despite the rapid growth of the national car industry, the multiple goals of the Malaysian national car project led to conflicts between the imperative of growth and efficiency on the one hand and the demands of distribution on the other. The industry had been established to accomplish three objectives. First, it was set up to promote the development of an integrated industrial sector with greater technological depth. Second, and related to the first objective, the project was part of Mahathir's vision to take Malaysia into the ranks of developed countries possessing an indigenous manufacturing and technological capability. Finally, the national car project was expected to catalyse the emergence of an ethnic Malay business community to fulfil the country's New Economic Policy goal of creating a Malay commercial and industrial class. Although ethnic Malay capital was involved in automobile manufacturing through the national car project, this was confined to the business elite with strong links to the political elite. The creation of a more broad-based ethnic Malay business community was to be achieved through stimulating the growth of ethnic Malay automotive component suppliers to the national car project.

Distribution occurred at two levels. First, the preferential policies supporting the national car project, including the high tariff wall, redistributed income to the national car firms from existing producers, namely the local assemblers who were not part of the national car project and from consumers who had to pay exorbitant prices for car purchases. For instance, tariffs on CBU ranged from 140 to 300 per cent while tariffs of 42 per cent were slapped on CKD imports (Tyndall 1999: 47). The national car project was also said to enjoy effective protection rates that were ten times that enjoyed by the non-national cars.[63] The resultant gains or rents were redirected to the national car project. At a second level, there was a further distribution of income, including monopoly rents, from the national car firms like Proton to the automotive component suppliers who were largely ethnic Malay.

The government had instituted a Vendor Development Programme (VDP) that required Proton and Perodua to procure component parts from domestic auto-parts suppliers. The VDP involved nurturing vendors, especially ethnic Malay vendors with little experience in the industry. It was the main vehicle to achieve the ethnic restructuring objective of the national car project, and it was responsible for increasing the proportion of ethnic Malay component suppliers in the country from 23 per cent in 1985 to 49 per cent by 1998 (Tyndall 1999: 14). The national car firms, however, have had to share their considerable rents with their vendors by paying high prices for components, which were often of poor quality. The guaranteed market did not provide sufficient incentive for domestic vendors to improve efficiency, as they could still enjoy substantial returns. Although most auto parts were placed on the fast-track schedule of the CEPT, many vendors were not adversely affected as Proton and Perodua guaranteed purchase of the output from their stable of vendors (Tyndall 1999: 14, 24).

The Malaysian national car project and liberalisation

Even as early as 1995, market analysts predicted that the national car sector would be unable to withstand global market competition and that early liberalisation was inadvisable.[64] The Malaysian government too failed to clarify its position on the industry's liberalisation schedule under the CEPT.[65] Moreover, Proton, Perodua and the auto-parts suppliers were all badly affected by the 1997 financial crisis due to the combined effects of the weakened ringgit, the reduced purchasing power and cautious attitude of consumers, and domestic credit tightening measures (Tyndall

1999: 21). Although tariffs were raised in 1998 to help the industry cope,[66] it was clear that the government had to come to a decision with regard to CEPT liberalisation. Malaysia was due to lower CEPT tariffs on automobiles to 20 per cent in 2000.

The government's ambiguous attitude to automobile tariff liberalisation stems from the growing conflict between the government's developmental approach to the national car project and market realities in ASEAN. On the one hand, the Prime Minister's aim had always been to develop through infant-industry protection, an export-oriented, efficient Malaysian automobile industry able to survive in the global market. He had never been interested in nurturing an inefficient auto industry operating permanently behind protectionist walls.[67] This was entirely consistent with his Vision 2020 goals, which called for Malaysian industries to be globally competitive. On the other hand, it was clear that regional liberalisation would pit Proton, which was yet to be internationally competitive, against the global automobile giants like Ford, General Motors, Honda, Toyota and Nissan. These firms had set up, or were planning to establish manufacturing plants in Thailand to supply to the ASEAN and wider Asian market. These players were also expanding their plants in Malaysia in the run-up to AFTA's completion.[68] Proton especially was not expected to survive what was effectively global market competition within a liberalised ASEAN market, nor in its home market given its history of protected development. Proton's share of the domestic market was expected to shrink to about 30 per cent from its 65 per cent share in 2000 once auto tariffs were reduced under AFTA disciplines.[69] Industry analysts predicted that Thailand's TNC-driven industry would have a competitive edge over subsidised industries like Proton, which would place Thai automobile firms well ahead of Proton once AFTA liberalisation was in place.[70]

Although constantly castigating the national car firms to improve their efficiency and competitiveness, and warning them that the government would not protect them indefinitely, the Prime Minister, nevertheless, acknowledged that temporary protection was necessary to develop an indigenous manufacturing capability in the country beyond mere vehicle assembly.[71] Dr Mahathir maintained that the Thai automobile industry was merely an assembly industry relying on foreign capital and foreign inputs producing foreign cars, contrasting it with the Malaysian strategy of developing an indigenous technological and engineering capability in automobile production.[72] The dispute between Malaysia and Thailand over automobiles stemmed from the distinct nature of the industry in the two countries, with their incompatible priorities. Thailand emphasised growth and efficiency through foreign capital while Malaysia focused on nurturing domestic capital for both economic and political reasons, and thus emphasised both growth and distribution. Although both countries shared broadly similar goals for the CEPT – as a means to attract foreign capital to the region – differences emerged in the specific case of automobiles.

Despite delaying the liberalisation of automobiles in AFTA, it soon became clear that the Malaysian government was preparing for eventual liberalisation of the industry. Additional steps were taken to improve the efficiency of the national car firms. Proton expanded its programme to develop an in-house engineering capability by making plans to purchase a second foreign automobile engineering firm, this time from the US.[73] Proton's purchase in 1996 of an 80 per cent stake in British carmaker, Lotus Cars, had paid dividends. Proton had used the engineering capability of Lotus to develop its own proprietary engine, which was unveiled in 2000 at the Lotus plant in the UK. This development was expected to enable Proton to reduce its 15-year dependence on Mitsubishi for engines, thereby saving Proton about 25 per cent in costs.[74] Industry analysts also endorsed Proton's plans to sell the 1.3 and 1.6 litre petrol engines to other carmakers with assembly operations in the region, given the growing demand for inexpensive engines. The engine's modular design also meant that high volume production runs were not needed to recoup investment costs.[75]

Both Proton and Perodua also began global sourcing of component parts,[76] departing from their previous policy of obtaining high-cost supplies from their stable of domestic, especially ethnic Malay vendors. The VDP, which had been the key instrument to implement the ethnic policy in the automotive sector, was clearly being placed on the back-burner. This move suggests that the efficiency imperative had become dominant. This was reflected in the government's refusal to delay liberalising tariffs on automotive parts in AFTA, despite expectations by vendors that the government would protect them.[77] By 2002, 60 per cent of automotive parts and components were already at tariff rates of between 0 and 5 per cent, while the remaining 40 per cent were subject to tariffs of between 11 and 20 per cent.[78] This was well in line with the requirements of the CEPT scheme.

Finally, and most interestingly, the Prime Minister agreed to allow Proton to sell a further equity stake in the company to foreign automobile firms, provided this was not more than 30 per cent.[79] Proton's need for foreign technical expertise to stay in the game, notwithstanding its ownership of Lotus, overcame Dr Mahathir's traditional resistance to the idea of selling Proton to foreign carmakers.[80] Sources claimed that two US auto firms had expressed interest in the deal – Ford and Daimler Chrysler,[81] although nothing had been finalised at the time of writing. Nevertheless, the point to note is that this *volte-face* on the part of the Prime Minister suggests that the goal of developing an efficient and internationally competitive national automotive industry had become overwhelming, with the Prime Minister also warning Proton, 'we cannot protect you anymore'.[82]

Failure of Proton, Mahathir's favoured project, would likely reflect badly on the Prime Minister and would add to the growing voices of opposition against him, especially in the ethnic Malay community. While it was clear that the need to emphasise the efficiency of Proton had become compelling, a pure growth and efficiency strategy that left outcomes to market forces was not adopted. The market was being kept in abeyance for a period of time through the CEPT delay to allow time for the national car project to try and meet international competitiveness standards, and thus to ensure its survival as well as vindicate Mahathir's vision of developing an indigenous Malaysian national car industry.

Conclusion

This chapter confirms the second proposition advanced in the book, namely that when domestic distributive imperatives became overwhelming, national governments chose to shield particular segments of domestic capital from regional liberalisation, including developmental regionalism. Despite the ambitious commitments that had been made to advance the regional project, and indeed despite the general success in implementing the CEPT, delays and difficulties were encountered in sectors like services, petrochemicals, agriculture and automobiles as a result of domestic political and economic concerns. Fairly serious disputes emerged in agriculture and automobiles, often involving threats of retaliation and counter-threats as member governments sought to re-negotiate their original commitments. These cases in particular clearly illustrate the sensitivities involved when regional liberalisation touched sectors in which politically important domestic firms, or those with strong ties to the political elite, were dominant.

How member governments addressed these disputes is a question that has yet to be adequately answered in the literature. As noted in the introductory chapter, many scholars not only expected such disputes to emerge in AFTA, they also predicted that the disputes would lead to a breakdown of the regional project. This clearly did not happen, as the discussion so far shows. The next chapter attempts to answer this question by analysing how member governments attempted to re-balance the growth-distribution trade-off at the regional level, in the process ensuring AFTA's continuation.

6 Implementation as a political process

Taking care of growth and distribution

Although external pressures stemming from globalisation drove ambitious commitments in AFTA towards open and developmental regionalism, the previous chapter reveals that sustaining regionalism itself became an onerous task due to domestic political priorities that emphasised distribution over growth. The latter led to disputes among member governments, particularly over agriculture and automobiles that threatened to stall the AFTA project. Yet, AFTA did not collapse. This was because member governments managed to address these conflicts through regional-level processes that helped to diffuse tensions, which in turn allowed cooperation to proceed. Specifically, the ASEAN governments bargained over implementation in order to address the growth-distribution conflicts within, and consequently between, member countries. Thus, implementation of AFTA became a political process rather than merely a technical one of complying with the commitments already made. Nevertheless, this process, which led to a downward revision of original AFTA targets and partial institution building, was valuable because it allowed the AFTA project to continue as a result of the compromise worked out between the growth and domestic distributive priorities of the project's different members.

The literature on international cooperation emphasises either the role of hegemonic power in maintaining cooperative processes or the role of institutions in sustaining cooperation (Keohane 1989). Yet, AFTA has made some fairly significant advances in regional economic cooperation despite the absence of a regional leader and even though the institutional structures considered to be necessary to ensure implementation were not put in place when the project was initiated.[1] The institutional argument is not rejected outright, however. One of the insights from the literature on post-agreement or compliance bargaining, which is well suited to explaining implementation in settings lacking a clear leader or a hegemonic power as in ASEAN, is that institutional structures can emerge out of the implementation process itself rather than simply prior to implementation. These emergent institutions, in turn, structure the game in ways that help to advance the cooperative process. The rest of this chapter draws on insights from the compliance bargaining literature to analyse implementation processes in AFTA, focusing especially on how member governments addressed the two major disputes that had emerged over the course of regional cooperation – agriculture and automobiles.

Implementation as a political process: the role of compliance bargaining

Compliance bargaining between states refers to all those bargaining and negotiation processes that follow from the conclusion of international agreements, a trend that is quite common in international negotiations (Jonsson and Tallberg 1998: 376–97). This perspective recognises that a cooperative agreement does not solve all problems once and for all, but instead creates a new bargaining situation once an agreement has been adopted. It provides useful insights on implementation as a political process, particularly with regard to what happens in the event of non-compliance. In compliance bargaining situations, bargaining strategies are adopted by both the 'guardians' and 'violators' of agreements to advance their respective positions during implementation. As already noted, this is particularly true for self-help situations in non-hegemonic settings where a third party enforcer or prosecutor is absent, a situation that characterises ASEAN. In such settings, compliance bargaining processes are likely to emphasise managerial approaches to address the problem at hand rather than sanctioning approaches that regard compliance purely as a technical problem of enforcement (Jonsson and Tallberg 1998: 376).[2]

The management school does not regard non-compliance as a deliberate decision by governments to violate an agreement, unlike the enforcement school.[3] Instead, non-compliance is viewed as the outcome of either ambiguities in the agreement, the limited technical capacity of governments to comply with the agreement, or unexpected social, economic or political developments that make compliance difficult to achieve (Chayes and Chayes 1993: 188; Jonsson and Tallberg 1998: 382–3). The use of in-built sanctioning or punishment measures in agreements, which features in enforcement approaches, is rejected in favour of managerial solutions that emphasise persuasion or 'jawboning' – the effort to persuade the violator to alter its behaviour (Chayes and Chayes 1995: 25). Thus, compliance bargaining strategies adopted by treaty guardians may include persuasion in addition to or instead of threats to impose sanctions or the mobilisation of social and political pressure. The violator's main bargaining strategy may also consist of persuasion, apart from promises of rewards in return for tolerance of deviant behaviour or threats of retaliation.

In such instances, the search for mutually acceptable solutions may entail compromises that do not fully conform to the original agreement. This will be especially true when partners in the agreement lack the means of forcing violators into compliance, as in the case of ASEAN. In such instances, partners may decide to accept a lower level of compliance rather than risk the cooperative agreement in total (Chayes and Chayes 1993: 184). Compliance bargaining processes generally also lead to some form of institutional strengthening. Apart from revisions to original commitments, members often attempt to enhance transparency of the cooperative process, tighten rules and procedures and improve dispute resolution mechanisms (Jonsson and Tallberg 1998: 375). The work of Martin and Simmons (1998: 739–42) on international institutions is instructive in this regard. They suggest that institutions can help to advance cooperation in two ways – they provide information to overcome cheating among members of the agreement and they help members to resolve distributional conflict among themselves.

Information improves transparency of government actions, thus facilitating the negotiation of cooperative agreements, the monitoring of agreements made, and allows compliance (or non-compliance) to be more easily observed. While the literature emphasises the primary audience to be other governments, this chapter suggests that informational institutions can also be directed at influencing non-state actors, business actors for instance, by signalling to the latter that the commitments made by governments are credible. Institution building is likely to be especially important when the downward re-negotiation of original commitments raises some doubts with regard to the future of the cooperative project.

Distributional institutions, on the other hand, address the problem of the unequal distribution of gains and losses between countries that impedes cooperation. Drawing on insights from legislative politics at the domestic level, particularly from the American experience, Martin and Simmons (1998: 741) argue that cooperation can be advanced through institutional structures that allow participants to link issues and cut deals with each other. Following a similar line of argument, this chapter suggests that institutions emerging out of compliance bargaining processes that accept lower commitments facilitate cooperation by allowing gains and losses to be traded between countries. Negotiating a lower level of compliance transfers gains to the violator from the offended party and from others for whom the original commitment was superior. In the process, the violating government is able to address domestic concerns with distribution. Nevertheless, all parties gain over the long run since this act allows the cooperative project to be maintained, provided of course that the project is valuable to all parties. The alternative may well have been the breakdown of the project.

The rest of the chapter examines in some detail the compliance bargaining processes in AFTA in two specific issue areas – agriculture and automobiles – that caused considerable tensions and appeared set to jeopardise the future of the regional project.

Compliance bargaining in AFTA

Two of the most notable disputes in AFTA – over liberalising trade in agriculture and automobiles – arose out of problems certain member governments had with implementing commitments already adopted. This was discussed in the previous chapter. Although inter-governmental bargaining that was set in motion as a result of these disputes was protracted, it eventually allowed the problem to be addressed. Members accepted downward revisions to original commitments but also engaged in institution building, albeit of a partial nature, as they attempted to re-balance growth and distributive concerns at the regional level.

Compliance bargaining and agricultural trade liberalisation

Indonesia triggered the dispute in ASEAN over agriculture when in early 1995 the Indonesian government backtracked on its earlier decision to liberalise trade in fifteen unprocessed agricultural products by 2003. The said items, notably cloves, sugar, wheat and rice had initially been placed in Indonesia's Temporary Exclusion List in 1994, which would have required the government to liberalise trade in these items at the latest from 2000 and to remove associated NTBs. In early 1995, Indonesia transferred the fifteen products to its Sensitive List, which effectively provided indefinite protection for these items. The domestic political sensitivities associated with these particular items, discussed in the previous chapter, explain the Indonesian government's action on the issue and its subsequent refusal to budge from this position.

Indonesia's move provoked a sharp response from Thailand, a major agricultural exporter. The Thai government then threatened to withdraw forty-four agricultural products from AFTA in retaliation. After intense discussion, a compromise was finally reached later that year. The Eighth AFTA Council meeting in December 1995 allowed Indonesia to shelter the fifteen items until 2010 by creating a new Temporary Exclusion List specific to agricultural products.[4] To lend some order to this process, only agricultural items regulated by state-trading enterprises would qualify for inclusion in the new Temporary Exclusion List in agriculture, which was consistent with GATT/WTO practices. In fact, Indonesia had cited this particular GATT clause when it initially transferred the fifteen products to its Sensitive List. The items excluded by Indonesia were at that time regulated by state-trading agencies, namely BULOG for rice, sugar and wheat and the BPPC for cloves.

The Thai government was placated by the move, which would have extended the exemption period for these items, including the all-important rice, to 2010 instead of indefinitely as Indonesia had originally intended.[5] The Thai Finance Minister stressed that his government could 'accept a lateral reclassification of the Indonesian products to another temporary exclusion category, but not a negative transfer of the items to Indonesia's Sensitive List'.[6] Unfortunately, the Indonesian officials at the meeting changed their minds only a day after the compromise had been adopted, and expressed reservations about meeting the new 2010 deadline.[7] The issue remained unresolved until the following April when the Ninth AFTA Council meeting confirmed that the deadline for agricultural tariff liberalisation would remain January 2010. Member governments were, however, allowed to determine the ending tariff rates on those agricultural products in the parallel Temporary Exclusion List, which could be higher than 5 per cent.[8]

The Indonesian government was still keen to delay liberalisation of the fifteen items until 2020. The Philippine government, wishing to delay liberalising trade in rice and sugar, backed the Indonesian position. Both governments were reported as having refused to accept the 2010 deadline adopted by the Ninth AFTA Council.[9] Indonesia later declared, in September 1996, that it would agree to accept the 2010 deadline for all the said items, except rice and sugar that the government deemed to be highly sensitive products. Indonesia wanted a 2020 deadline for CEPT liberalisation for these two items. This did not please the Thai government.[10]

This episode is clearly an instance of compliance bargaining in which the disputants, notably Thailand and Indonesia, employed both persuasion and threats. In the end, a compromise was reached when ASEAN member governments agreed to allow Indonesia until 2010 to finalise CEPT liberalisation of the fifteen products it had initially withdrawn from AFTA. This represented a lower level of compliance over the original commitment, and was to Indonesia's benefit although the government still attempted to extend the exemption period to 2020 for sugar and rice. The compromise allowed Indonesia to preserve domestic monopoly arrangements involving firms and individuals with strong connections to the political elite.

Member governments, nevertheless, attempted to tighten up loopholes and introduced rules and procedures to govern the treatment of agricultural products. Negotiations continued for the next three years over the issue, which ended in the adoption of the *Protocol on Sensitive and Highly Sensitive Products* in September 1999. Indonesia classified only rice as a highly sensitive product in the Protocol, as did the Philippines and Malaysia, for which final tariff rates had to be reduced to between 0 and 20 per cent by 2010.

Thailand was unfortunately the loser in the short term, since it could not export rice to Indonesia at preferential rates until 2010, and then only if Indonesia adhered to the Protocol. Thailand was compelled to compromise on the issue since AFTA had become a vital part of Thailand's economy. The AFTA market was vital to Thailand, second only to the US market in 1998 when these negotiations were in full swing.[11] Thailand was, therefore, unwilling to jeopardise the entire AFTA project by refusing to compromise over agriculture.[12] Thailand attempted to safeguard its growth priorities over the longer term by agreeing to compromise on this issue.[13] Although the formal Protocol benefits Thailand by stipulating deadlines and ending tariff rates by all parties, it does not guarantee that members will adhere to them. Compliance by Indonesia has, nevertheless, been made easier by the crisis-induced domestic economic reforms that removed the monopoly interests behind much of Indonesia's attitude to agricultural trade liberalisation in the CEPT over the previous five years.

Compliance bargaining and the dispute over automobiles

In early 1999, Malaysia requested that it be allowed to delay until 2005 the transfer of automobiles from the Temporary Exclusion List to the inclusion list, citing the problems experienced by Malaysia's national car project as a result of the 1997–98 financial crisis. All the ASEAN countries were dismayed by this development, particularly Thailand. The previous chapter shows how Thailand was poised to be the regional hub for global automobile producers planning to produce and export to the rest of ASEAN from Thailand if a free trade area in automobiles were in place. As in agriculture, this episode of compliance bargaining also involved threats of retaliation being made between Thailand and Malaysia, as well as persuasion and offers of rewards.

The dispute over automobiles was far more threatening to the core ASEAN countries than agriculture. Unlike agriculture, the automobile issue was more relevant to the creation of a single regional market for manufacturing activity, in which foreign investors in particular were interested. Moreover, Malaysia's delay request, made right in the throes of the financial crisis, raised questions among foreign investors about the future of the single regional market. The delay issue was a key item of discussion during the joint ASEAN investment promotion missions to the US and Europe in 1999–2000.[14] Business actors wanted some assurance that the regional project would proceed.[15]

It was understandable that business leaders, particularly those from the US and Japan, were worried. American automobile firms, like their Japanese counterparts, had invested substantially in Thailand with the intention of exporting to the regional market once AFTA commitments in automobiles came into force from 2000. Gerald Kania, President of ASEAN Operations for Ford Motor Company warned, 'implementation of AFTA is central to this region's ability to attract large-scale capital flows'.[16] Other US firms in the telecommunications, air express and pharmaceutical sectors acknowledged that they were holding off investing further in the ASEAN region due to the uncertainty raised by the automobile issue. These firms were also weighing the benefits of committing their regional investments to China, which had re-emerged as an attractive investment site with its impending entry into the WTO.[17] Japanese firms with substantial investments in the ASEAN countries were also worried that Malaysia's move might open the floodgates with more members clamouring to withdraw other products from AFTA.[18]

Thailand, the country with the most to lose from Malaysia's move, began a series of bilateral discussions with the Malaysian government to seek a solution to the impasse, but these were unsuccessful. As in the case of agriculture, the Thai government was in a weak bargaining position. It was noted in the previous chapter that the Malaysian automobile market constituted the largest segment of the potential regional market for automobiles. For Thailand, an open Malaysian automobile market was, therefore, the superior option.[19] On the other hand, the Thai government had nothing to offer the Malaysian government as a *quid pro quo*.

Although the Thai government threatened to delay reducing tariffs on imports of palm oil products,[20] a key export item for Malaysia, if Malaysia insisted on exempting automobiles, the Thai threat was ineffectual. Malaysia's main export markets for palm oil products lay outside ASEAN, in Pakistan and China (Malaysia 1998: xxvii). In an interesting twist, Malaysia reportedly lobbied the Thai government to delay liberalising tariffs on palm oil products so that it could proceed likewise for automobiles.[21] In the end, the Thai government decided not to exclude palm oil products from CEPT disciplines irrespective of the Malaysian position on automobiles. This was for purely internal reasons, to avoid disadvantaging domestic food manufacturers who would have otherwise had to pay higher prices for palm oil inputs, although the mostly small farmers who produce palm oil were likely to be hurt by tariff reduction in this sector.[22]

The Thai government instead urged the Malaysian trade authorities to use the emergency safeguard clause in the CEPT to protect the automobile industry. Malaysian officials refused, however.[23] Under the terms of the CEPT, the emergency safeguard clause could only be invoked if CEPT implementation caused injury to import-competing sectors. In other words, the Malaysian government would have had to first liberalise automobile tariffs under the CEPT and then demonstrate injury to the domestic industry before it could use the safeguard provision. The Malaysian government was not prepared to do so, given the political importance of the national car project.[24] In the end, ASEAN economic and foreign ministers agreed to allow Malaysia to defer automobile tariff reduction. They had little choice, because Malaysian trade officials had made it clear that the government was prepared to leave the AFTA project if its 'request' to delay tariff reduction on automobiles was not granted. Thai foreign minister, Surin Pitsuwan, admitted that if the other ASEAN governments did not acquiesce to the Malaysian demand, Malaysia 'might say "then to hell with AFTA"'.[25]

Although none of the ASEAN governments wished to scupper what had become a crucial economic project for them, and were therefore willing to go along with the Malaysian position, they were also keen to place the entire exercise within a rule-based framework to ensure the process was transparent and predictable. The ASEAN governments were especially keen to reassure business actors, particularly foreign investors that AFTA remained on track.[26] A decision was made to formulate a protocol on the modification of CEPT concessions that would be based on GATT Article XXVIII and would incorporate a clause on compensation by the offending party. In November 2000, the *Protocol Regarding the Implementation of the CEPT Scheme Temporary Exclusion List* (ASEAN 2000) was formally adopted by ASEAN.

While Malaysian trade officials rejected monetary forms of compensation, they were prepared to provide other forms of compensation including compensatory tariff reduction or technical assistance, which is similar to GATT Article XXVIII.[27] Thai trade officials admitted, however, that compensation was a second best offer for Thailand.[28] Malaysian tariffs were already low, while Thailand did not require development assistance. Nevertheless, the Thai government planned to ask for compensatory tariff reduction in agricultural commodities like sugar, rice and flour on which Malaysia retained high tariffs.[29] In any case, the compensation clause was also inserted to deter other governments in ASEAN from following the Malaysian example, and for whom compensation would significantly raise the costs of withdrawing from AFTA disciplines.[30] Malaysia has, in fact, rejected Thailand's right to compensation by claiming that Thailand was not a principal supplier of automobiles to Malaysia.[31] Article 3(3) of the CEPT Protocol allows 'member states having principal or substantial supplying interest' to ask for compensation from the offending party (ASEAN 2000). Negotiations between Thailand and Malaysia on compensation are continuing on the matter.

ASEAN officials and ministers are sufficiently realistic to acknowledge that they have very little means of preventing any further delays by Malaysia in liberalising the automobiles sector under AFTA, even though the Protocol aims to raise the costs of doing so.[32] Although member governments have little rule enforcement powers apart from diplomacy, they were clearly attempting to limit new requests for delays from members through the Protocol by making the process of modifying concessions sufficiently restrictive and costly to members. They were also aiming to make the CEPT more transparent to business actors. In doing so, they were attempting to ensure that the conditions for growth were maintained in AFTA, while also enabling a fellow member to address its particular concerns with domestic distribution.

Institution building in AFTA: an outcome of compliance bargaining

The outcome of bargaining over implementation in both the agriculture and automobile cases led to the downward revision of commitments from those previously agreed. They also led to a process of institutional strengthening through the tightening of rules and procedures governing regional economic cooperation. The *Protocol on Sensitive and Highly Sensitive Products* in the case of agriculture and the *Protocol Regarding the Implementation of the CEPT Scheme Temporary Exclusion List* are clear examples of this process. Rules and procedures are a key dimension of institutionalisation, functioning as constraints on the actions of member governments and to provide greater transparency in cooperation. In AFTA, they were important not only to convince other governments in the project to continue cooperation but also useful as signalling devices aimed at convincing investors that the regional project remained viable. These two protocols were part of a broader process of institution building in AFTA that took place throughout the 1990s, triggered by problems and setbacks with implementation.

A framework of institutionalisation

The extent and nature of institution building in AFTA as a result of compliance bargaining processes may be assessed using the following four-dimensional framework of institutionalisation (Table 6.1). In adopting this particular conception of institutions, the study goes beyond conventional approaches in studying institutional structures associated with ASEAN economic cooperation. These approaches tend to regard institutions as synonymous with organisational structures, and thus focus exclusively on administrative structures as well as decision-making hierarchies (Ch'ng 1991; Pelkman 1992).

While organisational structures clearly have a role to play in cooperation, and constitute two of the four dimensions included in the framework employed here, institutions in general are best conceptualised more broadly as sets of practices, rules and procedures that constrain activity, shape expectations and prescribe acceptable forms of behaviour (Keohane 1989: 3). This broader conception of institutions is captured in the four dimensions of institutionalisation identified in the framework below. Each of these four features can be presumed to vary in two ways, respectively reflecting low and high levels of institutionalisation depending on whether they impose weaker or stronger constraints on, as well as more explicit prescriptions for national behaviour. How these constraints work is explained below, which is followed by an assessment of institution building in AFTA.

Nature of the constitutional documents

Depending on the extent of their formality, whether they are binding on signatories, and the degree of detail provided, the constitutional documents that frame any cooperative project help to shape the nature of constraints imposed on participating members.

Table 6.1 A framework of institutionalisation

Dimensions of institutionalisation	*Level of institutionalisation*	
	Low	*High*
Nature of constitutional documents		
• Degree of formality	Informal	Formal
• Nature of commitments	Non-binding	Binding
• Form of the agreement	Joint communiqué or vaguely worded statement of intent	Detailed agreement
Decision-making procedures		
• Voting style	Consensus	Majority voting or partial easing of consensus requirements
Modality of cooperation		
• Substantive policy targets (rules)	Absent or ambiguous	Present and transparent
• If present	Nationally determined	Multilaterally/jointly determined
• Procedural rules	Absent or ambiguous	Present and transparent
Nature of coordination		
• Decision-making	Ad-hoc or crisis-driven	Regularised and/or centralised
• Monitoring	Decentralised/ inter-governmental	Third-party/centralised
• Enforcement	Decentralised/ inter-governmental	Third-party/centralised with delegated powers

Source: Nesadurai (2001: 203).

Compared to institutions based on formal agreements, which are defined to require ratification (Lipson 1991), institutions governed by informal agreements are presumed to reflect a lower level of institutional constraint on national governments. Informal agreements can, in theory at least, be more easily abandoned at lower cost than formal agreements. Although formal, ratified treaties do not in any way legally bind states to their promises in an anarchic international setting, they, nevertheless, tend to impose greater constraints on institutional members. The language of 'binding commitments' that is found in formal agreements are instances of diplomatic communication aimed at other signatories or third parties, revealing states' intentions to adhere to a particular commitment (Lipson 1991: 508). Such agreements raise the costs of non-compliance. These costs are incurred largely in terms of the loss of reputational capital if parties are seen to be reneging on 'binding' agreements to which they had committed themselves, making future cooperation less likely as other governments become increasingly wary of engaging in cooperation with the recalcitrant partner. In the case of economic agreements designed to influence the behaviour of economic actors, governments also incur economic costs when they renege on such agreements because reneging sends signals to crucial economic actors that the agreement is not likely to be fully implemented. For similar reasons, the presence of binding commitments imposes greater constraints on members, particularly if adequate monitoring and enforcement mechanisms are also present. Likewise, detailed agreements that are clear and transparent represent a higher level of institutionalisation compared to vaguely worded agreements or simple joint statements of intent, imposing a bigger constraint on signatories by specifying more clearly promises about future national behaviour.

International agreements are, nevertheless, also designed to be flexible, since governments, often being uncertain about the distribution of future benefits under a particular agreement, are naturally reluctant to conclude long-term, inflexible agreements (Lipson 1991: 518–19). For instance, international agreements, whether formal or informal, may be designed to be of limited duration in order to allow signatories to calculate their costs and benefits more confidently and to legitimately allow parties to reassess their commitment in the future. Agreements could also be devised in ways that allow signatories to partially withdraw without risk to their reputations, a prime example being the GATT escape clause that allows for post-agreement protection. While flexibility is an important attribute of institutions, flexible agreements in which caveats or escape clauses are well defined and clearly expressed, including the conditions under which they can be invoked, reflect a higher level of institutionalisation.

Decision-making procedures

Decision-rules within institutions can affect the constraints that an institution imposes on its members. Consensus decision-making allows the least inclined party to accept constraints on its behaviour to veto other parties that are willing to accept more stringent constraints. Mechanisms such as majority voting, easing consensus requirements for particular decisions, delegating responsibilities to technical experts, setting clear time limits for particular procedures especially in dispute settlement and establishing a clear organisational core to which some collective responsibilities could be devolved enhance institutional control on members' behaviour (Kahler 1995). Such forms of decision-making reflect a higher level of institutionalisation, while consensus decision-making involves weaker constraints on national behaviour.

Modality of cooperation

Coordination within an institution can follow substantive or procedural rules (Kahler 1995: 4). The former feature explicit and detailed rules on substantive policy targets, such as an ending tariff, the date by which a particular tariff has to be reached, or a precise timetable for tariff reductions. Procedural rules prescribe a course of action under certain specified conditions.

At one level, the presence of substantive policy targets may be said to reflect a higher level of institutionalisation since the degree of constraint imposed on members will be higher in such instances. At another level, institutions in which substantive policy targets or rules are jointly determined rather than decided unilaterally by each member tend to impose a higher degree of constraint upon members relative to unilaterally determined targets, since joint determination is more likely to consider the needs of the system as a whole (Padoa-Schioppa 1985: 266–8). When national governments are allowed to determine substantive policy targets unilaterally, they are not obliged to consider joint gains for the system. The presence of consensus decision-making qualifies this argument, however, because a party unwilling to accept a higher degree of constraint on its behaviour will be able to determine the agenda for all members.

The adoption of procedural rules generally reflects a higher degree of institutionalisation since such rules compel members to pursue a course of action in the event of disruption or potential disruption to cooperation. Thus, procedural rules may trigger either dispute settlement processes or at least an obligation for members to consult each other to address problems that arise in the course of cooperation. In such instances, institutional members must, at the very least, jointly consider or debate any departures from the cooperative agreement.

Nature of coordination

The three key aspects of institutional coordination, namely decision-making, monitoring and enforcement, can vary along the centralised – decentralised continuum, reflecting respectively higher and lower levels of institutionalisation. Stronger institutions are defined as those that display regularised and centralised decision-making in which decisions on collaboration are made jointly rather than on an *ad hoc* basis or only when crises strike. The assumption is that regularised decision-making meetings raise the chances for cooperative outcomes over purely *ad hoc* forums since the former raise the shadow of the future (Kahler 1988: 388). Decentralised or inter-governmental monitoring and enforcement usually reflect weaker institutions compared to third party or centralised arrangements provided with delegated or independent powers. The former raises the possibility that institutional constraints on behaviour may be negotiated downwards through inter-governmental compromises. Third party arrangements like panels of technical experts rarely allow for the downward re-negotiation of institutional commitments. Instead, such panels usually uphold institutions by providing rulings on whether institutional commitments have been breached and often also specify the countervailing actions that need to be taken in the event of such breaches.

Institution building in AFTA

While compliance bargaining processes led to the downward re-negotiation of original commitments, they also led to a limited form of institutional strengthening. Using the above framework of institutionalisation, the study reveals that partial institution building has taken place in AFTA since 1995. While consensus decision-making and the decentralised nature of coordination limit the constraints imposed on member governments, members have engaged in tightening existing rules and procedures as well as articulating new rules and procedures to govern issues where none existed previously. These rules and procedures were articulated through fairly detailed, binding protocols that required domestic ratification, and included clearly specified agendas for negotiations as well as negotiated timetables. While flexibility continues to be a feature, the conditions governing flexibility were made more transparent. Although decision-making, monitoring and enforcement remain decentralised, decision-making processes, in particular, have been regularised.

Nature of the constitutional documents

Apart from the initial agreements made among the ASEAN governments, in 1992, that launched AFTA and the Summit Declarations of 1992, 1995 and 1998, all other agreements signed between the ASEAN member governments are formal and binding requiring domestic ratification by national legislatures. Table 6.2 shows a progressive increase in the level of institutionalisation associated with AFTA when we focus on the nature of its constitutional documents.

It was noted in Chapter 2 that the original CEPT agreement of 1992 provided few specific details. Member governments quickly returned to the negotiating table to work out the necessary rules and procedures to govern the workings of the CEPT. Moreover, protocols on procedural matters were also adopted, notably on dispute settlement in 1996, on notification procedures in 1998 and on modification of CEPT concessions in 2000. In services and investment, initial statements of intent in the form of framework agreements were followed by negotiations to firm up commitments. Contrary to popular perception, this approach to AFTA – cynically dubbed '*A*gree *F*irst *T*alk *A*fter'[33] – is not unique to AFTA. Many international agreements are developed from general framework agreements that move to become increasingly specific protocols through a sequence of bargaining processes (Jonsson and Tallberg 1998: 372).

The point to note is that from 1995, the constitutional documents underpinning AFTA became formal and binding on signatories, while the level of detail provided also increased. This represented one dimension of the increasing institutionalisation of AFTA, as these agreements and protocols increased the degree of constraint on members' actions. Although members could easily renege on their commitments despite the formal, binding and detailed nature of the agreements and protocols they had committed themselves to, this would come at a cost to their reputations, particularly in the eyes of business actors.

Table 6.2 Nature of the constitutional documents

Agreements (signed)[a]	*Degree of formality*[b]	*Type of commitments*[c]	*Form of agreement*[d]
Framework Agreement on Enhancing Economic Cooperation (28-1-92)	Informal	Not clearly stated	Vague; Few specifics
Agreement on the Common Effective Preferential Tariff Scheme for AFTA (28-1-92)	Informal	Not clearly stated	Some details provided
Protocol to Amend the Framework Agreement on Enhancing ASEAN Economic Cooperation (15-12-95)	Formal	Binding	Additional details provided
Protocol to Amend the Common Effective Preferential Tariff Scheme for AFTA (15-12-95)	Formal	Binding	More details provided than original CEPT Agreement
ASEAN Framework Agreement on Services (15-12-95)	Formal	Binding	Statement of Intent
Protocol on Dispute Settlement Mechanism (26-11-96)	Formal	Binding	Detailed procedures provided
Protocol to Implement the Initial Package of Commitments Under ASEAN Framework Agreement on Services (15-12-97)	Formal	Binding	Commitment details provided in annexes
Framework Agreement on the ASEAN Investment Area (8-10-98)	Formal	Binding	Statement of intent, providing procedures for future negotiations
Protocol on Notification Procedures (8-10-98)	Formal	Binding	Detailed procedures provided
Protocol to Implement the Second Package of Commitments Under the ASEAN Framework Agreement on Services (16-12-98)	Formal	Binding	Commitment details provided in annexes
Protocol on the Special Arrangement for Sensitive and Highly Sensitive Products (30-9-99)	Formal	Binding	Substantive targets and procedures outlined

Protocol Regarding the Implementation of the CEPT Scheme Temporary Exclusion List (23-11-2000)	Formal	Binding	Detailed procedures provided on modification of CEPT concessions
Protocol to Implement the Third Package of Commitments Under the ASEAN Framework Agreement on Services (31-12-01)	Formal	Binding	Commitment details provided in annexes

Notes

a Other agreements signed but excluded from this table are the three Summit Declarations (1992, 1995, 1998), agreements on intellectual property rights, facilitation of goods in transit within ASEAN, industrial cooperation, customs harmonisation, electronic commerce, and mutual recognition arrangements.

b Ratification is required for formal agreements while informal agreements do not require ratification.

c Whether binding or non-binding.

d Whether detailed or vaguely worded/statement of intent.

As the previous discussion showed, the credibility of AFTA itself was questioned in the wake of Malaysia's withdrawal of automobiles from CEPT disciplines. The adoption of the CEPT modification protocol was aimed at reassuring investors about the future of AFTA. It was a necessary step. Although Malaysia's move had upset investors, particularly the US automobile producers, US investors considered the decision to frame a set of rules and procedures to govern the action a positive step forward that 'strengthens the AFTA mechanism and allows a transparent and rules-based process for countries to modify their concessions with compensation, hence providing a system of checks and balances'.[34]

Strengthening rules and procedures

Although some policy targets were initially indicated in AFTA for the liberalisation of goods trade, these were not clearly specified with individual member governments able to determine their respective rates of reduction within the end tariff rates and the fifteen year time period stipulated in the original CEPT Agreement. Annual tariff reduction schedules were thus nationally rather than jointly determined. Moreover, no clear procedures governed the treatment of exclusions. In 1994–95, ASEAN member governments introduced and tightened rules and procedures for the CEPT that set a common date for commencing tariff liberalisation, as well as stipulated how tariffs on products in the Temporary Exclusion List would be liberalised. Although the specifics of tariff liberalisation, such as the particular commodities to be liberalised and their respective rates of tariff reduction, were nationally determined, as is generally the case in the WTO, some regularity and transparency were introduced by stipulating common start and end dates and by the obligation for member governments to issue annual tariff reduction packages.

Neither did the 1992 CEPT Agreement include a mechanism for dispute settlement, only specifying in Article 8 that member states should try to amicably settle any disputes arising from implementation of AFTA through consultations. This was rectified in November 1996 when member countries adopted a *Protocol on Dispute Settlement Mechanism* (ASEAN 1996b). Comprising twelve Articles, this Protocol specifies in some detail the procedures that member governments need to follow in the event of a dispute. Thus far, the DSM has yet to be invoked, although a number of disputes have arisen in the course of AFTA. ASEAN member governments preferred to address these disputes through diplomatic consultations and bargaining. Senior officials from Indonesia, Singapore, Thailand and Malaysia interviewed by the author between July and September 2000 reiterated that invoking the DSM could jeopardise political relationships in ASEAN, something that all member governments wished to avoid. Nevertheless, members saw the need for a DSM, to at least make available a framework of procedures and rules in the event it became needed.[35]

Although the member governments' preference for diplomatic consultations to resolve disputes in AFTA seemingly reflects an Asian cultural aversion to legalistic forms of cooperation,[36] the cultural argument should not be exaggerated. The evidence in this chapter suggests that the ASEAN governments were not averse to adopting more formal rules and procedures to guide regional economic cooperation. Kahler (1995: 99), moreover, notes that a preference for diplomacy in dispute resolution exists in many international forums. The European experience in the European Free Trade Area (EFTA) is strikingly similar. Although a Ministerial Council had been established in EFTA to rule on disputes between members, only very minor conflicts were brought to the Council for resolution. Major disagreements between EFTA members were settled among the disputants concerned through bilateral or joint consultations so as not to jeopardise the political relationships between these countries (Curzon 1974: 51–5).

The original CEPT Agreement also failed to provide details on procedures to be adopted should members wish to nullify the concessions they originally offered to regional partners (ASEAN 1992c). The Notification Protocol adopted in 1998 attempted to address this gap in AFTA (ASEAN 1998b). Its adoption creates a more predictable AFTA as member governments and economic actors can now be warned in advance of possible changes to AFTA concessions. Member governments decided to adopt such a procedure largely in response to Indonesia's actions in raising import tariffs on a number of petrochemical items in 1996 and 1997 without informing other members or the ASEAN Secretariat.[37] This created problems for firms in the other ASEAN countries who were unaware of the alteration until actually confronted with the new rates at Indonesian customs borders. The Malaysian government had, in fact, threatened to lodge a complaint against Indonesia at the WTO over the latter's intransigence over petrochemicals. Supported by the other members, Malaysia pushed for the adoption of a Notification Protocol to limit similar 'surprises' in the future.[38]

The ASEAN economic ministers also signed a Protocol in November 2000 that provides rules and procedures to govern a more flexible implementation of the CEPT. The Protocol, closely based on Article XXVIII (Modification of Schedule) of the GATT 1994, was developed in response to Malaysia's request that it be allowed to delay shifting automobiles into the inclusion list and subjecting them to CEPT tariff reductions. The Protocol enables member governments facing real economic difficulties to delay the transfer of a product from the Temporary Exclusion List to the inclusion list or to temporarily suspend concessions on products already transferred to the inclusion list (ASEAN 2000). Modifications were, however, limited to the final tranche of Temporary Exclusion List products moved to the inclusion list on 1 January 2000. The Protocol also provides for compensatory adjustment from the offending party to other members on a most-favoured nation (MFN) basis through Article 5. This ASEAN-level multilateral agreement, nevertheless, sanctions negotiations on a bilateral or plurilateral basis between those members most affected to resolve the issue at hand.

Both the notification and modification protocols introduced transparency and predictability into the AFTA process, at least in theory. This was also the central aim of the *Protocol on Sensitive and Highly Sensitive Agricultural Products* (ASEAN 1999) adopted in September 1999 to govern agricultural trade liberalisation. This protocol not only focused on procedural issues, it also outlined substantive policy targets. The protocol provides for two categories of exemptions – a list of sensitive products and a list of highly sensitive items. The core six ASEAN members were to begin phasing into the CEPT scheme agricultural products on their Sensitive Lists between January 2001 and January 2003, with the deadline set at 2010 when tariffs on these products would have to be at the 0–5 per cent range. Governments had to begin tariff reductions on their 'highly sensitive products' anytime between January 2001 and January 2005. The protocol also required products categorised as highly sensitive to be officially submitted to the ASEAN Secretariat, which Indonesia, Malaysia and the Philippines did for rice and rice-related products. The protocol also allowed them the flexibility to determine the final tariff rates for these products, although this was capped at 20 per cent.

Decision-making procedures and institutional mechanisms for coordination

Although member governments were prepared to subject regional cooperation to more rules and procedures, they preferred to retain consensus decision-making procedures for all levels of cooperation. Moreover, decision-making, monitoring and enforcement remain decentralised, revealing ASEAN's preference for inter-governmental mechanisms as opposed to third party or centralised modes of coordination. This approach to cooperation is, however, not unique to ASEAN (Kahler 1995: 121).

Decision-making in AFTA occurs at three principal levels, namely the senior economic officials meeting (SEOM), the economic ministers meeting (AEM) and the leaders' summits. Prior to 1995, leaders' summits were held infrequently, with only four held between 1967 when ASEAN was formed and 1992. In 1992 at the Singapore Summit, the leaders decided to regularise their summits, agreeing to hold formal summit meetings once every three years. At the Bangkok Summit in 1995, ASEAN leaders agreed to meet annually on an informal basis to help advance AFTA. Thus, leaders now meet either formally or informally at least once each year.

The AEM meets at least twice annually, once formally and the second time informally, while the SEOM meet more frequently each year, with eleven such meetings held between July 1998 and June 1999 (ASEAN Annual Report 1998–99: 113). The AEM and SEOM meetings involve serious negotiations, consultations and ultimately decision-making on outstanding issues, including implementation issues. The process can be cumbersome and time consuming though, with issues on which decisions are difficult to reach transferred to the higher level meeting. Nevertheless, there is clearly a commitment to working through problems and outstanding issues in AFTA rather than avoiding or deferring them altogether, a charge sometimes levelled at ASEAN.

Monitoring is also carried out in a decentralised manner, with firms and national governments providing the main source of information on implementation problems in AFTA. Firms may notify the AFTA Units located within each national government or directly to the AFTA Unit in the ASEAN Secretariat of any problems they may have experienced in AFTA. Enforcement is also decentralised, with the SEOM or the AEM, the final arbiters on disputes. In addition, the ASEAN Secretariat has itself been tasked with the overall monitoring of all aspects of AFTA, although the Secretariat has no sanctioning powers.

While coordination in AFTA is carried out in a decentralised manner, the inter-governmental mechanisms for decision-making, monitoring and enforcement are well institutionalised rather than being ad-hoc or crisis-driven. At the very least, they provide an institutionalised arena for negotiations and bargaining that have helped to advance the AFTA process on many occasions. This does not always guarantee that decisions made in such forums will always hasten implementation of AFTA. On a number of occasions, these institutionalised mechanisms have served as the arena where compromises were worked out resulting in a lower level of compliance. Nevertheless, as all ASEAN senior officials and scholars of ASEAN interviewed between July and September 2000 pointed out, it is unlikely that AFTA could have advanced as far as it has done without these compromises. Stubbs makes a similar point on the value of compromises, although he argues that this was primarily the result of the regional political culture, namely the 'ASEAN Way' (Stubbs 2000: 312). The fact that many international agreements are advanced through similar processes of consultations, compromises and flexibility weakens the cultural basis of these processes in ASEAN, however, a point noted in the introductory chapter. This chapter advances an interest-based explanation of institution building in AFTA, rather than a cultural account.

Institutional strengthening in AFTA, notably through rule building, was a process phenomenon, the outcome of compliance bargaining and a means to balance the competing interests of member governments. When problems with regard to implementation of commitments already adopted emerged, a process of negotiations and bargaining between these countries was set in motion. The presence of regularised intergovernmental mechanisms for decision-making – such as the meetings of senior officials, ministers and leaders – facilitated this process by providing an institutionalised arena where negotiations could take place. While persuasion was the principal means employed to resolve problems, threats of retaliation were also used by one or another ASEAN member government, in a clear departure from the 'ASEAN Way' of inter-state relations.

This last point has wider relevance beyond this book. Scholars writing on ASEAN argue that this regional grouping works on the basis of a limited form of institutionalisation that stresses processes of socialisation and consensus building, employing minimal rules (Achayra 1999: 18–19). The governments of ASEAN member states are said to prefer such institutional forms owing to their preoccupation with national sovereignty and domestic policy autonomy (Henderson 1999: 42). ASEAN institutions are, therefore, expected to remain weak and informal, with little prospect for a shift to rule-based or centralised institutional forms (Sheridan 1998). This chapter challenges this contention.

AFTA has involved a steady process of institutionalisation in order to (a) signal the credibility of AFTA to foreign investors and (b) raise the costs to members of non-compliance. Both these issues became important when domestic distributional imperatives hindered the regional trade liberalisation process. The discussion suggests, however, that the process of institutionalisation itself and its impact on improving cooperative outcomes is only as strong as the convergent interests that drove the regional project in the first instance. In the AFTA case, these common interests emerged out of a shared threat – the diversion of foreign direct investment away from regional economies, notably to China. Although institutions were mediating variables only in AFTA, they helped to advance regional tariff liberalisation by shaping expectations and prescribing/proscribing behaviour of member governments in AFTA.

Conclusion

The discussion in this chapter confirms the book's third proposition – that implementation was itself a political process that attempted to take care of both growth and domestic distributive concerns in AFTA. This was accomplished through bargaining processes that attempted to address non-compliance of AFTA commitments. Two outcomes resulted. First, bargaining generally led to a re-negotiation of the original commitment and the adoption of revised, lower targets. This took care of the domestic distributive concerns of affected member countries, and thus, prevented the collapse of the entire project. Second, partial institution building occurred, largely through the tightening of rules and procedures in AFTA. The latter raised the costs to members of reneging on their original and re-negotiated AFTA obligations. They were also a means to signal to business actors, notably foreign investors, that AFTA remained a credible project despite the re-negotiations and setbacks.

This process of compliance bargaining allowed the ASEAN member governments to manage disputes between themselves over particular AFTA agenda items. Although a lower level of compliance prevailed than the original commitments would have entailed, intra-ASEAN tensions were diffused. The ASEAN Secretary General, Mr Rodolfo Severino, Jr used the metaphor of 'safety valves' to illustrate the role played by such processes.[39] Compromises were necessary in AFTA because they helped to defuse the tensions that often emerged due to divergent domestic political priorities, but they also helped to advance the regional project as a result. Far from being the product of regional cultural norms, these processes of working out a *modus vivendi* were driven by the respective interests of member governments in creating a balance between the imperatives of growth and domestic distribution. It was clearly not an ideal arrangement for all members, but it was the best available under the circumstances that allowed the core ASEAN governments to maintain what was for them a valuable project of economic regionalism.

Conclusion

Globalisation, domestic politics and regionalism

This book set out to explore three sets of empirical issues centred on the following research questions. (i) Why did the ASEAN countries, already committed to open trade and investment regimes since the end of the 1980s and which were already trading extensively worldwide and participating in international investment flows, engage in forming a regional free trade area? (ii) How are we to interpret the initial discriminatory treatment between ASEAN and non-ASEAN investors in the regional investment liberalisation programme if AFTA was adopted as a means to help attract global investment capital? (iii) What accounts for the subsequent shift to a more cautious programme of liberalisation in sectors like agriculture, automobiles, petrochemicals and services?

To briefly summarise, the study leads one to conclude that AFTA encompassed two forms of regionalism, both of which were stimulated by the forces of globalisation that the core ASEAN economies were confronted with during the 1990s. On the one hand, the CEPT programme to liberalise trade in goods was an exercise in open regionalism, designed to attract globally mobile foreign capital to the region. On the other hand, the investment liberalisation programme displayed the features of what I call 'developmental regionalism' designed to nurture the development of domestic-owned capital in anticipation of global market competition by according domestic investors temporary privileges ahead of foreign investors in the AFTA market. Nevertheless, domestic concerns with distribution sometimes overwhelmed the concern with growth that had driven the turn to both open and developmental regionalism, and consequently led to departures from some of the original commitments made. This made implementation of AFTA commitments a political process rather than merely a technical one, and involved a great deal of negotiations and bargaining that sought to balance the growth priorities of member governments with their concerns with domestic distribution.

Globalisation, domestic politics and AFTA

Both open regionalism and developmental regionalism were stimulated by the structural forces of globalisation, and were ultimately about engaging with these forces. Structural change in the pace, nature and pattern of global investment flows led to fears in the region about the possibility of investment diversion to other parts of the world, most notably to China. This was a major concern among ASEAN leaders and policymakers during the 1990s, providing the primary stimulus to adopting and sustaining AFTA as a project of open regionalism.

The shift in global capital flows was not the only systemic force impinging on these countries. Globalisation manifested itself in other ways as well, through changes in its institutional underpinnings and as an emerging hegemonic cognitive structure. The ASEAN member countries were confronted with the possibility that new multilateral rules would be written to allow TNCs maximum freedom of operation in all countries, particularly through the WTO that was already endowed with increased authority and responsibilities in new issue areas. ASEAN leaders and policymakers also perceived an unrelenting globalisation centred on intense international competition involving global/foreign firms. While these additional pressures of globalisation did, to some extent, reinforce open regionalism in ASEAN as an instrument to attract global capital flows, they also raised additional concerns in some countries with regard to the future of domestic-owned capital. Chapters 3 and 4 discussed these arguments in detail.

Although domestic capital was important in all the core ASEAN countries, it was especially important in Malaysia and Indonesia, often enjoying close political relationships with incumbent political elites and thereby helping to sustain elite coalitions and the stability of the prevailing regime. Domestic-owned firms were also important in fulfilling wider socio-economic and ultimately political goals in these two countries. Concern over the future of domestic firms in global market competition was, therefore, especially pronounced in Malaysia and Indonesia. Malaysia spearheaded the idea of using regionalism as a developmental tool to secure the future of domestic firms amidst impending global market competition, to which idea Indonesia gave its support. The idea of developmental regionalism was especially salient in sectors outside manufacturing, particularly in the category termed 'services incidental to manufacturing'. None of the other ASEAN countries challenged the idea, since there appeared to be little conflict, at least at that time, between the FDI dynamic of regionalism and the developmental dynamic. The former was centred on the CEPT and the latter on the AIA. Developmental regionalism, moreover, did not contradict the interests of the other ASEAN governments, particularly in Singapore and Thailand, which was to create the conditions for Singaporean and Thai domestic capital to expand through regionalism.

Thus, the ASEAN member countries endorsed the privileging of ASEAN investors over foreign investors in the AIA programme, intending the investment preferences to stimulate the growth through regional expansion of domestic firms into larger enterprises able to compete with TNCs, including through forming ASEAN multinationals. All the core ASEAN governments were broadly united on the importance of domestic firms becoming large and/or multinational as a means for them to survive global market competition. Chapter 4 discussed these points in detail. While the idea of developmental regionalism is theoretically plausible, underpinned by insights from strategic trade theory, whether the idea was a workable one in practice is a separate issue and beyond the focus of the book.

The point to be stressed is that different forms of regionalism emerged out of the forces of globalisation due to the mediation of domestic political economic dynamics in the core member countries that centred on the growth-distribution tension. Both open regionalism and developmental regionalism were driven by the growth imperative, and were about engaging with globalisation. Nevertheless, proponents of developmental regionalism did not fully accept the hegemonic position of foreign/global firms associated with globalisation, and attempted to nurture domestic firms and capabilities in an environment that was considered to be harshly competitive to developing country capital. The growth imperative was infused with a need to accommodate to domestic distributive priorities centred on elements of domestic capital that were considered to be important to the political elite and for the security and legitimacy of the ruling regime. Despite these concerns over domestic capital, the growth and FDI imperative became overwhelming by the middle of 2001 in the face of an expected slowdown in the global economy and the decline in FDI flows to regional economies. Member governments, consequently, gave up their three-year attempt at developmental regionalism, and open regionalism once again became the only form of economic regionalism in AFTA.

The tension between growth and distribution at the domestic level, which was especially evident in Malaysia and Indonesia, also had additional effects. They led, unsurprisingly, to these two countries being involved in major disputes in AFTA over implementation. Although these governments had committed themselves to all three component programmes in AFTA, the reality of the domestic political economy meant that the imperative of distribution overcame the concern with growth on a number of occasions that led to departures during implementation from the CEPT, AFAS and the AIA. Chapter 5 elaborated on this point. Notwithstanding an excellent track record in the CEPT, Malaysia chose in 1999 to delay liberalising tariffs on automobiles and was also responsible for some of the delays in negotiating liberalisation in the financial services and telecommunications sectors. Indonesia was involved in two major disputes in AFTA over agriculture and petrochemicals. This chapter thus demonstrated that the domestic level was a significant level of analysis. It was, however, the *interaction* between the systemic and the domestic that was, and remains, key in explaining developments in AFTA.

The tussle between growth and domestic distributive concerns within member countries, which consequently led to tensions and disputes between them, meant that implementation became a political process that attempted to balance both growth and distributive concerns among members. It was not simply a technical exercise of complying with commitments already made. Chapter 6 revealed that this was accomplished through bargaining processes that took place to address non-compliance during AFTA implementation. Two outcomes resulted. First, bargaining generally led to a re-negotiation of the original commitment and the adoption of revised, lower targets. This took care of domestic concerns with distribution in affected member countries. By consequently preventing the collapse of the entire project, it also took care of the growth concerns of other members for whom AFTA was believed to be important in sustaining a key source of growth – global capital. Second, partial institution building occurred, largely through the tightening of rules and procedures in AFTA, which raised the costs to members reneging on their original and re-negotiated AFTA obligations while also signalling to business actors, notably foreign investors, that AFTA remained a credible project despite the re-negotiations and setbacks. Institution building, therefore, also addressed the growth imperative.

AFTA and the wider literature: conceptual insights on the globalisation–regionalism relationship

This book also set out to address a conceptual question with broader analytical significance: how does economic regionalism relate to globalisation? Scholars of regionalism have begun to ask whether structural factors in the world economy associated with globalisation are primarily responsible or whether local dynamics, both intra-state and intra-region also influence the course of regionalism. A secondary concern was to explore whether regionalism offers state actors a means to escape the structural constraints of the neoliberal practices and ideas underpinning globalisation.

The empirical discussion on AFTA summarised above clearly points to the salience of regional and especially domestic dynamics in shaping regional outcomes. The conceptual discussion in Chapter 1 made a similar point in its discussion of the two main models of the globalisation–regionalism relationship currently found in the literature. The dominant model of this relationship, the model of open regionalism, is underwritten by a liberal political economy perspective and neoclassical ideas about economic efficiency and the benefits of engaging with market competition. This model takes global market outcomes as a given and beneficial to all, with regionalism merely a means to subordinate national economies to these beneficial forces of globalisation. In the liberal reading of regionalism, therefore, regionalism involves very little purposive political action by governments of states to alter global market outcomes. In short, it privileges structural or systemic factors in explanation, while marginalising domestic-level political economic dynamics.

The theoretical literature also identified a second model of regionalism based on resistance by domestic social groups to globalisation. The latter is a useful corrective to the highly economistic liberal economic reading of the globalisation–regionalism relationship. Chapter 1 criticised the second model for adopting a Euro-centric version of domestic level dynamics, however, one that repeats some of the shortcomings of the neoliberal model, notably the separation of economics and politics in explaining the drivers behind this resistance model of regionalism.

A major conceptual innovation made in this book is its explicit consideration of domestic-owned capital as a key analytical variable. This was based on a rejection of a strict form of methodological individualism, which allowed business actors to be identified as part of domestic society rather than simply as atomistic profit-maximising agents responding to price signals only with no social identity. The dominant liberal model does not make an adequate distinction between foreign-owned and domestic-owned capital, focusing instead on globally oriented businesses whose competitive position regionalism helps advance. If a distinction is made at all, it is usually to view domestic businesses as agents of protectionism likely to resist regional liberalisation. Chapter 1 also suggested that this was because of the model's focus on the industrial world where domestic capital is likely to be well developed, unlike in the developing world. In settings where domestic capital is not as well developed as foreign capital but plays crucial political and social roles, governments may well respond to globalisation in ways that attempt to preserve and especially to nurture emerging domestic capital. By emphasising this dynamic, politics and economics are explicitly integrated in analysis.

Paying close attention to the nature of domestic politics also means specifying the broad interests of domestic actors and how and why they form coalitions with other actors *independently of the phenomenon being studied* (Moravcsik 1993: 477). In other words, government responses to globalisation, including the policy choice of regionalism, are argued to be shaped primarily by domestically derived priorities that are prior to the matter under study. Although this book emphasises the interaction of systemic and domestic factors in explaining regional outcomes, domestic interests are, nevertheless, treated as prior. International forces only acquire 'political significance' through domestic politics (Jacobsen 1996: 94).

In the book's study of AFTA, the preferences of ASEAN member governments with regard to both globalisation and AFTA agenda items are shaped by domestic political priorities given by domestic state–society relations, and centred on the imperatives of growth and/or distribution. Both these imperatives are ultimately linked to political concerns centred on the legitimacy and security of governing regimes in ASEAN, and are the product of historical and social realities in these political communities. These domestic priorities shape the way external events and developments are interpreted by domestic actors as well as influence government responses to these external forces, which in turn serve as a set of constraints and opportunities for the attainment of these domestic priorities.

Apart from its treatment of the domestic level, a second conceptual innovation this book makes is in its use of the economic realist perspective in modelling the relationship between globalisation and regionalism. In theoretical terms, the economic realist perspective offers substantial analytical purchase over the liberal political economy perspective in explaining regionalism as a response to globalisation. Chapter 1 elaborated on these points. The value of economic realism as a theoretical tool comes from its recognition that state actors view global market forces in conflictual or zero-sum terms, and importantly, that these actors can, and often do, consciously manipulate inter-state relations to try and alter the structures and processes in the world economy in line with domestic interests. Regionalism can be interpreted as one such instrument for states to pool their resources in order to influence the international political economy.

Using the economic realist perspective on IPE allowed a third conceptual model – developmental regionalism – to be advanced, which draws on insights from strategic trade theory in economics rather than neoclassical economics. This model of regionalism is distinct from notions of 'development integration' and the like that were common during the 1960s and 1970s that attempted to overcome the limits of import-substitution industrialisation by using regionalism to create larger markets, often also involving state allocation of industrial projects among regional states. In contrast, the model of developmental regionalism outlined here, like open regionalism, is premised on engagement with globalisation in the long-term but offers emerging, *domestic* firms some form of temporary shelter from global competition or some advantage to meet competition in the medium-term. This, coupled with the larger market obtained through regionalism, offers significant scale advantages to emerging domestic firms over foreign rivals that enables the former to realise dynamic and 'learning by doing' benefits, at least theoretically. It is, therefore, not a model of resistance to globalisation, but neither is it a model of complete acquiescence to global market forces. Developmental regionalism, in short, represents a means through which state actors attempt to challenge one particular aspect of globalisation – the dominance of TNCs in the world economy – by carving out a space that is partially and temporarily insulated from the structures and processes of globalisation.

Economic realist insights, moreover, allowed a subtle distinction to be made within the dominant open regionalist model to reveal two variants, neoliberal regionalism and the FDI model of regionalism, the latter more likely to reflect embedded or limited neoliberalism encompassing elements of state intervention in markets. The distinction between the two variants is not a trivial one. The discussion in Chapter 1 suggested that the two variants of open regionalism were likely to display distinct features and crucially for this discussion, to project different future trajectories for regionalism. This last point is extremely pertinent to the discussion that follows on the future of Southeast Asian economic regionalism.

The conceptual framework adopted in the study also helped towards addressing the divide between structure and agency, a key conceptual issue in IPE. The combined economic realist-domestic politics analytical framework allowed for the possibility of agency on the part of key actors in two possible ways. First, domestic actors, principally but not exclusively governments, interpreted and responded to specific aspects of globalisation in ways that were shaped by prior domestic social and political priorities. In short, globalisation did not manifest itself as an objective structure meaning the same thing to everyone, nor to be taken purely as given. Moreover, governments displayed agency to the extent that they attempted to alter the structures and processes of the global economy through inter-state cooperation in fulfilment of these domestically derived priorities or interests. Governments were driven to this action by their zero-sum view of global market forces where benefits for some are at the expense of others.

In the case of AFTA, this dynamic was revealed by the concern in ASEAN with FDI diversion to other countries, notably China. It was also implicit in the notion of developmental regionalism in which its proponents aimed at nurturing domestic capital by providing them temporary advantages over foreign capital in the regional market in anticipation of global market competition. It is clear that there is a strong redistributive element associated with AFTA, both in terms of re-directing FDI to the region and in conferring privileges, albeit on a temporary basis, to domestic/ASEAN capital over foreign capital as a way to challenge the growing dominance of foreign firms in the economy.

Both these arguments share the fundamental notion that ASEAN leaders and policymakers did not accept the prevailing structures of globalisation and attempted to use regionalism to alter the outcomes of global market forces. This was evident in both open regionalism and developmental regionalism. Open regionalism, initiated as a means to re-direct globally mobile FDI to the ASEAN region, may be considered to be an activist response by national governments seeking to influence the worldwide allocation of FDI. Available studies of AFTA do not emphasise this particular point, although they do recognise it as a project of open regionalism designed to remain engaged with global markets. Theirs is an implicit liberal interpretation of AFTA. Although their argument that

AFTA was specifically about countering the FDI threat from China is correct, it cannot be fully accommodated within liberal perspectives that see global market forces in essentially beneficial and non-zero-sum terms. This reflects the lack of explicit attention to theorising in these generally atheoretical studies of AFTA, a point that was noted in the introductory chapter.

The present study does not challenge the broad notion of AFTA as a project of open regionalism. Nevertheless, by adopting a modified economic realist theoretical perspective combined with the elite governance model of domestic politics, the study offers a more nuanced reading of open regionalism in AFTA as well as advances the argument that AFTA also displayed the features of developmental regionalism, albeit for a limited period. Apart from the fact that only two members were strong advocates of developmental regionalism, the severe pressures on growth as a result of cyclical forces in the world economy led member governments to re-evaluate the purposes of AFTA and emphasise once again the project's role in stimulating the inflow of FDI to the region.

While a developmental approach to economic regionalism was evident in Southeast Asia, it does not as yet feature in other parts of the world. It remains, nevertheless, a theoretically plausible model of regionalism based on economic realist insights, strategic trade theory and the privileging of domestic capital. Interestingly, a Europeanist faction of the transnational business elite in Western Europe lobbied for a somewhat similar project in Europe, what Van Apeldoorn (2000) terms a neo-mercantilist regional project. Although Van Apeldoorn does not suggest that this particular project sought to specifically privilege domestic-owned capital over foreign-owned capital, which is a principle feature in developmental regionalism, the attempt at neo-mercantilist regionalism in Europe was aimed at promoting European business champions amidst the threatening forces of globalisation. This practical project thus incorporated ideas and approaches that are broadly similar to those underpinning the model of developmental regionalism advanced in this book. It failed to take root in the EU due to the growing power of the globalist faction of the transnational business elite over the Europeanist faction, which resulted in a strong neoliberal regionalist project becoming consolidated from the 1990s.

That developmental regionalism is a limited practical feature in the contemporary world economy is, perhaps, not surprising, given the strong neoliberal trend in the industrial world as well as in large parts of the developing world, particularly Eastern Europe and Latin America. It is not unexpected that it found expression in Southeast Asia, where in particular countries the preoccupation with domestic-owned capital for political reasons was strongest. Even though its only expression thus far, in Southeast Asia, was of limited duration, there is always the possibility that it may emerge as an empirical feature in some part of the world under different conditions. As with the resistance project, it is not unreasonable to expect a form of developmental regionalism to emerge as a backlash against globalisation, although we may not see an exact replica of the ASEAN version.

If developmental regionalism is characterised by a kind of developmentalist ambition informed by a unique perception of how the world works,[1] then it reveals a particular interventionist approach to economics in Southeast Asia that endures despite the restructuring processes set in motion by the Asian financial crisis. Although developmental regionalism was a short-lived phenomenon in ASEAN, it has revealed the complex nature of domestic political economies in the region that are missed in the open regionalist story of AFTA, notably the continued political salience of domestic-owned capital in these societies and an implicit, if not explicit, economic nationalism.

It was already noted in Chapter 4 that despite agreeing to dispense with a developmental approach to the AIA, Malaysia continues to emphasise the building up of domestic-owned firms and the need to avoid relying on FDI as a source of growth. The Malaysian Prime Minister continues to caution developing countries against globalisation and the unrestricted acceptance of FDI, which he believes will lead to foreign control of the domestic economy. For Dr Mahathir, 'while foreign direct investments should be welcomed . . . local investors are our true partners . . . [with] a stake in the prosperity of the country'.[2] This theme was continued in the Prime Minister's 2003 budget speech in parliament delivered in September 2002 when he also revealed his continued preference for a developmental approach to economic policy and the importance of building up domestic firms to be global players through industrial policy.[3] Indonesia's pressing need for foreign capital notwithstanding, growing domestic opposition to IMF requirements to privatise state-owned enterprises and domestic resistance to increasing foreign participation in the economy suggests that economic nationalism remains a potent force in the country.[4] Even in Singapore, the government has thus far resisted domestic demands even from members of its own party to sell off the government-linked corporations (GLCs) that are alleged to be crowding out private entrepreneurs, maintaining instead that these corporations are all the more necessary to face global market competition.[5] Philippine President, Gloria Arroyo, recently pronounced 'unbridled globalisation is no longer in vogue' when declaring a renewed focus on domestic industries.[6] These episodes reflect socially embedded and historical approaches and attitudes to economics that remain salient despite, or perhaps because of, the structral push towards a neoliberal economic model.

The future of ASEAN economic regionalism

An economic realist reading of AFTA, specifically the FDI model of regionalism, offers useful insights into the future of ASEAN economic regionalism. It suggests that ASEAN member governments would be cautious about any development that threatens to blunt the contours of the ASEAN region as a distinct functional space of investment/production. The case for ever-widening processes of regionalism is, from the economic realist point of view, far more contingent than liberal readings would suggest. On the other hand, it also suggests that regionalism will only be as strong as the self-interests of its member states. Of the most significant of recent developments in wider regionalism in the Asia-Pacific region to date, ASEAN responses to the ASEAN–China FTA and the spate of bilateral FTAs involving Singapore, both reveal an economic realist dynamic at work.

The ASEAN–China free trade area

The cautious response of all the ASEAN leaders and policymakers to China's proposal made in late 2000 to form a free trade area between China and ASEAN is completely understandable from the economic realist point of view.[7] China by itself potentially offers foreign capital a 'regional' site of production by virtue of its size and internal industrial complementarities. China's attraction is, of course, magnified when its overall lower cost of production is factored into the equation. China's regional market potential, moreover, is strengthened through the 'Greater China' configuration that includes Hong Kong. In short, China offers a range of complementarities that producers can take advantage of, that smaller countries as in ASEAN are only able to do through pooling their complementarities via regional cooperation.

At one level, an ASEAN–China FTA would tend to blur the distinction between the two regional sites because the FTA would allow producers locating in China to sell at preferential rates in both China and ASEAN and vice versa for those locating in ASEAN. At another level, this could well enhance the attraction China displays relative to ASEAN as a site for investment as it means that an investor preferring to locate in China would be assured of preferential market access to ASEAN, assuming that selling in ASEAN is considered to be important. In short, if AFTA had been salient because it offered an investment site for FDI searching for a *regional* economic space in the Asia-Pacific, then an ASEAN–China FTA has the potential to weaken the salience of the AFTA region as a distinct regional space for investment.

Although the ASEAN countries initially side stepped the issue of a free trade area with China by agreeing to a one-year feasibility study on the proposal, the project was formally endorsed by ASEAN in November 2001 despite the ambivalence of a number of member governments on the matter. It would have been difficult to reject the Chinese proposal, given the ASEAN countries' desire to engage with China on political and security issues. This explains why a fully operational ASEAN–China free trade area was scheduled for 2010 at the earliest. ASEAN is clearly proceeding cautiously on implementation of the proposal.[8] This is not to suggest that ASEAN policymakers and leaders are against the idea of closer economic integration with China. On the contrary, all the ASEAN leaders, including those hesitant about the project, recognise the gains to their respective economies from investment opportunities for local firms in China, from preferential market access, and from access to lower priced final products and intermediate inputs from China.

In fact, a China–ASEAN FTA may well provide the ASEAN side with a 'regional space of consumption' to supplement AFTA as a 'regional space of production' given the enormity of the Chinese market. While the share of intra-regional trade is not the relevant indicator of progress in AFTA for reasons that will be discussed below, the stability of this figure for the AFTA region, at between 20 and 25 per cent, nevertheless does suggest that AFTA remains for the present only a partial economic space. AFTA is most significant as a region of investment/production, while its capacity as a significant consuming region is limited until such time that economic growth and development raise regional consumption demand for a wider range of goods and services produced within ASEAN. It is, therefore, not surprising that the ASEAN region's major markets remain outside ASEAN, notably in the US, notwithstanding the rise in absolute levels of intra-regional trade since the mid-1990s. As such, global market developments and the prospects for the US economy would have considerable bearing on how ASEAN members calculate the costs and benefits of a free trade area with China. The uncertainties surrounding the global economy in the closing months of 2002, particularly with economists fearing that the US could linger for a few years in a post-bubble recession[9] may well render the ASEAN–China FTA more attractive to those ASEAN members currently most hesitant about this project. While ASEAN members would not be the only countries turning to the China market in the event of a prolonged global downturn, a functioning ASEAN–China FTA is more likely to provide the ASEAN members with preferential access.

For the present, however, there is considerable ambivalence about this project in the region as leaders recognise the competitive and cooperative nature of an ASEAN–China free trade area.[10] The ten-year delay is, therefore, seen to be necessary to allow ASEAN to consolidate itself as a regional site for production.[11] In fact, Malaysia, the Philippines and Indonesia are said to prefer the project to become fully operational only by 2012 or 2014 rather than the 2010 deadline for precisely this reason.[12] Although this is not to suggest that a wider free trade zone with China will never materialise in the future, the argument put forward is that the ASEAN governments will probably proceed extremely cautiously for so long as they regard China as a major rival for FDI and as a competing producer of goods now being manufactured in ASEAN. ASEAN member governments may not concur with liberal expectations that wider regionalism, particularly with China, would necessarily be a good thing on economic grounds.

Thus, the *Framework Agreement on ASEAN-China Comprehensive Economic Cooperation* signed at the ASEAN–China Summit in November 2002 will only flag off negotiations on the FTA, which are scheduled to begin in 2003. Although the idea of an 'early harvest package' has been proposed as a means of accelerating implementation of the project by focusing initially on a limited number of liberalisation commitments, this package is only scheduled to be implemented from 2004 and then over a three-year period, taking it to 2007. It is clearly with much caution that the ASEAN countries are approaching the ASEAN–China FTA. These sentiments could change, however, if there is expectation of a prolonged global economic downturn, a point already alluded to above.

Bilateral free trade areas

Bilateral free trade areas are increasingly the norm in the region, with Singapore the most active proponent of this instrument.[13] At least seven bilateral FTAs involving Singapore have apparently been considered, with the most notable being the Japan–Singapore FTA signed in January 2002 and the US–Singapore FTA to be signed in 2003. Apart from concern over the future of multilateral trade liberalisation (Desker 2002), Singapore's frustration over the slow pace of services liberalisation in AFTA also explains its preference for bilateralism. Thus, the services component of the Singapore–Japan free trade area[14] is highly significant for Singapore, enabling the country to gain access to Japan's notoriously closed but large services market.[15] In the forthcoming US–Singapore free trade area, all service sectors will be liberalised automatically unless specifically excluded.[16] Singapore's bilateralism in trade policy, which has generated some tensions within ASEAN over its potential to 'dilute AFTA', clearly reflects the kind of economic realism that paradoxically prompted the ASEAN countries to form AFTA in the face of an external threat from China to FDI inflows to the region. Singapore's foreign economic policy is based on the search for economic security and achieved at various levels – bilateral, regional and multilateral (Dent 2001). That the bilateral instrument was pursued given the slow pace of regional services liberalisation is unsurprising.

There are two potential problems with the growing bilateralism in trade policy in the region. While bilateral arrangements provide economic gains for participating countries, economic simulations reveal that those excluded would suffer losses, particularly if these arrangements involve a major economic power such as the US or Japan (Scollay and Gilbert 2001: 115–16). On the one hand, this may prompt excluded countries to either get on board existing bilateral arrangements or to negotiate their own bilateral free trade areas. The attraction here is the seemingly better prospect for negotiating bilateral FTAs on an *a la carte* basis, with the cooperating parties opting to exclude particular sectors that are sensitive for one or both parties from the arrangement, as Singapore and Japan recently did with goldfish and cut flowers in their bilateral FTA. Shifting towards a bilateral route may lead to what economist Richard Baldwin calls the 'domino effect' in regionalism (Baldwin 1999). This suggests some potential for trade tensions in the region. Thailand and Malaysia, for instance, have already expressed concern over Singapore's bilateral free trade areas.[17]

The second source of concern stems from any mushrooming of bilateral arrangements that will lead to what Jagdish Bhagwati and his colleagues call a 'spaghetti bowl' phenomenon, and to the fragmentation of the regional economy (Bhagwati *et al.* 1998). Fragmentation could arise if overlapping arrangements involved mutually inconsistent rules, which mean that products could be traded under a range of different rules and tariffs. This is especially likely during the period when the free trade area provisions are being implemented. In such instances, firms are likely to suffer directly from the increased costs of complying with distinct trading arrangements. Under these conditions, firms will have to comply with a range of requirements depending on which FTA partner they are trying to do business with. Such effects will be especially pronounced for overlapping free trade areas even if these are designed to be WTO consistent. A mere difference in tariff phasing schedules and in rules of origin could mean that the same product would be subject to quite different treatment, depending on its origins and where it is destined for (Scollay and Gilbert 2001: 17). For these reasons, the bilateral route, while offering a way out of the difficulties in obtaining further progress in AFTA, might itself introduce economic inefficiencies and add to the cost of doing business in the region.

Moreover, to the extent that firms are interested in regional divisions of labour, as mentioned at various points in this book, and are increasingly engaging in regional production networks, then a 'spaghetti bowl' framework of market access arrangements may not be in their best interests. This is why in the US–Singapore free trade area still under negotiation, a provision has been included to extend the juridical reach of the free trade area to include two Indonesian islands, Batam and Bintan for the category of electronics and information technology items.[18] Because production of final goods in Singapore involves extensive use of components produced in other parts of the region, like Bintan and Batam, local content rules would effectively exclude Singapore-made final products from the US market unless crucial portions of Singapore's hinterland are included within the ambit of the free trade area. While the US–Singapore approach is one way to address this structural issue, the exercise repeated over a number of bilateral FTAs will only raise the costs of negotiating, monitoring and enforcing agreements, while increasing fragmentation in the regional economy. There is, in a sense, a tension or incongruence between the institutional framework for organising economic activity that appears to be increasingly dominating the regional landscape – the bilateral framework – and the logic of capital, which is seeking *regional* spaces for organising production.

AFTA in perspective

Despite setbacks in AFTA, the project appears to have the potential to alter the dynamics of regionalisation in Southeast Asia and the wider Asia-Pacific region. Intra-ASEAN trade averaged around 20–25 per cent of total trade during the 1990s, and remained at this share in the early years of the new century. The share of intra-regional trade is not, however, the relevant indicator of progress in AFTA, which many assessments of AFTA tend to be based on, incorrectly in this author's opinion. Not only was the regionalist project primarily aimed at boosting FDI to the region, the ASEAN governments have always maintained that their attempt at economic cooperation was a means to ensure their continued participation in the global economy rather than to increase intra-regional trade *per se*. Even if intra-ASEAN trade levels rose, the relative share will not change dramatically if ASEAN's trade with the world continued to also rise. Interestingly, intra-ASEAN trade has grown slightly faster than ASEAN's trade with the rest of the world, at an average annual rate of 9.4 per cent over the 1993–2000 period compared to the 7.3 per cent growth in ASEAN's global trade over the same period. Moreover, intra-ASEAN trade grew by 21.4 per cent in 2000 from the previous year, which again is much faster than the 15.2 per cent annual increase in ASEAN's global trade flows in 2000.[19]

Investment flows to the region were fairly stable during the 1990s, at least until 1997, despite the growing competition posed by China. Investment inflows averaged about 20 per cent of global FDI flows to developing countries and about 30 per cent of global FDI flows to Asian developing countries until the financial crisis (ASEAN Secretariat 1999a: 131). Although foreign investment registered a marked decline from a high of US$32 billion in 1997 to US$14 billion in 2000, almost 80 per cent of this is accounted for by the fall in FDI to Indonesia.[20] In fact, FDI levels have remained fairly stable in ASEAN since the crisis, albeit at lower levels compared to the high growth era. Moreover, intra-ASEAN investment flows strengthened significantly during the 1990s, particularly flows from the core members to the newer members (ASEAN Secretariat 1999a: 13). Macro data on investment flows is, however, limited because it does not reveal whether the flows were influenced by the AFTA project.

Neither does macro data indicate the prospects for an ASEAN regional division of labour as a result of AFTA's facilitating effect. There is, in fact, a gap in the empirical literature on the extent to which a Southeast Asian regional division of labour exists and its future trajectory. There is some initial evidence that Southeast Asian regional production networks are a growing feature, especially in automobiles, electronic and electrical products, and food manufacturing, but more concrete empirical evidence of recent trends is lacking. This suggests a promising line of future enquiry, one that can help address the question of whether ASEAN economic regionalism through AFTA has indeed led to changing regional patterns of production.

Surveys of business decisions by corporate leaders suggest that AFTA has had an impact on corporate activity, although the question of whether a significant reorganisation of production has taken place requires further study. A survey of 150 firms in the East-Asian region conducted for the Economist Intelligence Unit in late 1996 revealed that these firms regarded AFTA as the regional project most likely to be realised or implemented compared to APEC. More significantly, a third of those surveyed admitted that AFTA had had a major impact on their business operations, while 41 per cent believed the impact was moderate. Only 6 per cent admitted that AFTA made no difference to their business operations. Moreover, almost 62 per cent of corporate leaders surveyed acknowledged that they had incorporated AFTA as a factor in their future regional production strategies.[21] A 1997 survey conducted among Asian regional business executives by the *Far Eastern Economic Review* revealed essentially similar results.[22] It revealed that more than three quarters of Asian executives surveyed made investment decisions that took the AFTA regional market into account. Studies by Japan's Export–Import (EXIM) Bank, the Japan External Trade Organisation (JETRO) and the Nomura Research Institute also revealed that an increasing number of Japanese firms were stepping up regional operations in view of the AFTA market, especially in the automobiles, automotive components, and electrical and electronic sectors.[23]

A more recent JETRO survey of Japanese TNCs producing in ASEAN revealed that almost all the companies surveyed would continue to invest and produce in ASEAN.[24] Fewer than 8 per cent of corporations surveyed had plans to relocate part of their operations to China, while only about 2 per cent planned to completely cease operations in ASEAN in favour of China. These firms cited the completion of the single AFTA market, at least of its first phase, as a major reason for their remaining in ASEAN. Not only was AFTA expected to result in an expansion of the regional market, it was also seen to facilitate regional production operations in ASEAN. Japanese firms also wished to avoid the risk of concentrating their operations in China, and were instead adopting a two-pronged strategy in East Asia – establishing production bases in both China and ASEAN, since both 'regions' were regarded as potentially significant consumer markets. This is an interesting point, although it raises the question of whether other investors are adopting a similar strategy. Japanese investors could well be hesitant about investing extensively in China given prickly China–Japan relations and historical animosities between the two countries.

In fact, the ASEAN region is said to continue to offer significant advantages to TNCs over China. Felker argues that 'Southeast Asia offers leading MNCs an environment in which they can articulate their global production strategies with maximum flexibility', unlike China (Felker 2002: 28). Governments' ongoing efforts to upgrade their policy and institutional infrastructures are, according to Felker, critical in positioning the ASEAN countries to successfully exploit the regional logic of global capital. The full realisation of the single AFTA market, with the first phase virtually in place at the end of 2002, will be a significant contributory factor in that process, although it will not be the only factor. Both the fate of Indonesia and the spectre of regional terrorist networks will unfortunately also influence economic actors evaluating the prospects of AFTA.

AFTA is perhaps ASEAN's most successful regional cooperation project to date, notwithstanding the setbacks and tensions experienced in the project through the decade since its formal inception in 1992. Compared to cooperation over security, transnational crime and the environment, the very real accomplishments of AFTA described in this book cannot be dismissed. It points to the need to consider different issue areas separately when assessing regional projects like ASEAN, and in particular, to take seriously the salience of domestic political dynamics when explaining outcomes in regional cooperation. Not every external force will necessarily result in meaningful regional action in ASEAN, unless it has significant repercussions on domestic politics. Likewise, the latter itself will shape the manner in which governments respond to external events. As a growing number of IR scholars argue, external events acquire 'political significance only as they are factored into national politics in ways that accommodate the interests, strategies and ideologies of dominant local players' (Jacobsen 1996: 94–5). AFTA has demonstrated members' willingness to engage in concrete joint actions in the face of a perceived serious external threat to their economic well being, which also had implications for the security and legitimacy of domestic political regimes in a number of member states.

Nevertheless, the easier phase of liberalisation – in manufactured goods – is over. Although ASEAN will continue to work towards full implementation of AFTA, progress in liberalising services trade, especially financial and telecommunications services is likely to be slow because this will affect entrenched domestic interests. While AFTA will remain a key feature of the regional economic architecture, it will increasingly be in competition with other regional configurations, a point already discussed in this chapter. Perhaps, in the end, it is this very threat to the distinctiveness of ASEAN as a region of investment/production that will spur members to complete the next phase of AFTA, provided the latter continues to be regarded as crucial to the economic well being of its member states.

Notes

Introduction

1 ASEAN was formed in 1967 by Indonesia, Malaysia, the Philippines, Singapore and Thailand. Brunei joined the grouping in 1984 on its independence from Britain. Vietnam joined in 1995, Laos and Myanmar in 1997, while Cambodia joined the Association in April 1999, bringing ASEAN's total membership to ten.
2 Intra-ASEAN exports among the six core members in 1990 stood at about 20 per cent, while their exports to the industrial countries totalled 58 per cent of total exports. Calculated from the IMF, *Direction of Trade Statistics Yearbook 1996*.
3 Detailed analyses of ASEAN economic cooperation between 1976 and 1990 are found in ASEAN Secretariat (1997a: 1–88); Frost (1990: 7–14); Suriyamongkol (1988); Ch'ng (1985) and Tongzon (1998: 64).
4 The core or founding members of AFTA are Brunei, Indonesia, Malaysia, the Philippines, Singapore and Thailand. New members of ASEAN acceded to AFTA on joining the Association.
5 The latter include customs initiatives, standards harmonisation and mutual recognition programmes, as well as information sharing arrangements that facilitate the free movement of goods and services within the region.
6 The term 'open regionalism' originally meant a form of regionalism that was based on the principles of unilateral liberalisation as well as non-discrimination in tariff preferences between members and outsiders (Drysdale and Garnaut 1993: 187–8). Today, the term is used in a broader sense, to describe regionalist projects that aim at enhancing the participation of their members in global economic activities. This is in contrast to the 'closed' regionalist projects of the 1960s and 1970s (Gamble and Payne 1996a: 252; Grugel and Hout 1999: 10).
7 Although Menon (1998: 18) and Tham (1998: 32–3) question the wisdom of such a distinction, they offer no explanation on why member governments were prompted to adopt this particular policy for the AIA. Their implicit argument is that policymakers were not acting rationally since the distinction made between ASEAN and foreign investors was redundant and inconsistent with national policies towards FDI.
8 The literature defines 'economic regionalism' as a project of states, or their governments, to coordinate economic policies, instruments and arrangements within a given region (Wyatt-Walter 1995: 77). It is often differentiated from regionalisation, which is a market-driven process of economic integration within a region driven by corporate actors and individuals (Hurrell 1995: 39). Notwithstanding their conceptual and practical interrelationships, this book is primarily concerned with explaining economic regionalism, or the political decisions of governments within a geographically delimited area to cooperate.

In this book, the term 'economic regionalism' is used inter-changeably with the term 'regional economic cooperation'.

9 Of an extensive literature, see Gamble and Payne (1996a), Hveem (2000) and Mittelman (2000: 4).

10 The seminal contribution to customs union theory is that of Viner (1950).

11 Low (1996) provides a comprehensive review of the various empirical studies that yield this conclusion. See also Australia (1994).

12 APEC presently groups together the United States, Canada, Mexico, Chile, Australia, New Zealand, Papua New Guinea, China, Japan, Hong Kong, Taiwan, South Korea, the six core ASEAN members, Russia, Vietnam and Peru.

13 These are characterised by constant returns to scale, a large number of small firms that are price takers in the market, unchanging demand and tastes, costless access to technology and perfect information.

14 It also depends on what factors it can create through policy, such as human resources and infrastructure availability, giving rise to the notion of dynamic comparative advantage.

15 The interpretation is termed 'strategic' realist to distinguish it from the economic realist perspective on IPE.

16 The notion of 'national resilience', a core doctrine in ASEAN, reflects the centrality of domestic politico-economic priorities. It emphasises the crucial role of domestic economic development as a means to a materially satisfied citizenry who would then be less vulnerable to internal and external subversion. See Leifer (1989: 3–4).

17 Compare, for instance, Ariff (1994, 1998).

18 The 'ASEAN Way' is a regional code of conduct that is characterised by informality, aversion to formal institutions, flexibility, pragmatism, expedience, the practice of consensus, a high degree of discreteness and non-confrontational bargaining styles developed through a process of elite socialisation over a period of time (Acharya 1997: 329).

19 This constitutes the supply-side of Mattli's model for successful economic integration. Leadership is the critical supply condition, with centralised institutions only a weak condition for successful integration (Mattli 1999: 42–3).

20 On this last point, see Martin and Simmons (1998: 739–42).

21 Breslin and Higgott (2000) provide a comprehensive review of these works, as well as a critical commentary on the state of research and theorising on contemporary regionalism. Hurrell (1995) and more recently, Ravenhill (2001: 6–40) also offer useful surveys and insightful critiques of the IR literature on regional collaboration.

22 See especially Hurrell (1995); Grugel and Hout (1999); Hettne *et al.* (2000); and the edited volumes by Gamble and Payne (1996b) and Coleman and Underhill (1998b).

23 Some of the chapters in the edited volume by Mansfield and Milner (1997) continue to emphasise parsimony in theorising, and thus, tend to focus on single-level variables, whether power relations/hegemony, institutional forms or domestic interest group politics.

24 The weaknesses of methodological individualism are discussed in Murphy and Tooze (1991).

25 See Gourevitch (1978), for instance.

26 Although Brunei is a founding member of AFTA, its domestic political economy will not be examined in detail. Being an oil-rich state whose major economic activities are oil production, refining and export, its domestic political economy relates very differently to the AFTA project compared to the other ASEAN countries. The Brunei government has, nevertheless, always been a strong advocate of AFTA.

1 Globalisation and economic regionalism

1 See Scholte (2000: 44–6).
2 Even the European Union, the most advanced regionalist project in the world economy cannot yet be termed a super-state or political entity. It continues to remain an inter-governmental project although it has a high level of institutionalisation and supranational governance mechanisms.
3 Ohmae (1990, 1995) is the most notable advocate of this thesis.
4 The notion of 'de-territorialisation' comes from Scholte (1997b: 431).
5 Other interpretations see globalisation as a continuing process of the last 100 years (Hirst 1997: 410), a development dating from 1945–50 (Amin 1996: 244–5), or emerging in its 'fully-fledged' form since around 1960 (Scholte 1997a: 19).
6 See the Research Agenda of the Centre for the Study of Globalisation and Regionalisation (CSGR) at the University of Warwick available at: http://www.csgr.org/agenda.html and accessed in July 2001.
7 Flexible production systems emphasise flexibility of the production process, of its organisation within the factory and of relationships with customers and with supplier firms. Dicken (1998: 165–72) and Oman (1994: 86–9) provide useful overviews of flexible and fordist production systems.
8 Hirst and Thompson (1992), and Weiss (1998: 176–7) employ this line of argument.
9 Scholte (2000: 34–5) sets out the neoliberal underpinnings of globalisation.
10 As at 1 January 2002.
11 Challenges have increasingly been mounted against globalisation through street protests, for instance during the WTO Ministerial in Seattle in 1999, the 2000 IMF/World Bank meetings, the 2001 World Economic Conference at Davos and the June 2001 EU Summit in Sweden.
12 See Van Apeldoorn (2000) who discusses neoliberal regionalism in relation to the European Union.
13 See Phillips (2000: 286, fn 7) who attributes the idea of 'meso-globalisation' to Richard Higgott.
14 See, for instance, Mittelman (2000: 112–13, 126).
15 On the European Union, see Van Apeldoorn (2000).
16 See the work of James Jesudason (1989) on this point.
17 Gilpin refers to this perspective as economic nationalism.
18 The economic realist perspective on IPE derives from the classical realist tradition in IR, specifically state-centric realism rather than system-centred realism or Waltzian neorealism. Hans Morgenthau and E.H. Carr are the contemporary intellectual pioneers of classical realism.
19 The structural power of capital rests on the ability of capital owners to deny investment (Lindblom 1977).
20 While the relationship between efficiency and growth is a close one, growth can, nevertheless, proceed in the presence of some level of economic inefficiency by simply increasing inputs of the factors of production, notably labour or capital. Efficiency pertains to maximising output and returns from a given amount of inputs. Paul Krugman's claim about the myth of the East-Asian miracle rests on this distinction. See Krugman (1994).
21 This does not necessarily stop TNCs from lobbying for neoliberal policies, particularly through multilateral organisations.
22 The notion of 'embedded neoliberal' regionalism is borrowed from Van Apeldoorn (2000: 241) who uses it to describe the emerging European regional order in which the state continues to play a role in the provision of

public goods like education and infrastructure. The original term, embedded neoliberalism, comes from Ruggie (1998: 72–6).

23 See, for instance, Gourevitch (1978).

24 The notion of the developmental state goes beyond this, of course. The developmental state is often conceptualised in terms of a set of institutional features of the state and its relationship to society. See Woo-Cumings (1999).

25 Strategic trade theory derives its conclusions from assumptions that depart from those of neoclassical trade theory: that markets display increasing returns to scale, that learning effects or the experience of firms is important, and that technological innovations matter (Helpman and Krugman 1985: 3; Brander 1986: 25; Krugman 1986: 8). Under these imperfect market conditions, an interventionist trade policy is shown to secure welfare gains for the country (Krugman 1986: 12–14; McCulloch 1993: 49–50).

26 Although Gamble and Payne (1996a: 252) advance the idea of 'strategic trade' regionalism, this model is fundamentally distinct from the model of developmental regionalism advanced in this book. Crucially, the former does not make a distinction between domestic and foreign firms. In Gamble and Payne's model, whatever sheltering of firms producing within the regional scheme comes from the higher effective price of extra-regional imports. It is fundamentally a model of open regionalism, as the authors themselves acknowledge. Likewise, Mittelman's (2000: 116–17) development integration model of regionalism is also fundamentally distinct from the notion of developmental regionalism advanced here. Mittelman's model involves explicit state allocation of regional industrial projects among regional members, which is *not* a feature of developmental regionalism. Mittelman's model was a central feature of more 'closed' regionalist schemes of the 1960s and 1970s based on import-substitution industrialisation.

27 See the discussion in Ayoob (1998: 39–40) and Williams (1996: 215). Morgenthau emphasises the importance of domestic context in shaping state interests in international politics.

28 The concept of distribution used in this book does not incorporate any normative connotation. It is not to be seen as an egalitarian act, as something that is inherently 'progressive' involving the allocation of material and other benefits from rich to poor. As Susan Strange notes, distribution may well involve the 'regressive' reallocation of wealth, from the poor to the rich (Strange 1988/94: 212–13), and in the context of this book, to partners of ruling elites as the latter attempt to maintain elite cohesion and their power base.

29 In the ASEAN countries, as in most developing countries, internal vulnerabilities are considered to be far more threatening to state structures and to the governing regime than are external, military challenges. See Ayoob (1995).

30 Ayoob (1995: 9–15).

31 Elite governance is most usefully viewed as a project whose principal aim is to maintain elite power, autonomy and exclusivity (Case 1996: 20; McCargo 1998: 127).

32 See Crouch (1996) for Malaysia and Habir (1999) for Indonesia.

33 Thus, the terms 'capital' and 'business' are used interchangeably in the book.

2 The unfolding of a regional economic cooperation project: AFTA, 1991–2002

1 The annual series of ASEAN Economic Ministers Meetings (AEM) began in 1969 when member governments first decided to explore the possibility of economic cooperation.

2 The SEOM is a meeting of senior civil servants, usually at the level of permanent secretaries or their equivalent from the economic or related ministries from each ASEAN member country.
3 *AWSJ*, 'ASEAN nations endorse plans for free trade zone', 9 October 1991.
4 Article 7 of the CEPT Agreement provides for the establishment of the AFTA Council, an inter-governmental ministerial council comprising one nominee from each ASEAN member country. The Council is tasked with supervising, coordinating and reviewing the implementation of the CEPT Agreement. It also handles dispute resolution. Although the AFTA Council and the AEM are distinct organisational entities, the same minister often participates at both Council and Ministerial meetings. While the AEM oversees ASEAN economic cooperation broadly defined, the AFTA Council focuses entirely on matters pertaining to AFTA more specifically.
5 See Press Statement, *Third AFTA Council Meeting*, Indonesia, 11 December 1992.
6 See *AWSJ*, 'ASEAN moves closer to paring group tariffs', 26 October 1992.
7 Thailand, however, reduced tariffs under the CEPT scheme on selected items in February 1993. See *Business Times*, 'Anand, the white knight of Thai politics', 8 March 1993.
8 *Business Times*, 'Industries hit by AFTA scheme', 10 April 1993.
9 See *New Straits Times* (*NST*), 'KL may consider delaying tariff cuts', 16 July 1993.
10 *NST* 'ASEAN needs transitional period', 26 March 1993.
11 For administrative reasons, Brunei was to begin CEPT tariff cuts in June 1994. See the ASEAN *Annual Report 1993–94*.
12 The foundational AFTA agreements of 1992 covered only about 16 pages. The NAFTA Agreement, in contrast, came up to more than 1,000 pages.
13 See Joint Press Statement, *Fifth AFTA Council Meeting*, Thailand, 21 September 1994.
14 See Joint Press Statement, *Sixth AFTA Council Meeting*, Thailand, 27 April 1995.
15 See Joint Press Statement, *Seventh AFTA Council Meeting*, Brunei Darussalam, 6 September 1995 and ASEAN *Annual Report 1995–96*.
16 Joint Press Statement, *Seventh AFTA Council Meeting*, Brunei Darussalam, 6 September 1995.
17 See ASEAN *Annual Report 2001–02*.
18 See ASEAN *Annual Report 1996–97*.
19 Tongzon (1998: 58–65) discusses the AIJV and the BBC in some detail.
20 See Press Statement, *Second ASEAN Informal Meeting of Heads of State/Government of the Member States of ASEAN*, Kuala Lumpur, 15 December 1997.
21 Joint Press Statement, *Twelfth AFTA Council Meeting*, 6 October 1998, Manila.
22 See *Bangkok Post*, 'Tariff reductions may be delayed', 26 September 1998; and *Bangkok Post*, 'AFTA tariff cut delays likely if neighbours can't agree', 19 May 1999. Nevertheless, Thailand, Malaysia and the Philippines temporarily raised import tariffs and introduced other import measures on selected items in 1997 and 1998 as a way of dealing with the 1997–98 Asian financial crisis. See Shimizu (2000: 83) for details. Also see *Jakarta Post*, 9 February 1999.
23 Vietnam's deadline to reduce tariffs to 0–5 per cent is 2006, Laos and Myanmar have until 2008 while Cambodia is required to reach a 0–5 per cent tariff target by 2010.
24 Joint Press Statement, *Thirteenth Meeting of the AFTA Council*, 29 September 1999, Singapore. The target date for new members was set at 2018.
25 The deadline for new members was also advanced from 2018 to 2015 although some sensitive products would be allowed to follow the original 2018 deadline. See Chairman's Press Statement, *ASEAN Third Informal Summit*, Manila, 28 November 1999.

26 See ASEAN *Annual Report 2001–02*.
27 For the purposes of the AIA Agreement, an ASEAN investor is deemed to be one who is accorded the status of a national or home country investor in each of the ASEAN countries.
28 See Joint Press Statement, *Second Meeting of the AIA Council*, Singapore, 29 September 1999. A formal protocol to this effect was signed in September 2001. See ASEAN *Annual Report 2001–02*.
29 See Chairman's Press Statement, *ASEAN Third Informal Summit*, Manila, 28 November 1999.
30 These lists were compiled and published by the ASEAN Secretariat in July 1999. See ASEAN Secretariat (1999b).
31 The AIA Council, established under the auspices of the 1998 Framework Agreement on the AIA, is a ministerial-level council overseeing matters pertaining to the investment agreement.
32 See Press Statement, *Fourth Meeting of the ASEAN Investment Area Ministerial Council*, Vietnam, 14 September 2001. The new 2010 deadline applied to the founding six members; new members would be required to liberalise investment flows only in 2015.
33 Since 1997, most of the ASEAN countries have enacted legislation covering the entire period of CEPT tariff reduction. Annual legal enactments continue, however, for products being moved from the Temporary Exclusion or Sensitive Lists to the Inclusion List (ASEAN Secretariat 1998a: 6).
34 Calculated from data in the 1996 and 1998 CEPT packages. See Press Statement, *Eleventh AFTA Council Meeting*, Malaysia, 15 October 1997.
35 Joint Press Statement, *The Sixteenth Meeting of the ASEAN Free Trade Area (AFTA) Council*, Bandar Seri Begawan, Brunei Darussalam, 11 September 2002. The figure for 2001 was obtained from the ASEAN Secretariat website (www.aseansec.org), accessed on 31 August 2002.
36 See *Business Times*, 'No delay in the implementation of AFTA', 12 September 2002.
37 See the Joint Press Statement, *The Sixteenth Meeting of the ASEAN Free Trade Area (AFTA) Council*, Bandar Seri Begawan, Brunei Darussalam, 11 September 2002.
38 From the CEPT tariff database of the ASEAN Secretariat, accessible at its website (www.aseansec.org).
39 The relationship between unilateral and CEPT/AFTA tariff reductions is discussed in Chapter 3.
40 The then ASEAN Secretary General, Ajit Singh, pointed out in late 1996 that CEPT and MFN tariff rates were the same in about half of all tariff lines. See *Jakarta Post*, 10 October 1996.
41 Interview in Jakarta in July 2000 with Dr Robert Teh Jr, Director of the Bureau of Trade, Industry and Services at the ASEAN Secretariat.
42 Interview in Bangkok in August 2000 with Ms Chularat Suteethorn, Director of the International Economic Policy Division, Ministry of Finance, Thailand.
43 Under the new tariff structure, import tax on raw materials and primary goods is set at 0–5 per cent, 7 per cent for intermediate goods, and 15 per cent for final goods. See *Bangkok Post*, 'Protection remains for strategic sectors', 7 June 1999.
44 These unilateral MFN tariff cuts were part of the May 1995 trade liberalisation package announced by the Indonesian government.
45 These figures on the proportion of HS-9 tariff lines in Thailand, Malaysia, Indonesia and the Philippines displaying MFN–CEPT differentials were calculated by the author from the 2001 CEPT tariff database maintained by the ASEAN Secretariat, and accessible at its website (www.aseansec.org). Latest MFN rates are also available in this database.

46 In contrast, the products in the 1994 CEPT Inclusion List for manufactured products accounted for 85 per cent of the total intra-ASEAN trade value. See Joint Press Statement, *Fifth AFTA Council Meeting*, Thailand, 21 September 1994.
47 See the *ASEAN Annual Report 1996–97*.
48 See the *ASEAN Annual Report 2001–02*.
49 See ASEAN Secretariat (1998a: 21–7).
50 See the *ASEAN Annual Report 1996–97*.
51 See the *ASEAN Annual Report 2001–02*.
52 *Bangkok Post*, 'FTI: AFTA spirit being threatened', 19 June 2002.
53 See *The Nation*, 'ASEAN told to speed up AICO to lure investors', 10 April 1998.
54 See Joint Press Statement, *Thirtieth ASEAN Economic Ministers Meeting*, Makati City, Philippines, 7–8 October 1998.
55 *Business Times*, 'Obstacles to AICO implementation', 17 December 1997; and *Business Times*, 'Companies doubt ASEAN scheme', 23 August 1997.
56 *The Nation*, 'Government encouraged to accelerate AFTA time-frame', 24 January 1998.
57 See the *ASEAN Annual Report 2001–2002* and the Joint Press Statement, *The Thirty-Fourth ASEAN Economic Ministers Meeting*, Bandar Seri Begawan, Brunei Darussalam, 12 September 2002.
58 See the Joint Press Statement, *The Thirty-Fourth ASEAN Economic Ministers Meeting*, Bandar Seri Begawan, Brunei Darussalam, 12 September 2002.
59 The Coordinating Committee on Services reports to the SEOM.
60 Interview with Mr Rodolfo C. Severino Jr, Secretary General of ASEAN in July 2000 in Jakarta.
61 Interview with Dr Suthad Setboonsang, then Deputy Secretary General of ASEAN, in July 2000 in Jakarta.
62 Interview with Dr Suthad Setboonsang.
63 From an ASEAN press release, 'ASEAN Economic Ministers Sign Protocol to Implement Initial Package of Commitments under the ASEAN Framework Agreement on Services', Kuala Lumpur, 15 December 1997.
64 Interview in Jakarta with Mr Lim Hong Hin, Assistant Director in the Bureau of Trade, Industry and Services at the ASEAN Secretariat, July 2000.
65 See ASEAN *Annual Report 1999–2000*.
66 Interview in August 2000 with Mr Kong Mun Pew, Director of International Operations (Southeast Asia), Singapore Trade Development Board (now International Enterprise, Singapore).
67 Unlike the AIA agreement, the AFAS did not exclude foreign providers of services from the benefits of ASEAN liberalisation in services if they were engaged in substantive business operations in a member country (ASEAN 1995d). In other words, foreign service providers already operating in an ASEAN country would be accorded similar privileges as a domestic service firm.
68 Confidential interview, August 2000.
69 Details are found in the respective lists found in ASEAN Secretariat (1999b).
70 Joint Press Statement, *Fifth ASEAN Investment Area Ministerial Council*, Bandar Seri Begawan, Brunei Darussalam, 11 September 2001.
71 *Ibid*.
72 *Bangkok Post*, 'AFTA agenda has long way to go', 22 February 2002.
73 Buszynski (1997: 566) notes that a number of economists in the region held this view.
74 Many of the projects initiated under the earlier phase of economic cooperation continued for some years even after AFTA was initiated, although they were eventually absorbed into the AFTA framework. Thus, the Preferential Trading

Arrangement (PTA) was absorbed into the CEPT scheme of AFTA while two industrial cooperation projects (AIJV and the BBC) were replaced by the AICO.

75 Comprehensive discussions of ASEAN economic cooperation between 1976 and 1990 are found in ASEAN Secretariat (1997a: 1–88); Frost (1990: 7–14); Suriyamongkol (1988) and Ch'ng (1985).

3 Foreign capital and open regionalism

1 *New Straits Times*, 'Delegate: Thai proposal not viable', 25 July 1991.
2 *Business Times*, 'Japan throws weight behind AFTA scheme', 13 January 1993.
3 Interview in Kuala Lumpur in August 2000 with Mr Razak Ramli, then Deputy Secretary-General of the Ministry of International Trade and Industry, Malaysia, and currently its Secretary General.
4 *Business Times*, 'Stepped-up liberalisation of trade can be expected: Chuan', 8 January 1993.
5 *Business Times*, 'Indonesia seeking closer collaboration with Singapore', 25 June 1994.
6 *Business Times*, 'KL poised to take centre stage in AFTA', 18 September 1993.
7 *Business Times*, 'Domestic investments paying off', 11 July 1994.
8 The governing elite in Malaysia had always included politicians from the major political parties in the ruling National Front coalition representing the three major ethnic groups in the country. By the late 1980s, prominent businesspersons, especially those from the majority ethnic Malay and minority ethnic Chinese communities, became closely allied with political elites to form the dominant elite coalition in Malaysia. See Case (1996).
9 UMNO is the United Malays National Organisation, the dominant Malay political party in the ruling multiethnic National Front coalition that has governed Malaysia since independence. Its President and Deputy President become respectively the Prime Minister and Deputy Prime Minister of Malaysia.
10 *Business Times*, 'Indonesia seeking closer collaboration with Singapore', 25 June 1994.
11 *Business Times*, 'Indonesia seeking closer collaboration with Singapore', 25 June 1994.
12 See *NST*, 'Thailand takes on regional leadership', 1 October 1994.
13 Interview in Bangkok in August 2000 with Ms Doojduan Sasanavin of the Thai Ministry of Agriculture and Cooperatives.
14 *Business Times*, 'Need to address problems in ASEAN's farm sector', 26 August 1994.
15 See the press release from the ASEAN Secretariat, 'ASEAN to send investment missions to the US and Europe', 14 April 1999.
16 See, for instance, Clad (2000).
17 Interview in July 2000 with Dr Robert Teh Jr, of the ASEAN Secretariat, Jakarta. Also see *Business Times*, 'No delay in the implementation of AFTA', 12 September 2002.
18 *Jakarta Post*, 7 April 1999.
19 *Business Times*, 'AFTA will force Manila to change economic policies', 15 December 1993.
20 Interview in August 2000 with Ms Chularat Suteethorn, Director of the International Economic Policy Division, Ministry of Finance, Thailand.
21 *The Nation*, 'Textile group pushes for cut in input duties', 9 November 1999.
22 *Bangkok Post*, 'Protection remains for strategic sectors', 7 June 1999.

23 See Rinakit and Soesastro (1998) and Murphy (1999) on Indonesia; Gochoco-Bautista (1998) on the Philippines; Chantana (1998) and Hamilton-Hart (1999) on Thailand; and Welsh (1999) on Malaysia.

24 Nevertheless, the CEPT was designed to be sufficiently flexible, as Chapter 2 shows, to give firms time to adjust to the eventual removal of protection. In addition, both Thailand and the Philippines introduced financial support programmes to help domestic industries hurt by AFTA.

25 *FEER*, 'Thailand: trade and investment', 5 August 1993.

26 See *The Nation*, 'Coming to terms with free trade', 8 April 1997.

27 *Business Times*, 'Rafidah: open market can create resilience', 17 August 1992.

28 *Business Times*, 'Philippines unveils economic blueprint', 20 November 1992.

29 *Republika* (*Republic*), 27 September 1996.

30 Since the financial crisis, however, opposing discourses have become more prominent (Soesastro 1998).

31 See *FEER*, 'Thailand Incorporated', 18 January 2001.

32 *Business Times*, 'ASEAN set to liberalise investment within region', 30 September 1999.

4 Domestic capital and developmental regionalism

1 Menon (1998: 18) subscribes to this view.

2 These categories are described fully in ASEAN Secretariat (1998b: 1–3).

3 *The Nation*, 'Pressure grows to end Alien Business Law', 12 December 1997.

4 ABL-72 restricted foreign equity to 49 per cent unless a 50 per cent export condition was met. Majority foreign ownership was allowed in priority activities, however, but again, this required 50 per cent or more of the output to be exported.

5 Information on the Foreign Business Act 1999 and on Thai investment policy in general is available from the website of the Board of Investment (www.boi.gov.th).

6 According to Paisan Kumanwisai, panel chairman of the Senate committee for vetting aliens. See *The Nation*, 'Alien business law', 19 June 1999.

7 *The Nation*, 'Thailand to offer 100% bank equity', 3 December 1997.

8 *FEER*, 'Thaksin turns back the clock', 19 April 2001.

9 See Malaysia (1998).

10 Information on Malaysian investment policy is available on the website of the Malaysian Industrial Development Authority, the country's investment agency (www.mida.gov.my).

11 See ASEAN Secretariat (1998b: 34–40).

12 Austria (1998: 111–15) lists these restricted sectors/activities.

13 Foreign firms establishing joint ventures with the National Development Council can own land.

14 Interview in May 2001 with Mr Ong Hong Cheong, retired senior analyst, Institute of Strategic and International Studies (ISIS), Malaysia and former coordinator of Malaysian participation in the OECD-sponsored workshops that brought together OECD members and 'dynamic non-member economies'.

15 From the *Report of the WTO General Council Meeting 1998*. See WTO (1998). All reports and minutes of General Council meetings are available at the WTO website (www.wto.org).

16 Even after failure of the Seattle Ministerial in December 1999, industrial countries continued their attempts to include investment in the WTO, as part of a new development round for the next meeting, to which move Malaysia and Indonesia were opposed. See *Economic Times of India*, 'India opposes

proposals for investment agreement', 8 June 2001. Although investment was, in the end, relegated to the backburner at the November 2001 WTO Ministerial in Doha in view of the urgent need to reach an agreement on trade liberalisation amidst a global economic slowdown and the post-September 11 (2001) uncertainties, this was clearly not for want of trying.

17 See the Summary Report of the Proceedings, *Conference on the World Trade Organisation: Perspectives from the South*, 9–10 July 1996, Kuala Lumpur, Institute of Strategic and International Studies (ISIS), Malaysia (mimeo).

18 *Business Times*, 'Malaysia, seven others jointly oppose new WTO rules', 5 November 1996.

19 *Business Times*, 'Thais not ready for EU pact', 12 March 1996.

20 *The Nation*, 'Cabinet to set stance on WTO issues', 20 November 1999.

21 The Washington Consensus refers to a set of orthodox economic ideas that advocate, among other things, trade and investment liberalisation, deregulation as well as privatisation as a way to achieving competitiveness and maximising economic welfare (Williamson 1994).

22 Speech to the Inaugural Plenary of the Sixth G-15 Summit made on behalf of the Asian members of the G-15, in Harare, Zimbabwe on 3 November 1996. Available on the website of the Prime Minister's Department, Malaysia (www.smpke.jpm.my).

23 Mahathir's speech on 'Globalisation – what it means to small nations', quoted in Welsh (1999: 273).

24 Author's emphasis.

25 Interview with Razak Ramli of the Ministry of International Trade and Industry, Malaysia, August 2000.

26 Interview with Karun Kittisataporn, Director General, Department of Business Economics of the Thai Commerce Ministry, August 2000.

27 Interview with Dr Wee Kee Hwee of the ASEAN Secretariat, July 2000.

28 See *Bangkok Post*, 'Hopes vary for investment area', 11 September 1996.

29 See the argument put forward by economists at these meetings (Chia 1996: 20).

30 *Bulletin KADIN Indonesia* (Bulletin of the Indonesian Chamber of Commerce and Industry), No. 11/XIII, 30 September 1995.

31 *Business Times*, 'ASEAN firms urged to tap potential in region', 19 March 1997.

32 *The Nation*, 'Regionalism scope needed under AFTA', 21 August 1997.

33 *Bangkok Post*, 'Investment area plan proceeding', 9 January 1998.

34 *Bangkok Post*, 'BOI backs 30% as level for national treatment', 17 January 1998.

35 Discussion with then ASEAN Deputy Secretary General, Dr Suthad Setboonsang, July 2000.

36 Comment by Abdullah Tahir, quoted in Felker (1998: 247).

37 Interview with Karun Kittisataporn, Ministry of Commerce, Thailand in August 2000.

38 See the comment by a senior Malaysian investment official in *Business Times*, 'Don't ask for many exemptions, industries told', 26 March 1999.

39 *New Straits Times*, 'Set up ASEAN consortiums, urges Rafidah', 13 March 1997; and *Business Times*, 'Bumi economic shares won't fall', 11 April 1998.

40 *Business Times*, 'ASEAN to boost liberalisation, address dwindling FDI', 10 October 1998.

41 *Bisnis Indonesia* (Indonesian Business), 10 October 1998.

42 Interview with Mr Karun Kittisataporn of Thailand.

43 Interview with Ms Lim Bee Suan of the Singapore Trade Development Board (now known as International Enterprise, Singapore), conducted via e-mail in June 2001.

44 *Bangkok Post*, 'Region's ministers reaffirm plan', 6 March 1999.

45 The Philippine case will not be discussed here. The overwhelming concern in the country during this period was whether Philippine business would be able to survive the CEPT and the influx of more competitive imports from the ASEAN region.

46 Reproduced in *Speeches*, May–June 1993: 15.

47 Interview with Mr Rodolfo Severino Jr, Secretary General of ASEAN, July 2000.

48 Interview with Dr Wee Kee Hwee of the ASEAN Secretariat, July 2000.

49 *Bangkok Post*, 'Region's ministers reaffirm plan', 6 March 1999.

50 Interview with Mr Manasvi Srisodapol, Counsellor in the Department of ASEAN Affairs, Ministry of Foreign Affairs, Thailand in August 2000.

51 See Brown (1998: 188) on the redistribution imperative.

52 The 1990s witnessed growing cooperation between the ethnic Chinese business elite and the indigenous business elite, although this was mostly limited to alliances between Chinese businesses and Suharto family businesses (Habir 1999).

53 Small and medium-scale indigenous businesses also gained through patronage provided through the government political party, Golkar. See Robison (1996: 90–1).

54 Since the 1997 financial crisis and the sacking of Deputy Prime Minister Anwar Ibrahim in 1998, Malay support for UMNO has declined, channelled instead to the opposition Islamic party and to the new party begun by Anwar's supporters.

55 Interview via e-mail.

56 E-mail interview with Ong Hong Cheong.

57 Joint Press Statement, *Thirty-third ASEAN Economic Ministers Meeting*, 15 September 2001.

58 *Business Times*, 'ASEAN set to liberalise investment within region', 30 September 1999.

59 *International Herald Tribune*, 'Investment in Southeast Asia plunges', 27 July 2000. Later information revealed a higher FDI figure for 1999 of US$16 billion. See UNCTAD (2000).

60 *Financial Times*, 'Foreign investors desert Southeast Asia for China', 13 October 2000.

61 Interview with a senior Malaysian trade official, December 2001.

62 See *Chairman's Statement, Seventh ASEAN Summit*, 11 November 2001.

63 Press Release of the US-ASEAN Business Council, 13 September 2001.

64 See *Press Statement, Fourth AIA Council Meeting*, 14 September 2001.

65 The 'training ground' argument advanced by economists studying AFTA is distinct from the concept of developmental regionalism advanced in this book. Ariff (1998: 10) suggests that AFTA provides a 'training ground where ASEAN manufacturers will learn to compete with one another in the regional market before they can penetrate into the world market'. The training ground metaphor, which is implicitly associated with the CEPT, does not make any distinction between foreign-owned and domestic-owned capital, which is central to the notion of developmental regionalism. It also fails to specify how preferential trade liberalisation through the CEPT 'will enable local manufacturers to spread their wings regionally first and globally afterwards' (Ariff 1998: 10). The CEPT by itself does not prevent production within ASEAN by international firms, and consequently, does not restrict global market competition in the regional market, except by raising the prices of competing imports from non-ASEAN sources.

5 Re-negotiating AFTA commitments

1 *Review Indonesia*, 8 April 1992.
2 *Suara Karya*, 9 August 1995.
3 *Bisnis Indonesia*, 7 December 1992.
4 See Stubbs (2000: 307–8).
5 *Jakarta Post*, 17 November 1992; and Suara *Karya*, 30 March 1992.
6 *Merdeka*, 13 August 1992; *Jakarta Post*, 16 December 1993; and *Bangkok Post*, 'FTI asked to submit tariff cut list', 20 May 1999.
7 *Jakarta Post*, 25 February 1993.
8 See *Business Times*, 'Bangkok sets up fund to help local industries', 14 June 1993; and *Business Times*, 'Philippine government to help industry compete in region', 19 November 1992.
9 *Jakarta Post*, 'Local businessmen want implementation of AFTA delayed', 12 July 2000.
10 *Business Times*, 'Philippine industries want tariff freeze until 2003', 4 September 1998.
11 *Business Times*, 'No delay in the implementation of AFTA', 12 September 2002.
12 Interview with Ms Chularat Suteethorn of the Thai Ministry of Finance, August 2000.
13 Confidential interview with a Malaysian trade official, August 2000.
14 Interview in June 2001 via e-mail with Ms Lim Bee Suan, Singapore Trade Development Board (now International Enterprise, Singapore).
15 Interview with Dr Suthad Sethboonsang, Deputy Secretary General of ASEAN, July 2000.
16 Details of the episode are found in *FEER*, 'Changing lanes', 8 June 2000.
17 Renong was, in fact, the former business arm of UMNO. See Gomez and Jomo (1997: 69).
18 See Lee (1998).
19 Confidential interview with a Malaysian trade official, August 2000.
20 Singapore already possessed a petrochemical industry that had its roots in the petroleum refining and petroleum products industries begun in the late 1960s (Rodan 1989: 96–101).
21 *Bangkok Post*, 'Thai PET resin firms worry over duty cuts', 9 September 1996.
22 *Bangkok Post*, 'Industry ministry lobbies against plastic duty cuts', 4 December 1997.
23 *Bangkok Post*, 'Agencies in two camps over tariff cut delay', 17 December 1996.
24 *Ibid*.
25 *Bangkok Post*, 'Free trade goal under pressure', 10 July 2000.
26 See the ASEAN Secretariat's 2001 CEPT database (www.aseansec.org).
27 *Inquirer News Service*, 'Petrochem players told to show financial muscle', 27 January 2002.
28 Interview with Robert Teh Jr, ASEAN Secretariat, July 2000.
29 *Inquirer News Service*, 'Push for retention of 15% resin tariff now, DTI urged', 17 January 2002.
30 *Inquirer News Service*, 'Petrochem players told to show financial muscle', 27 January 2002.
31 *Inquirer News Service*, 'Govt. asked to protect resin beyond 2003', 31 December 2001.
32 See the ASEAN Secretariat's 2001 CEPT database (www.aseansec.org).
33 *Agence France Presse*, 'Philippines mulls shielding petrochemicals despite AFTA', 11 September 2001.

34 *Business Times*, 'Protection for petrochem products will be temporary', 19 September 1992.
35 *Business Times*, 'Association: Review protective duty on polyethylene', 26 February 1994.
36 Interview with Dr Leong Choon Heng, Director of Research, Malaysian University of Science and Technology, August 2000.
37 *Business Times*, 'Rafidah: 40,000 permits issued for import of resins', 25 May 1994.
38 *Malaysian Business*, 'Pioneering the big play', 16 October 1993.
39 Interview with Dr Hadi Soesastro, Executive Director of the Centre for Strategic and International Studies (CSIS), Jakarta, July 2000.
40 *AWSJ*, 'ASEAN defuses trade dispute with Jakarta', 11 December 1995.
41 *AWSJ*, 'ASEAN fine tunes services liberalisation', 12 December 1995.
42 *AWSJ*, 'ASEAN defuses trade dispute with Jakarta', 11 December 1995.
43 This was despite the declining political and economic salience of rice since the 1970s, the result of structural economic transformation and rural income growth (Tomich 1992: 25).
44 The Finance Ministry, nevertheless, set the unofficial maximum MFN rice tariff at 160 per cent.
45 The share of agriculture in GDP declined from 23 per cent in 1980 to 16 per cent in 1992. In contrast, the share in the Philippines remained at close to a quarter of GDP in 1992. See McFarlane (1998: 152).
46 PAS is the Pan-Malaysian Islamic Party (or *Partai Agama Islam Se-Malaysia*).
47 Although the MFN tariff on rice between 1990 and 1995 was low, set at 0.3 per cent, import prohibitions and licensing regulations, many of them not fully transparent, offered substantial protection to domestic rice farmers. See Acosta (1998: 39).
48 A later decision by the SEOM stipulated that all NTBs are to be removed by 2003. Confidential interview with a Malaysian trade official, August 2000.
49 Interview with Ms Doodjuan Sasanavin, Ministry of Agriculture and Cooperatives, Thailand, August 2000.
50 In fact, the government had initially targeted the wheat flour sector for deregulation in the mid-1990s, but after Liem pointed out to government officials that Suharto's daughter also owned a flour mill, the wheat sector was removed from the deregulation agenda. See *FEER*, 'Depth of connections', 16 October 1997.
51 The discussion in this sub-section benefited from the author's interview with Hadi Soesastro of CSIS, Jakarta.
52 Interview with Hadi Soesastro.
53 Malaysia had the highest number of automotive sector tariff lines – 246 – in the Temporary Exclusion List, compared to Thailand's 7, Indonesia's 45 and 56 for the Philippines. Information is from the ASEAN Secretariat.
54 Details are found in Borsuk (1999: 147–9) and Aswicahyono *et al.* (2000).
55 The Indonesian Automobile Industry Association, GAIKINDO had raised this issue a number of times since 1999. See *Bisnis Indonesia*, 8 December 1999; *Jakarta Post*, 28 June 2000; and *Jakarta Post*, 6 July 2000.
56 Interview with Dr Haryo Aswicahyono, Centre for Strategic and International Studies, Jakarta, July 2000.
57 Abdulsomad (1998) provides a comprehensive discussion of the Malaysian and Thai auto industries.
58 These were removed in 2000 in line with Thailand's commitment to the WTO (Thailand 2000: 7).
59 Interview with Mr Manasvi Srisodapol of the Ministry of Foreign Affairs, Thailand, August 2000.
60 *NST*, 'BMW: expansion of Thai unit hinges on AFTA', 13 October 2000.

61 Data calculated from information from the respective national automobile industry associations.
62 From a survey by Automotive Resources Asia Ltd, reported in *Bernama*, 'Delay to include CKD, CBU items in CEPT only 2.1% of auto products', 3 September 2002.
63 Interview with Mr Paramjit Singh Tyndall, Research Fellow, Malaysian Institute of Economic Research, August 2000.
64 *Investors Digest*, 'On the horns of a dilemma', 16 March 1995.
65 *Business Times*, 'Automotive industry must be profitable on its own: PM', 24 September 1997.
66 The 1998 national budget exercise raised import duties from 140–200 per cent on CBU to 140–300 per cent, and from 42 per cent on CKD to 42–80 per cent. See Tyndall (1999: 47). This further hurt domestic assemblers of foreign (non-national) vehicles.
67 *Business Times*, 'Automotive industry must be profitable on its own: PM', 24 September 1997.
68 *Business Times*, 'Big boys are beefing up Malaysian operations', 4 July 2000.
69 According to market analyst Valuer Dresdner Kleinwort Benson, reported in *Business Times*, 'Proton share of domestic car mart to shrink: study', 8 September 2000.
70 *Bangkok Post*, 'Thai car industry a key to sustainable growth', 13 June 1997.
71 *Business Times*, 'Automotive industry must be profitable on its own: PM', 24 September 1997.
72 See *NST*, 'PM: Malaysia seeks delay in opening auto sector', 31 May 2000.
73 *Financial Times*, 'Proton uses its delay in liberalisation to prepare for rise in foreign competition', 11 October 2000.
74 *Ibid.*
75 *Business Times*, 'S-ENG will give Proton more mileage', 9 October 2000.
76 Interview with Razak Ramli, Ministry of International Trade and Industry, Malaysia, August 2000.
77 *Business Times*, 'Local car part makers to face foreign competition', 8 September 1999.
78 Speech by Minister of International Trade and Industry, Rafidah Aziz, reported in *Bernama*, Delay to include CKD, CBU items in CEPT only 2.1% of auto products', 5 September 2002.
79 *NST*, 'Foreign firms to hold not more than 30pc stake in national car', 7 October 2000.
80 *NST*, 'Attempts to take over Proton revealed', 19 July 2000.
81 From *Associated Press*, 'Malaysia's Proton narrows search for partner', 9 October 2000.
82 *NST*, 'Gear up to face AFTA challenges, PM tells Proton', 17 February 2001.

6 Implementation as a political process

1 See Mattli (1999: 170–71) and Ravenhill (1995: 859).
2 Works belonging to the management school are Chayes and Chayes (1993, 1995) and Keohane (1984). The enforcement school includes the work of Martin (1992) and Yarborough and Yarborough (1992).
3 The enforcement school treats non-compliance as a deliberate decision by a member state to violate its commitments under the cooperative agreement. In this approach, cooperation is facilitated by the provision of effective enforcement and sanctioning mechanisms that deter potential violators. A study of 125 international treaties showed that sanctioning authority is

rarely granted by treaty, rarely used when granted and likely to be ineffective when used (Chayes and Chayes 1995: 32).

4 See the *Joint Press Statement of the Eighth AFTA Council Meeting* held on 10 December 1995 in Bangkok.

5 *AWSJ*, 'ASEAN defuses trade dispute with Jakarta', 11 December 1995.

6 *Ibid.*

7 *AWSJ*, 'ASEAN fine tunes services liberalisation', 12 December 1995.

8 *NST*, 'Council sets deadline for tariff reduction', 27 April 1996.

9 *Business Times*, 'Officials deadlocked on farm issue', 11 September 1996; *Jakarta Post*, 11 September 1996.

10 *Jakarta Post*, 11 September 1996.

11 While the US market took 22 per cent of Thai exports in 1998, almost 18 per cent went to the ASEAN-10 market, still a significant share given the crisis-induced recession in the region. Trade data was obtained from the IMF, *Direction of Trade Statistics Yearbook, 2000*.

12 Interview with the Secretary General of ASEAN, Mr Rodolfo Severino Jr.

13 Interviews in August 2000 with Mr Manasvi Srisodapol, Ministry of Foreign Affairs, Thailand, and Ms Doodjuan Sasanavin, Ministry of Agriculture and Cooperatives, Thailand.

14 *Bangkok Post*, 'Group must get serious about backing free trade', 2 October 2000.

15 *NST*, 'US firms seek assurance', 14 April 1999.

16 *Business Times (Singapore)*, 'Why US firms find ASEAN less appealing', 6 October 2000.

17 *Ibid.*

18 Interview with Mr Kong Mun Pew, Singapore Trade Development Board (now International Enterprise, Singapore), August 2000.

19 Interviews with Mr Rodolfo Severino Jr, the ASEAN Secretary General and Mr Karun Kittisataporn of Thailand.

20 *The Nation*, 'Tariff reduction set despite Malaysia move', 30 September 1999.

21 This was pointed out by Mr Cherdpong Siriwit, Director General of the Office of Industrial Economics, Thailand. See *The Nation*, 'Tariff reduction set despite Malaysia move', 30 September 1999.

22 *The Nation*, 'Palm oil producers have most to lose', 22 October 1999.

23 This point was confirmed by a Malaysian trade official in a confidential interview. Article 6 of the CEPT Agreement is the safeguards clause (ASEAN 1992c).

24 Confidential interview with a Malaysian trade official, August 2000.

25 *Financial Times*, 'Malaysia trade exemption won through threat', 27 July 2000.

26 Interview with Mr Kong Mun Pew.

27 Interview with Mr Karun Kittisataporn.

28 Interview with Mr Karun Kittisataporn.

29 *Business Times*, 'Malaysia under pressure over automotive sector duties rollback', 3 October 2000.

30 Interview with Mr Karun Kittisataporn.

31 *Kyodo News Service*, 'Malaysia rejects Thailand's demand for compensation' 6 July 2002.

32 Interview with Mr Kong Mun Pew.

33 According to Narongchai Akrasanee, a prominent Thai corporate executive and a long-time advocate of closer economic cooperation in ASEAN (Baldwin 1997: 55).

34 From a US-ASEAN Business Council *Special Report Update on AFTA and Regional Economic Integration*, prepared by Pricewaterhouse Coopers, August 2000, available on the website of the US-ASEAN Business Council (www.us-asean.org/pwcreport1.htm).

35 Interview with Mr Razak Ramli, Ministry of International Trade and Industry, Malaysia, August 2000.
36 See Ravenhill (1998: 159).
37 See the discussion on Indonesia and petrochemicals in Chapter 5.
38 *Jakarta Post*, 16 October 1997.
39 Interview in July 2000.

Conclusion

1 On this point, see the discussion in Loriaux (1999).
2 From the Prime Minister's speech at the Global 2001 Smart Partnership Dialogue held in Kampala, Uganda (www.smpke.jpm.my).
3 The 2003 Malaysian budget speech is available at the website of the Prime Minister's Department (www.smpke.jpm.my).
4 *Business Times (Singapore)*, 'Jakarta preparing to cut itself loose from IMF', 15 August 2002.
5 *The Straits Times*, 'Are GLCs crowding out businesses or do they give Singapore an edge?', 28 August 2002.
6 *Agence France Presse*, 'Philippine leader calls for slowdown of her tariff reduction policy', 26 September 2002.
7 These responses are detailed in *Business Times (Singapore)*, 'All eyes on China push for FTA', 24 November 2000.
8 *AWSJ*, 'ASEAN wants China trade zone', 5 November 2001.
9 See economist Paul Krugman's op-ed piece, 'The US economy needs leadership', in *The New York Times*, reproduced in *the International Herald Tribune*, 2 October 2002; *IHT*, 'Will the US follow Japan?', 3 October 2002.
10 *AWSJ*, 'China-ASEAN bloc faces snag', 7 November 2001.
11 Confidential interview with a Malaysian trade official, December 2001.
12 *Philippine Daily Inquirer*, 'ASEAN wants trade bloc with Japan before China', 18 September 2002.
13 Scollay and Gilbert (2001: 1–2) provide a list of negotiated and proposed bilateral and plurilateral free trade areas in the Asia-Pacific region.
14 The *Japan–Singapore Economic Agreement for a New Age Partnership* was signed in January 2002.
15 *Straits Times*, 'FTA opens door to Japan's huge services market', 14 January 2002.
16 *Sunday Times*, 'FTA customs union to benefit SEAsia', 17 March 2002.
17 *Bangkok Post*, 'AFTA tax incentives to be strictly local', 11 February 2002.
18 *Ibid.*
19 Author's calculations using trade data from the ASEAN trade database, available at the ASEAN Secretariat website (www.aseansec.org).
20 Based on calculations from UNCTAD figures on investment.
21 The survey results are reported in Baldwin (1997: 126).
22 *FEER*, 7 August 1997, p. 39.
23 Reported in ASEAN Secretariat (1999a: 16).
24 The survey was conducted in October 2001, and reported in *The Sunday Times*, 'Are Japanese businesses leaving for China?', 15 September 2002.

References

Books, chapters, journal articles, dissertations and conference/working papers

Abdulsomad, K. (1998) 'Promoting Industrial and Technological Development Under Contrasting Industrial Policies: The Automobile Industries in Malaysia and Thailand', in K.S. Jomo, Greg Felker and Rajah Rasiah (eds), *Industrial Technology Development in Malaysia*, London: Routledge, pp. 274–300.

Acharya, A. (1997) 'Ideas, Identity and Institution-Building: From the "ASEAN Way" to the "Asia-Pacific Way?"', *The Pacific Review*, 10(3): 319–46.

Acharya, A. (1999) 'Realism, Institutionalism and the Asian Economic Crisis' *Contemporary Southeast Asia*, 21(1): 1–29.

Acosta, L. (1998) *The Impact of ASEAN Free Trade Area (AFTA) on Selected Agricultural Products in ASEAN Countries*, Frankfurt: Peter Lang.

Akrasanee, N. and Stifel, D. (1992) 'The Political Economy of the ASEAN Free Trade Area', in Pearl Imada and Seiji Naya (eds), *AFTA: The Way Ahead*, Singapore: Institute of Southeast Asian Studies (ISEAS), pp. 27–47.

Alagappa, M. (1987) *The National Security of Developing States*, Dover, MA: Auburn House Publishing.

Alagappa, M. (1995) 'Seeking a More Durable Basis', in Muthiah Alagappa (ed.), *Political Legitimacy in Southeast Asia: The Quest for Moral Authority*, Stanford: Stanford University Press, pp. 293–334.

Ali Abul Hassan Sulaiman (1992) 'Long-term Economic Planning and Strategies in a Globalisation Era', Paper presented to the *Conference on Economic Globalisation: Issues, Challenges and Responses by Developing Countries*, 16–17 August 1992, Malaysia: Universiti Utara Malaysia (Northern University of Malaysia).

Amin, S. (1996) 'The Challenge of Globalisation', *Review of International Political Economy*, 3(2): 216–59.

Ariff, M. (1993) *AFTA: An Outward-Looking Free Trade Agreement*, Private Investment and Trade Opportunities (PITO) Economic Brief No. 14, Honolulu: East-West Centre.

Ariff, M. (1994) 'AFTA = Another Futile Trade Area?', *Syarahan Perdana (Inaugural Lecture)*, 3 February 1994, Kuala Lumpur: Universiti Malaya.

Ariff, M. (1998) 'Economic Regionalism Versus Multilateralism: Dilemmas for Southeast Asia', Paper presented to the *ISEAS 30th Anniversary Conference on Southeast Asia in the 21st Century: Challenges of Globalisation*, 30 July–1 August 1998, Singapore: Institute of Southeast Asian Studies.

Aswicahyono, H., Basri, M.C. and Hill, H. (2000) 'How Not to Liberalise Indonesia's Automotive Industry', *Bulletin of Indonesian Economic Studies*, 36(1): 209–41.

Athukorala, P. and Menon, J. (1997) 'AFTA and the Investment-Trade Nexus', *World Economy*, 20(2): 159–74.

Austria, M.S. (1998) 'The Emerging Philippine Investment Environment', *Journal of Philippine Development*, XXV(1): 79–126.

Ayoob, M. (1995) *The Third World Security Predicament*, Boulder, Colorado: Lynne Rienner Publishers.

Ayoob, M. (1998) 'Subaltern Realism: International Relations Theory Meets the Third World', in Stephanie Neuman (ed.), *International Relations Theory and the Third World*, Basingstoke: Macmillan, pp. 31–54.

Azarcon, C.J. (1997) 'Comparative Tariff Policies of ASEAN Member Countries', *Journal of Philippine Development*, XXIV(1): 93–135.

Baldwin, P. (1997) *Planning for ASEAN: How to Take Advantage of Southeast Asia's Free Trade Area*, London: The Economist Intelligence Unit.

Baldwin, R.E. (1999) 'A Domino Theory of Regionalism', in J. Bhagwati, P. Krishna and A. Panagariya (eds), *Trading Blocs: Alternative Approaches to Analysing Preferential Trade Agreements*, Cambridge, MA: MIT Press.

Barry Jones, R.J. (1995) *Globalisation and Interdependence in the International Political Economy*, London: Pinter Publishers.

Beeson, M. and Jayasuriya, K. (1998) 'The Political Rationalities of Regionalism: APEC and the EU in Comparative Perspective', *The Pacific Review*, 11(3): 311–36.

Bhagwati, J.N. (1982) 'Directly Unproductive, Profit-Seeking (DUP) Activities', *Journal of Political Economy*, 90(51): 988–1002.

Bhagwati, J., Greenaway, D. and Panagariya, A. (1998) 'Trading Preferentially: Theory and Policy', *Economic Journal*, 108: 1128–48.

Biersteker, T.J. (1992) 'The Triumph of Neoclassical Economics in the Developing World: Policy Convergence and Bases of Governance in the International Economic Order', in James N. Rosenau and Ernst-Otto Czempiel (eds), *Governance Without Government: Order and Change in World Politics*, Cambridge: Cambridge University Press, pp. 102–31.

Bolongaita, Jr, E.P. (2000) 'The Philippines in 1999', *Asian Survey*, 40(1): 67–77.

Borsuk, R. (1999) 'Markets: The Limits of Reform', in Donald K. Emmerson (ed.), *Indonesia Beyond Suharto*, New York: M.E. Sharpe, pp. 136–68.

Bowles, P. (2000) 'Regionalism and Development after (?) the Global Financial Crisis', *New Political Economy*, 5(3): 433–55.

Bowles, P. and MacLean, B. (1996) 'Understanding Trade Bloc Formation: The Case of the ASEAN Free Trade Area', *Review of International Political Economy*, 3(2): 319–48.

Brander, J.A. (1986) 'Rationales for Strategic and Industrial Policy', in Paul Krugman (ed.), *Strategic Trade Policy and the New International Economics*, Cambridge, MA: MIT Press, pp. 23–46.

Breslin, S. and Higgott, R.A. (2000) 'Studying Regions: Learning from the Old, Constructing the New', *New Political Economy*, 5(3): 333–52.

Brown, C. (1998) 'Indonesia: The Changing Balance of Commercial Power?', in Kyoko Sheridan (ed.), *Emerging Economic Systems in Asia*, Sydney: Allen & Unwin, pp. 180–207.

Buszynski, L. (1997) 'ASEAN's New Challenges', *Pacific Affairs*, 70(2): 555–77.

Case, W.F. (1996) *Elites and Regimes in Malaysia*, Clayton, Victoria: The Monash Asia Institute.

Case, W.F. (2002) *Politics in Southeast Asia: Democracy or Less*, Surrey, UK: Cuyrzon.

Castells, M. (1992) 'Four Asian Tigers with a Dragon Head: A Comparative Analysis of the State, Economy, and Society in the Asian Pacific Rim', in Richard P. Appelbaum and Jeffrey Henderson (eds), *States and Development in the Asian Pacific Rim*, London: Sage Publications, pp. 33–70.

Chantana, B. (1998) 'Thailand', in Charles E. Morrison and Hadi Soesastro (eds), *Domestic Adjustments to Globalisation*, Tokyo: Japan Centre for International Exchange, pp. 257–83.

Chayes, A. and Chayes, A.H. (1993) 'On Compliance', *International Organisation*, 47(2): 175–205.

Chayes, A. and Chayes, A.H. (1995) *The New Sovereignty: Compliance with International Regulatory Agreements*, Cambridge, MA: Harvard University Press.

Chia, S.Y. (1996) 'Intra-ASEAN Direct Investments', Paper presented at the *Seminar on the Promotion of Foreign Direct Investment in the Context of the ASEAN Investment Area*, 23–24 May 1996, Bangkok, Thailand.

Chia, S.Y. (1998) 'The ASEAN Free Trade Area', *The Pacific Review*, 11(2): 213–32.

Ch'ng, M.K. (1985) 'ASEAN Economic Cooperation: The Current Status', in Kernial Singh Sandhu (ed.), *Southeast Asian Affairs 1985*, Singapore: Institute of Southeast Asian Studies, pp. 31–53.

Ch'ng, M.K. (1991) 'Institutional Structures for Enhanced Economic Cooperation', in *ASEAN Economic Cooperation for the 1990s*, a report prepared by Seiji Naya for the ASEAN Secretariat.

Chung, S.P., Tan, H.Y., Goh, D. and Yang, C.C. (1998) 'Trade Policy Challenges and Issues', in Tan Teck Meng, Low Aik Meng, John Williams and Choo Teck Min (eds), *Business Opportunities in Indonesia*, Singapore: Prentice Hall, pp. 19–40.

Clad, J. (2000) 'Fin de Siecle, Fin de l'ASEAN?', *PacNet*, No. 9 (March 3, 2000) (www.nyu.edu/globalbeat/asia/Pacnet030300.html).

Coleman, W.D. and Underhill, G.R.D. (1998a) 'Introduction: Domestic Politics, Regional Economic Cooperation, and Global Economic Integration', in William D. Coleman and Geoffrey R.D. Underhill (eds), *Regionalism and Global Economic Integration*, London: Routledge, pp. 1–16.

Coleman, W.D. and Underhill, G.R.D. (1998b) (eds) *Regionalism and Global Economic Integration*, London: Routledge.

Cox, R.W. (1981/96) 'Social Forces, States and World Orders: Beyond International Relations Theory', in Robert W. Cox and Timothy J. Sinclair (eds), *Approaches to World Order*, Cambridge: Cambridge University Press, pp. 85–123.

Crouch, H. (1996) *Government and Society in Malaysia*, Sydney: Allen & Unwin.

Curzon, V. (1974) *The Essentials of Economic Integration: Lessons of EFTA Experience*, London: Macmillan.

Dent, C. (2001) 'Singapore's Foreign Economic Policy: The Pursuit of Economic Security', *Contemporary Southeast Asia*, 23(1): 1–23.

Desker, B. (2002) 'Keynote Address', *Joint IDSS-Harvard Workshop on the New Regional Economic and Security Architecture in East Asia*, 24 May 2002, Singapore: Institute of Defence and Strategic Studies (mimeo).

Dicken, P. (1998) *Global Shift: Transforming the World Economy* (Third Edition), London: Paul Chapman Publishing.

Dicken, P. and Yeung, H.W.-C. (1999), 'Investing in the Future: East and Southeast Asian Firms in the Global Economy', in Kris Olds, Peter Dicken, Philip F. Kelly, Lily Kong and Henry Wai-Chung Yeung (eds), *Globalisation and the Asia-Pacific*, London: Routledge, pp. 107–28.

Djidin, D.A. (1997) 'The Political Economy of Indonesia's New Economic Policy', *Journal of Contemporary Asia*, 27(1): 14–35.

Doner, R.F. (1997) 'Japan in East Asia: Institutions and Regional Leadership', in Peter J. Katzenstein and Takashi Shiraishi (eds), *Network Power: Japan and Asia*, Ithaca: Cornell University Press, pp.197–233.

Drysdale, P. and Garnaut, R. (1993) 'The Pacific: An Application of a General Theory of Economic Integration', in C. Fred Bergsten (ed.), *Pacific Dynamism and the International Economic System*, Washington, DC: Institute for International Economics, pp. 183–223.

Dunning, J.H. (1993) *Globalisation: The Challenge for National Economic Regimes*, Dublin: Economic and Social Research Council.

Ethier, W.J. (1998) 'The New Regionalism', *Economic Journal*, 108: 1149–61.

Evans, Peter (1993) 'Building an Integrative Approach to International and Domestic Politics: Reflections and Projections', in Peter B. Evans, Harold K. Jacobson and Robert D. Putnam (eds), *Double-Edged Diplomacy: International Bargaining and Domestic Politics*, Berkeley, California: University of California Press, pp. 397–430.

Fane, G. (2000) 'Survey of Recent Developments', *Bulletin of Indonesian Economic Studies*, 36(1): 13–44.

Fane, G. and Condon, T. (1996) 'Trade Reform in Indonesia, 1987–95', *Bulletin of Indonesian Economic Studies*, 32(3): 33–54.

Felker, G. (1998) *Upwardly Global? The State, Business and MNCs in Malaysia and Thailand's Technological Transformation*, PhD Dissertation, Princeton University, USA (unpublished).

Felker, G. (2002) 'Southeast Asian Industrialism and the Changing Global Production System', Paper presented to the Symposium on *Running on Empty? Politics, Markets and Southeast Asian Regionalism*, 17–18 January 2002, City University of Hong Kong.

Feridhanusetyawan, T. (1998) 'The Impact of Trade Liberalisation on Welfare and Employment in ASEAN', *ACIAR Working Paper 98.05*, Australia: Australian Centre for International Agricultural Research.

Frost, F. (1990) 'Introduction: ASEAN Since 1967 – Origins, Evolution and Recent Developments', in Alison Bronowski (ed.), *ASEAN into the 1990s*, London: Macmillan, pp. 1–31.

Gamble, A. and Payne, A. (1996a) 'Conclusion: The New Regionalism', in Andrew Gamble and Anthony Payne (eds), *Regionalism and World Order*, London: Macmillan, pp. 247–64.

Gamble, A. and Payne, A. (1996b) (eds) *Regionalism and World Order*, London: Macmillan.

George, J. (2000) 'Creating Globalisation: "Patriotic Internationalism" and Symbiotic Power Relations in the Post-WW2 Era', Coventry, UK: Centre for the Study of Globalisation and Regionalisation, University of Warwick (mimeo).

Gibbs, M. (1997) 'Policy Options in the Changing International Environment', in *Proceedings of the International Conference on East Asian Development: Lessons for a New Global Environment*, New York/Geneva: United Nations, pp. 181–93.

Gilpin, R. (1987) *The Political Economy of International Relations*, Princeton, NJ: Princeton University Press.

Gochoco-Bautista, M.S. (1998) 'Philippines', in Charles E. Morrison and Hadi Soesastro (eds), *Domestic Adjustments to Globalisation*, Tokyo: Japan Centre for International Exchange, pp. 207–27.

Gomez, E.T. (1996) 'Electoral Funding of General, State and Party Elections in Malaysia', *Journal of Contemporary Asia*, 26(1): 81–99.

Gomez, E.T. and Jomo, K.S. (1997) *Malaysia's Political Economy: Politics, Patronage and Profits*, Cambridge: Cambridge University Press.

Gourevitch, P. (1978) 'The Second Image Reversed: The International Sources of Domestic Politics', *International Organisation*, 32(4): 881–911.

Grugel, J. (1996) 'Latin America and the Remaking of the Americas', in Andrew Gamble and Anthony Payne (eds), *Regionalism and World Order*, London: Macmillan, pp. 131–67.

Grugel, J. and Hout, W. (1999) 'Regions, Regionalism and the South', in Jean Grugel and Wil Hout (eds), *Regionalism Across the North–South Divide: State Strategies and Globalisation*, London: Routledge, pp. 3–13.

Habir, A.D. (1999) 'Conglomerates: All in the Family', in Donald K. Emmerson (ed.), *Indonesia Beyond Suharto*, New York: M.E. Sharpe, pp. 168–202.

Haggard, S. and Kaufman, R.R. (1997) 'The Political Economy of Democratic Transitions', *Comparative Politics*, 29(3): 263–83.

Hamilton-Hart, N. (1999) 'Thailand and Globalisation', *Asian Perspective*, 23(4): 287–313.

Hay, S. (1996) 'The 1995 ASEAN Summit: Scaling a Higher Peak', *Contemporary Southeast Asia*, 18(3): 254–74.

Helpman, E. and Krugman, P. (1985) *Increasing Returns, Imperfect Competition and International Trade*, Cambridge, MA: MIT Press.

Henderson, J. (1999) *Reassessing ASEAN*, Adelphi Paper No. 328, London: International Institute for Strategic Studies.

Hettne, B., Inotai, A. and Sunkel, O. (2000) *National Perspectives on the New Regionalism in the South*, Basingstoke: Macmillan Press.

Hewison, K. (2000) 'Thailand's Capitalism and Economic Crisis', in Richard Robison, Mark Beeson, Kanishka Jayasuriya and Hyuk-Rae Kim (eds), *Politics and Markets in the Wake of the Asian Crisis*, London and New York: Routledge, pp. 192–211.

Higgott, R.A. (1997) 'Regional Integration, Economic Cooperation or Economic Policy Coordination in the Asia Pacific?', in Heribert Dieter (ed.), *The Regionalisation of the World Economy and Consequences for Southern Africa*, Marburg: Metropolis-Verlag, pp. 237–76.

Higgott, R.A. (1999) 'Economics, Politics and (International) Political Economy: The Need for a Balanced Diet in an Era of Globalisation', *New Political Economy*, 4(1): 23–36.

Higgott, R.A. (2000) 'Back from the Brink: The Theory and Practice of Globalisation at Century's End', in Mely C. Anthony and Jawhar Hassan (eds), *Beyond the Crisis: Challenges and Opportunities*, Kuala Lumpur: Institute of Strategic and International Studies, pp. 67–91.

Hill, H. (1992) 'Survey of Recent Developments', *Bulletin of Indonesian Economic Studies*, 28(2): 3–41.
Hill, H. (1994) 'The Economy', in Hal Hill (ed.), *Indonesia's New Order: The Dynamics of Socio-Economic Transformation*, Sydney: Allen & Unwin, pp. 64–120.
Hirst, P. (1997) 'The Global Economy – Myths and Realities', *International Affairs*, 73(3): 409–25.
Hirst, P. and Thompson, G. (1992) 'The Problem of Globalisation: International Economic Relations, National Economic Management and the Formation of Trading Blocs', *Economy and Society*, 21(4): 354–96.
Hirst, P. and Thompson, G. (1995) 'Globalisation and the Future of the Nation State', *Economy and Society*, 24(3): 408–42.
Hirst, P. and Thompson, G. (1996) *Globalisation in Question*, Cambridge: Polity Press.
Hobohm, S. (1995) 'Survey of Recent Developments', *Bulletin of Indonesian Economic Studies*, 31(1): 3–40.
Hobson, J. (1997) *The Wealth of States: A Comparative Sociology of International Economic and Political Change*, Cambridge: Cambridge University Press.
Hoogvelt, A. (1997) *Globalisation and the Postcolonial World*, London: Macmillan.
Hughes, C.W. (2000) 'Globalisation and Security in the Asia-Pacific: An Initial Investigation', *CSGR Working Paper No. 61/00*, Coventry, UK: Centre for the Study of Globalisation and Regionalisation, University of Warwick.
Hurrell, A. (1995) 'Regionalism in Theoretical Perspective', in Louise Fawcett and Andrew Hurrell (eds), *Regionalism in World Politics*, Oxford: Oxford University Press, pp. 36–73.
Hutchison, J. (1997) 'Pressure on Policy in the Philippines', in Garry Rodan, Kevin Hewison and Richard Robison (eds), *The Political Economy of Southeast Asia*, Oxford: Oxford University Press, pp. 64–92.
Hveem, H. (2000) 'Explaining the Regional Phenomenon in an Era of Globalisaton', in Richard Stubbs and Geoffrey R.D. Underhill (eds), *Political Economy and the Changing Global Order*, Oxford: Oxford University Press, pp. 70–81.
Imada, P. (1993) 'Production and Trade Effects of An ASEAN Free Trade Area', *The Developing Economies*, XXXI(1): 3–23.
James, W.E. (1995) 'Survey of Recent Developments', *Bulletin of Indonesian Economic Studies*, 31(3): 3–38.
Jacobsen, J.K. (1996) 'Are All Politics Domestic? Perspectives on the Integration of Comparative Politics and International Relations Theories', *Comparative Politics*, 29(1): 93–115.
Jesudason, J. (1989) *Ethnicity and the Economy: The State, Chinese Business and Multinationals in Malaysia*, Singapore: Oxford University Press.
Jonsson, C. and Tallberg, J. (1998) 'Compliance and Post-Agreement Bargaining', *European Journal of International Relations*, 4(4): 371–408.
Kahler, M. (1988) 'Organisation and Cooperation: International Institutions and Policy Coordination', *Journal of Public Policy*, 8(3/4): 375–401.
Kahler, M. (1995) *International Institutions and the Political Economy of Integration*, Washington, DC: The Brookings Institution.
Keohane, R.O. (1984) *After Hegemony: Cooperation and Discord in the World Political Economy*, Princeton: Princeton University Press.
Keohane, R.O. (1989) *International Institutions and State Power: Essays in International Relations Theory*, Boulder, Colorado: Westview Press.

Khoo, B.T. (1995) *Paradoxes of Mahathirism*, Kuala Lumpur: Oxford University Press.

Khoo, B.T. (2000) 'Economic Nationalism and its Discontents', in Richard Robison, Mark Beeson, Kanishka Jayasuriya and Hyuk-Rae Kim (eds), *Politics and Markets in the Wake of the Asian Crisis*, London: Routledge, pp. 212–37.

Khor, M. (2001) *Rethinking Globalisation*, London and New York: Zed Books.

Krongkaew, M. (1997) 'An Alternative Interpretation of Economic Policy Determination in Thailand: An Important Interplay of Bureaucracy, Political Power, and Private Business', *IDRI Occasional Paper*, No. 9, Tokyo: Foundation for Advanced Studies on International Development (FASID).

Krugman, P. (1984) 'Import Protection as Export Promotion: International Competition in the Presence of Oligopoly and Economies of Scale', in Henryk Kierzkowski (ed.), *Monopolistic Competition and International Trade*, pp. 180–93.

Krugman, P. (1986) 'Introduction: New Thinking about Trade Policy', in Paul Krugman (ed.), *Strategic Trade Policy and the New International Economics*, Cambridge, MA: MIT Press, pp. 1–22.

Krugman, P. (1994) 'The Myth of Asia's Miracle', *Foreign Affairs*, 73(6): 62–78.

Kurus, B. (1994) 'Agreeing to Disagree: The Political Reality of ASEAN Economic Cooperation', *Asian Affairs (American edition)*: 28–41.

Kurzer, P. (1993) *Business and Banking: Political Change and Economic Integration in Western Europe*, Ithaca, New York: Cornell University Press.

Lake, D. (1993) 'Leadership, Hegemony, and the International Political Economy: Naked Emperor or Tattered Monarch with Potential?', *International Studies Quarterly*, 37(4): 459–89.

Lee, K.Y. (1998) *The Singapore Story*, Singapore: Times Edition.

Leifer, M. (1989) *ASEAN and the Security of Southeast Asia*, London: Routledge.

Legewe, J. (2000) *The Political Economy of Industrial Integration in Southeast Asia: An Analysis of the Role of Japanese Firms for the Future of the Regional Automobile Industry*, Kuala Lumpur: Malaysian Institute of Economic Research (mimeo).

Liddle, R.W. (1999a) 'Regime: The New Order', in Donald K. Emmerson (ed.), *Indonesia Beyond Suharto*, New York: M.E. Sharpe, pp. 39–70.

Liddle, R.W. (1999b) 'Indonesia's Unexpected Failure of Leadership', in Adam Schwarz and Jonathan Paris (eds), *The Politics of Post-Suharto Indonesia*, Singapore: Raffles for the Council on Foreign Relations, pp. 16–39.

Liddle, R.W. and Mallarangeng, R. (1997) 'Indonesia in 1996: Pressures from Above and Below', *Asian Survey*, XXXVII (2): 167–74.

Lim, J. (1998) 'The Petrochemical Industry in the Philippines', in *ASEAN Selected Industries, Volume II*, Jakarta: ASEAN Secretariat, pp. 138–89.

Lim, L.Y.C. (1994) 'The Role of the Private Sector in ASEAN Regional Economic Cooperation', in Lynn K. Mytelka (ed.), *South–South Cooperation in a Global Perspective*, Paris: Organisation for Economic Cooperation and Development, pp. 125–68.

Lindblad, J.T. (1997) 'Survey of Recent Developments', *Bulletin of Indonesian Economic Studies*, 33(3): 3–33.

Lindblom, C. (1977) *Politics and Markets: The World's Political-Economic System*, New York: Basic Books.

Lipson, C. (1991) 'Why are Some International Agreements Informal?', *International Organisation*, 45(4): 495–538.

Loriaux, M. (1999) 'The French Developmental State as Myth and Moral Ambition', in Meredith Woo-Cumings (ed.), *The Developmental State*, Ithaca and London: Cornell University Press, pp. 235–75.
Low, L. (1996) 'The ASEAN Free Trade Area', in Bijit Bora and Christopher Findlay (eds), *Regional Integration and the Asia-Pacific*, Sydney: Oxford University Press, pp. 197–206.
Lucas, L.E. (1998) 'The Petrochemical Industry in Thailand', in *ASEAN Selected Industries, Volume II*, Jakarta: ASEAN Secretariat, pp. 70–137.
MacIntyre, A. and Sjahrir (1993) 'Survey of Recent Developments', *Bulletin of Indonesian Economic Studies*, 29(1): 3–33.
Mahathir, M. (1990) *Vision 2020: The Way Forward*, Kuala Lumpur: Institute of Strategic and International Studies.
Mahathir, M. (1998) *In the Face of Attack: Currency Turmoil*, Kuala Lumpur: Limkokwing Integrated.
Manning, C. and Jayasuriya, S. (1996) 'Survey of Recent Developments', *Bulletin of Indonesian Economic Studies*, 32(2): 3–43.
Mansfield, E. and Milner, H. (1997) (eds) *The Political Economy of Regionalism*, New York: Columbia University Press.
Mansfield, E. and Milner, H. (1999) 'The New Wave of Regionalism', *International Organisation*, 53(3): 589–627.
Mardjana, I.K. (1999) 'Public Enterprises under the New Order', in Richard W. Baker, Hadi Soesastro, J. Kristiadi and Douglas E. Ramage (eds), *Indonesia: The Challenge of Change*, Singapore: Institute of Southeast Asian Studies, pp. 41–57.
Martin, L. (1992) *Coercive Cooperation: Explaining Multilateral Economic Sanctions*, Princeton, NJ: Princeton University Press.
Martin, L.M. and Simmons, B.A. (1998) 'Theories and Empirical Studies of International Institutions', *International Organisation*, 52(4): 729–57.
Mattli, W. (1999) *The Logic of Regional Integration: Europe and Beyond*, Cambridge: Cambridge University Press.
McCargo, D. (1998) 'Elite Governance: Business, Bureaucrats and the Military', in Richard Maidment, David Goldblatt and Jeremy Mitchell (eds), *Governance in the Asia-Pacific*, London: Routledge/Open University, pp. 126–49.
McCulloch, R. (1993) 'New Perspectives on Foreign Direct Investment', in Kenneth A. Froot (ed.), *Foreign Direct Investment*, Chicago and London: University of Chicago Press, pp. 37–56.
McFarlane, B. (1998) 'The State and Capitalist Development in the Philippines', in Kyoko Sheridan (ed.), *Emerging Economic Systems in the Philippines*, Sydney: Allen & Unwin, pp. 144–79.
Means, G.P. (1995) 'ASEAN Policy Responses to North American and European Trading Agreements', in Amitav Acharya and Richard Stubbs (eds), *New Challenges for ASEAN: Emerging Policy Issues*, Vancouver: University of British Columbia Press, pp. 146–81.
Menon, J. (1998) 'The Expansion of AFTA: Widening and Deepening?', *Asia-Pacific Economic Literature*, 12(2): 10–22.
MIER (2001a) *Malaysian Economic Outlook 2001: First Quarter Update*, Kuala Lumpur: Malaysian Institute of Economic Research.
MIER (2001b) *Malaysian Economic Outlook 2001: Second Quarter Update*, Kuala Lumpur: Malaysian Institute of Economic Research.

Mittelman, J.H. (2000) *The Globalisation Syndrome: Transformation and Resistance*, Princeton, New Jersey: Princeton University Press.

Moravcsik, A. (1993) 'Preferences and Power in the European Community: A Liberal Intergovernmentalist Approach', *Journal of Common Market Studies*, 31(4): 473–524.

Morgenthau, H.J. (1948/85) *Politics Among Nations: The Struggle for Power and Peace* (Sixth Edition, Revised by Kenneth W. Thompson), New York: McGraw-Hill.

Murphy, A.M. (1999) 'Indonesia and Globalisation', *Asian Perspective*, 23(4): 229–59.

Murphy, C.N. and Tooze, R. (1991) 'Getting Beyond the "Common Sense" of the IPE Orthodoxy', in Craig N. Murphy and Roger Tooze (eds), *The New International Political Economy*, Boulder, Colorado: Lynne Rienner Publishers, pp. 11–31.

Nallappan, K., Ong, B.H. and Tee, S.J. (1998) 'Privatisation and Deregulation', in Tan Teck Meng, Low Aik Meng, John Williams and Choo Teck Min (eds), *Business Opportunities in Indonesia*, Singapore: Prentice Hall, pp. 41–61.

Negara, S.D. (1998) 'Foreign Direct Investment in Indonesia: Trends and Prospects', *Jurnal Ekonomi Pembangunan (Journal of Development Economics)*, VI (2): 1–24.

Nesadurai, H.E.S. (2001) 'Cooperation and Institutional Transformation in ASEAN: Insights from the AFTA Project' in Andrew T.H. Tan and Kenneth Boutin, J.D. (eds), *Non-Traditional Security Issues in Southeast Asia*, Singapore: Institute of Defence and Security Studies, pp. 197–226.

Ng, C.Y. and Sudo, S. (1991) *Development Trends in the Asia Pacific*, Singapore: Institute of Southeast Asian Studies.

Ohmae, K. (1990) *The Borderles World*, New York: Fontana.

Ohmae, K. (1995) *The End of the Nation State: The Rise of Regional Economies*, New York: The Free Press.

Oman, C. (1994) *Globalisation and Regionalisation: The Challenge for Developing Countries*, Paris: Organisation for Economic Cooperation and Development (OECD).

Oye, K. (1985) 'Explaining Cooperation under Anarchy: Hypotheses and Strategies', *World Politics*, 38: 1–24.

Oye, K. (1992) *Economic Discrimination and Political Exchange: World Political Economy in the 1930s and 1980s*, Princeton: Princeton University Press.

Padoa-Schioppa, T. (1985) 'Rules and Institutions in the Management of Multi-Country Economies', in Loukas Tsoukalis (ed.), *The Political Economy of International Money: In Search of a New Order*, London: The Royal Institute of International Affairs, pp. 261–81.

Palan, R. and Abbott, J. (with Deans, P.) (1996) *State Strategies in the Global Political Economy*, London: Pinter.

Panagariya, A. (1999) *Regionalism in Trade Policy*, Singapore: World Scientific Publishing.

Pangestu, M. (1995) 'Indonesia in a Changing World Environment: Multilateralism vs Regionalism', *The Indonesian Quarterly*, XXIII(2): 121–37.

Pangestu, M. (1996) 'Maintaining ASEAN's Competitive Edge: The Role of AFTA', Paper presented at the *Conference on Globalisation and Development: Lessons for the Malaysian Economy*, August 1996, University of Malaya, Kuala Lumpur.

Pangestu, M. and Azis, I.J. (1994) 'Survey of Recent Developments', *Bulletin of Indonesian Economic Studies*, 30(2): 3–47.

Parker, S. (1993) 'Trade and Investment in Southeast Asian Development', *Journal of Northeast Asian Studies*, XII(3): 49–65.
Parsonage, J. (1994) 'The State and Globalisation: Singapore's Growth Triangle Strategy', *Working Paper No. 23*, Perth, Australia: Asia Research Centre/ Murdoch University.
Payne, A. (1998) 'The New Political Economy of Area Studies', *Millennium: Journal of International Studies*, 27(2): 253–73.
Pelkman, J. (1992) 'Institutional Requirements of ASEAN with Special Reference to AFTA', in Pearl Imada and Seiji Naya (eds), *AFTA: The Way Ahead*, Singapore: Institute of Southeast Asian Studies, pp. 99–133.
Petrella, R. (1996) 'Globalisation and Internationalisation: The Dynamics of the Emerging World Order', in Robert Boyer and Daniel Drache (eds), *States Against Markets*, London: Routledge, pp. 62–83.
Petri, P. (1997) 'AFTA and the Global Track', *ASEAN Economic Bulletin*, 14(2): 190–201.
Phillips, N. (2000) 'The Future of the Political Economy of Latin America', in Richard Stubbs and Geoffrey R.D. Underhill (eds), *Political Economy and the Changing Global Order*, Oxford: Oxford University Press, pp. 284–93.
Phongpaichit, P. and Baker, C. (1995) *Thailand: Economy and Politics*, Kuala Lumpur: Oxford University Press.
Phongpaichit, P. and Baker, C. (1998) *Thailand's Boom and Bust*, Chiang Mai, Thailand: Silkworm Books.
Polanyi, K. (1944) *The Great Transformation*, Boston: Beacon.
Pricewaterhouse Coopers (2000) *Special Report: Update on AFTA and Regional Economic Cooperation* (www.us-asean.org/pwcreportr1.htm).
Rafidah Aziz (1996) 'Keynote Address', *Conference on the World Trade Organisation: Perspectives from the South*, 9–10 July 1996, Kuala Lumpur, Malaysia: Institute of Strategic and International Studies (ISIS) (mimeo).
Ravenhill, J. (1995) 'Economic Cooperation in Southeast Asia', *Asian Survey*, XXXV(9): 850–66.
Ravenhill, J. (1998) 'Australia and APEC', in Vinod K. Aggarwal and Charles E. Morrison (eds), *Asia-Pacific Crossroads: Regime Creation and the Future of APEC*, Basingstoke: Macmillan, pp. 143–64.
Ravenhill, J. (2001) *APEC and the Construction of Pacific Rim Regionalism*, Cambridge: Cambridge University Press.
Reich, R. (1991) *The Work of Nations: Preparing Ourselves for 21st Century Capitalism*, London: Simon & Schuster.
Rinakit, S. and Soesastro, H. (1998) 'Indonesia', in Charles E. Morrison and Hadi Soesastro (eds), *Domestic Adjustments to Globalisation*, Tokyo: Japan Centre for International Exchange, pp. 193–206.
Robison, R. (1996) 'The Middle Class and the Bourgeoisie in Indonesia', in Richard Robison and David S.G. Goodman (eds), *The New Rich in Asia*, London: Routledge, pp. 79–101.
Robison, R. (1997) 'Politics and Markets in Indonesia's Non-Oil Era', in Garry Rodan, Kevin Hewison and Richard Robison (eds), *The Political Economy of Southeast Asia*, Oxford: Oxford University Press, pp. 29–63.
Robison, R. and Rosser, A. (2000) 'Surviving the Meltdown: Liberal Reform and Political Oligarchy in Indonesia', in Richard Robison, Mark Beeson, Kanishka

Jayasuriya and Hyuk-Rae Kim (eds), *Politics and Markets in the Wake of the Asian Crisis*, London: Routledge, pp. 171–91.

Rodan, G. (1989) *The Political Economy of Singapore's Industrialisation*, KualaLumpur: Forum.

Rodan, G. (1993) 'Reconstructing Divisions of Labour: Singapore's New Regional Emphasis', in R. Higgott, R. Leaver and J. Ravenhill (eds), *Pacific Economic Relations in the 1990s: Cooperation or Conflict?*, Boulder, Colorado: Lynne Reinner Publishers, pp. 223–49.

Rodan, G. (1997) 'Singapore: Economic Diversification and Social Divisions', in Garry Rodan, Kevin Hewison and Richard Robison (eds), *The Political Economy of Southeast Asia*, Oxford: Oxford University Press, pp. 148–78.

Rosser, A. (2002) *The Politics of Economic Liberalisation in Indonesia: State, Market and Power*, Richmond, Surrey: Curzon.

Ruggie, J.G. (1998) *Constructing the World Polity*, London: Routledge.

Samuels, W.J. (1981) 'Interrelationships between Legal and Economic Processes', in Warren J. Samuels and A. Allen Schmid (eds), *Law and Economics: An Institutional Perspective*, Boston: Martinus Nijhof Publishing.

Scholte, J.A. (1997a) 'The Globalisation of World Politics', in John Bayliss and Steve Smith (eds), *The Globalisation of World Politics*, Oxford: Oxford University Press, pp. 14–30.

Scholte, J.A. (1997b) 'Global Capitalism and the State', *International Affairs*, 73(3): 427–52.

Scholte, J.A. (2000) *Globalisation: A Critical Introduction*, London: Macmillan.

Schott, J. (1996) *WTO 2000: Setting the Course for World Trade*, Washington, DC: Institute for International Economics.

Schwarz, A. (1994) *A Nation in Waiting: Indonesia in the 1990s*, St. Leonards: Allen and Unwin.

Scollay, R. and Gilbert, J.P. (2001) *New Regional Trading Arrangements in the Asia Pacific?*, Washington, DC: Institute for International Economics.

Sell, S.K. (2000) 'Big Business and the New Trade Agreements: The Future of the WTO?', in Richard Stubbs and Geoffrey R.D. Underhill (eds), *Political Economy and the Changing Global Order*, Oxford: Oxford University Press, pp. 174–83.

Sheridan, G. (1998) 'Where are Asia's Institutions?', *Asian Wall Street Journal*, 2 April.

Shimizu, K. (2000) 'The Asian Economic Crisis and Intra-ASEAN Economic Cooperation', *Economic Journal of Hokkaido University*, 29: 67–83.

Sjolander, C.T. (1996) 'The Rhetoric of Globalisation: What's in a Wor(l)d?', *International Journal*, LI(4): 603–16.

Smythe, E. (2000) 'State Authority and Investment Security: Non-state Actors and the Negotiation of the Multilateral Agreement on Investment at the OECD', in Richard A. Higgott, Geoffrey R.D. Underhill and Andreas Bieler (eds), *Non-State Actors and Authority in the Global System*, London: Routledge, pp. 74–90.

Soesastro, H. (1991) 'The ASEAN Free Trade Area and the Future of Asian Dynamism', *CSIS Discussion Paper M72/91*, Jakarta: Centre for Strategic and International Studies (CSIS).

Soesastro, H. (1998) 'Domestic Adjustments in Four ASEAN Economies', in Charles E. Morrison and Hadi Soesastro (eds), *Domestic Adjustments to Globalisation*, Tokyo: Japan Centre for International Exchange, pp. 24–36.

Soesastro, H. (1999) 'Economic Measures: How Bold, How Measured?', Paper presented at the *ASEAN-ISIS Conference on ASEAN 2020: Vision, Crisis and Change*, 21–22 July 1999, Singapore.

Soesastro, H. and Basri, M.C. (1998) 'Survey of Recent Developments', *Bulletin of Indonesian Economic Studies*, 34(1): 3–54.

Stone, Diane (2000) 'Knowledge, Power and Policy' in Diane Stone (ed.), *Banking on Knowledge: The Genesis of the Global Development Network*, London and New York: Routledge, pp. 241–58.

Stopford, J. and Strange, S. (1991) *Rival States, Rival Firms: Competition for World Market Shares*, Cambridge: Cambridge University Press.

Storper, M. (1997) 'Territories, Flows and Hierarchies in the Global Economy', in Cox K.R. (ed.), *Spaces of Globalisation: Reasserting the Power of the Local*, New York: The Guildford Press, pp. 19–44.

Strange, S. (1988/94) *States and Markets*, London: Pinter.

Stubbs, R. (1998) 'Asia Pacific Regionalism versus Globalisation: Competing Forms of Capitalism', in William D. Coleman and Geoffrey R.D. Underhill (eds), *Regionalism and Global Economic Integration: Europe, Asia and the Americas*, London and New York: Routledge, pp. 68–80.

Stubbs, R. (2000) 'Signing on to Liberalisation: AFTA and the Politics of Regional Economic Cooperation', *The Pacific Review*, 13(2): 297–318.

Stubbs, R. (2001) 'Performance Legitimacy and "Soft Authoritarianism"' in Amitav Acharya, Michael Frolic, B. and Richard Stubbs (eds), *Democracy, Human Rights and Civil Society in Southeast Asia*, Toronto: Joint Centre for Asia-Pacific Studies, York University, pp. 37–54.

Studer-Noguez, M.I. (2000) 'How Global is Ford Motor Company's Global Strategy?', in Richard A. Higgott, Geoffrey R.D. Underhill and Andreas Bieler (eds), *Non-State Actors and Authority in the Global System*, London: Routledge, pp. 174–92.

Surbakti, R. (1999) 'Formal Political Institutions', in Richard W. Baker, Hadi Soesastro, Kristiadi, J. and Douglas E. Ramage (eds), *Indonesia: The Challenge of Change*, Singapore: Institute of Southeast Asian Studies, pp. 61–98.

Suriyamongkol, M. (1988) *Politics of ASEAN Economic Cooperation: The Case of ASEAN Industrial Projects*, Singapore: Oxford University Press.

Tan, K.Y. (1993) 'Diversion of Direct Foreign Investments from Southeast Asia to China', *Working Paper on Contemporary Management No. 01/07/93*, Singapore: Faculty of Business Administration, National University of Singapore.

Teh, Jr, R. (1999) 'Completing the CEPT Scheme for AFTA', Paper presented at the *Conference on Beyond AFTA and Towards an ASEAN Common Market*, October, Manila.

Tham, S.Y. (1998) 'Competition and Cooperation for Foreign Direct Investment: An ASEAN Perspective', *Asia-Pacific Development Journal*, 5(1): 9–35.

Thomsen, S. (1999) 'Southeast Asia: The Role of Foreign Direct Investment Policies in Development', *Working Papers on International Investment (1999/1)*, Paris: Organisation for Economic Cooperation and Development.

Tomich, T.P. (1992) 'Survey of Recent Developments', *Bulletin of Indonesian Economic Studies*, 28(3): 3–39.

Tongzon, J.L. (1998) *The Economies of Southeast Asia: The Growth and Development of ASEAN Economies*, Cheltenham, UK: Edward Elgar.

Tori, T. (1997) 'The New Economic Policy and the United Malays National Organisation', *The Developing Economies*, XXXV(3): 209–39.

Turnbull, C.M. (1989) *A History of Singapore, 1918–1988*, Singapore: Oxford University Press.

Tyndall, P.S. (1999) 'The Malaysian Automotive Industry', Paper presented at the *Policy Workshop on the Malaysian Automotive Industry*, May 1999, Kuala Lumpur.

Underhill, G.R.D. (2000) 'Introduction: Conceptualising the Changing Global Order', in Richard Stubbs and Geoffrey R.D. Underhill (eds), *Political Economy and the Changing Global Order*, London: Macmillan, pp. 3–24.

Van Apeldoorn, B. (2000) 'The Political Economy of European Integration', in Richard Stubbs and Geoffrey R.D. Underhill (eds), *Political Economy and the Changing Global Order*, Oxford: Oxford University Press, pp. 235–44.

Van der Eng, P. (1993) 'Survey of Recent Developments', *Bulletin of Indonesian Economic Studies*, 29(3): 3–35.

Viner, J. (1950) *The Customs Union Issue*, New York: Carnegie Endowment for International Peace.

Vos, R. and Yap, J.T. (1996) *The Philippine Economy: East Asia's Stray Cat?*, London: Macmillan Press.

Walter, A. (2000) 'Globalisation and Policy Convergence: The Case of Direct Investment Rules', in Richard A. Higgott, Geoffrey R.D. Underhill and Andreas Bieler (eds), *Non-State Actors and Authority in the Global System*, London: Routledge, pp. 51–73.

Weiss, L. (1998) *The Myth of the Powerless State*, Cambridge: Polity Press.

Welsh, B. (1999) 'Malaysia and Globalisation: Contradictory Currents', *Asian Perspective*, 23(4): 261–86.

Williams, M.C. (1996) 'Hobbes and International Relations: A Reconsideration', *International Organisation*, 50(2): 213–36.

Williamson, J. (1994) 'In Search of a Manual for Technopols', in John Williamson (ed.), *The Political Economy of Policy Reform*, Washington, DC: Institute for International Economics, pp. 11–28.

Wong, P.K. and Ng, C.Y. (1997) 'Singapore's Industrial Policy to the Year 2000', in Seiichi Masuyama, Donna Vandenbrink and Chia Siow Yue (eds), *Industrial Policies in East Asia*, Singapore and Tokyo: Institute of Southeast Asian Studies and Nomura Research Institute, pp. 121–41.

Woo-Cumings, M. (1999) 'Introduction: Chalmers Johnson and the Politics of Nationalism and Development', in Meredith Woo-Cumings (ed.), *The Developmental State*, Ithaca, NY: Cornell University Press, pp. 1–31.

Wyatt-Walter, A. (1995) 'Regionalism, Globalisation, and World Economic Order', in Louise Fawcett and Andrew Hurrell (eds), *Regionalism in World Politics*, Oxford: Oxford University Press, pp. 74–121.

Yarborough, B.V. and Yarborough, R.M. (1992) *Cooperation and Governance in International Trade: The Strategic Organisational Approach*, Princeton, New Jersey: Princeton University Press.

Yeung, H.W.-C. (1999) *Singapore's Global Reach: An Executive Report*, Singapore: Department of Geography, National University of Singapore.

Official publications

APEC (1994) *Non-binding Investment Principles*, Singapore: APEC Secretariat.

ASEAN (1992a) *The Singapore Declaration*, Singapore, 28 January 1992.

ASEAN (1992b) *Framework Agreement on Enhancing Economic Cooperation*, Singapore, 28 January 1992.

ASEAN (1992c) *Agreement on the Common Effective Preferential Tariff Scheme for the ASEAN Free Trade Area*, Singapore, 28 January 1992.

ASEAN (1995a) *The Bangkok Summit Declaration of 1995*, Bangkok, 15 December 1995.

ASEAN (1995b) *Protocol to Amend the Framework Agreement on Enhancing ASEAN Economic Cooperation*, Bangkok, 15 December 1995.

ASEAN (1995c) *Protocol to Amend the Agreement on the Common Effective Preferential Tariff Scheme for the ASEAN Free Trade Area*, Bangkok, 15 December 1995.

ASEAN (1995d) *ASEAN Framework Agreement on Services*, Bangkok, 15 December 1995.

ASEAN (1995e) *ASEAN Framework Agreement on Intellectual Property Cooperation*, Bangkok, 15 December 1995.

ASEAN (1996a) *Basic Agreement on the ASEAN Industrial Cooperation Scheme*, Singapore, 27 April 1996.

ASEAN (1996b) *Protocol on Dispute Settlement Mechanism*, Manila, 26 November 1996.

ASEAN (1997) *Protocol to Implement the Initial Package of Commitments under the ASEAN Framework Agreement on Services*, Kuala Lumpur, 15 December 1997.

ASEAN (1998a) *Protocol to Implement the Second Package of Commitments under the ASEAN Framework Agreement on Services*, Hanoi, 16 December 1998.

ASEAN (1998b) *Protocol on Notification Procedures*, Makati, Philippines, 8 October 1998.

ASEAN (1998c) *Statement on Bold Measures*, Hanoi, 16 December 1998.

ASEAN (1998d) *Framework Agreement on the ASEAN Investment Area*, Manila, 8 October 1998.

ASEAN (1998e) *Short-term Measures to Enhance ASEAN Investment Climate*, Hanoi, 16 December 1998.

ASEAN (1998f) *ASEAN Framework Agreement on Mutual Recognition Arrangements*, Hanoi, 16 December 1998.

ASEAN (1999) *Protocol on the Special Arrangement for Sensitive and Highly Sensitive Products*, Singapore, 30 September 1999.

ASEAN (2000) *Protocol Regarding the Implementation of the CEPT Scheme Temporary Exclusion List*, Singapore, 23 November 2000.

ASEAN *Annual Report* (various issues), Jakarta: ASEAN Secretariat (www.asean.or.id).

ASEAN Secretariat (1993) *AFTA Reader: Volume 1*, Jakarta: The ASEAN Secretariat.

ASEAN Secretariat (1995) *AFTA Reader: Volume III*, Jakarta: The ASEAN Secretariat.

ASEAN Secretariat (1996) *AFTA Reader: Volume IV*, Jakarta: The ASEAN Secretariat.

ASEAN Secretariat (1997a) *ASEAN Economic Cooperation: Transition and Transformation*, Singapore: Institute of Southeast Asian Studies.

ASEAN Secretariat (1997b) *ASEAN Industrial Cooperation Scheme*, Jakarta: The ASEAN Secretariat.

ASEAN Secretariat (1998a) *AFTA Reader: Volume V*, Jakarta: The ASEAN Secretariat.

ASEAN Secretariat (1998b) *Compendium of Investment Policies and Measures in ASEAN Countries*, Jakarta: The ASEAN Secretariat.

ASEAN Secretariat (1999a) *ASEAN Investment Report 1999: Trends and Developments in Foreign Direct Investment*, Jakarta: The ASEAN Secretariat.

ASEAN Secretariat (1999b) *ASEAN Investment Area: Temporary Exclusion List and Sensitive List*, Jakarta: The ASEAN Secretariat.

Australia (1994) *ASEAN Free Trade Area: Trading Bloc or Building Block?*, Canberra: East-Asian Analytical Unit, Department of Foreign Affairs and Trade.

IMF, *Direction of Trade Statistics Yearbook* (various issues), Washington, DC: International Monetary Fund.

Malaysia (1998) *Economic Report 1998/99*, Kuala Lumpur: Ministry of Finance.

OECD (1999) 'Recent Trends in Foreign Direct Investment', *Financial Market Trends*, No. 73 (June), Paris: Organisation for Economic Cooperation and Development.

Singapore (1991) *Towards a Developed Nation: The Strategic Economic Plan*, Singapore: Ministry of Trade and Industry.

Singapore (1993) *Interim Report of the Committee to Promote Enterprise Overseas*, Singapore: Ministry of Finance.

Singapore (1998) *Report of the Committee on Singapore's Competitiveness*, Singapore: Ministry of Trade and Industry.

Thailand (2000) *Automotive Industry in Thailand*, Office of Industrial Economics, Ministry of Industry.

UNCTAD (1999) *World Investment Report 1999: Foreign Direct Investment and the Challenge of Development*, New York: United Nations.

UNCTAD (2000) *World Investment Report 2000: Cross-border Mergers and Acquisitions and Development*, New York: United Nations.

WTO (1998) *Report of the WTO General Council Meeting*, Geneva: WTO (www.wto.org).

WTO Secretariat (1999) *An Introduction to the GATS*, Geneva: Trade in Services Division.

Newspapers, Magazines and News Services (italics indicate local language)

Agence France Presse
Asian Wall Street Journal (AWSJ)
Associated Press
Bangkok Post
Bernama news service
Bisnis Indonesia
Bulletin KADIN Indonesia
Business Times (Malaysia, if country source unspecified)
Business Times (Singapore)
Far Eastern Economic Review (FEER)
Financial Times
Inquirer News Service
International Herald Tribune (IHT)
Investors Digest (Malaysia)
Jakarta Post
Kyodo News Service
Malaysian Business
Merdeka (Indonesia)
The Nation (Thailand)
New Straits Times (NST, Malaysia)
Philippine Daily Inquirer
Republika (Indonesia)
Review Indonesia
Straits Times (Singapore)
Suara Karya (Indonesia)

Index